# It's another Quality Book from CGP

This book is for anyone doing GCSE AQA French.

Whatever subject you're doing it's the same
old story — there are lots of facts and you've just got
to learn them. GCSE French is no different.

Happily this CGP book gives you all that important
information as clearly and concisely as possible.

It's also got some daft bits in to try and make the whole
experience at least vaguely entertaining for you.

# What CGP is all about

Our sole aim here at CGP is to produce the highest quality
books — carefully written, immaculately presented and
dangerously close to being funny.

Then we work our socks off to get them out to you
— at the cheapest possible prices.

# Contents

## SECTION 1 — GENERAL STUFF

Numbers ..................................................................................... 1
Times and Dates ......................................................................... 2
Asking Questions ........................................................................ 4
Being Polite ................................................................................ 5
Opinions ..................................................................................... 7
What Do You Think of...? ............................................................ 9
Writing Informal Letters ............................................................ 10
Writing Formal Letters ............................................................... 11
Revision Summary ..................................................................... 12

## SECTION 2 — LIFESTYLE (FOOD AND HEALTH)

Food .......................................................................................... 13
Mealtimes .................................................................................. 14
Feeling Ill .................................................................................. 16
Health and Health Issues ........................................................... 17
Revision Summary ..................................................................... 20

## SECTION 3 — LIFESTYLE (RELATIONSHIPS & CHOICES)

About Yourself ........................................................................... 21
Family and Pets ......................................................................... 22
Personality ................................................................................ 23
Relationships ............................................................................. 24
Marriage .................................................................................... 25
Social Issues and Equality ......................................................... 26
Revision Summary ..................................................................... 28

## SECTION 4 — FREE TIME AND THE MEDIA

Free time Activities ................................................................... 29
Television ................................................................................... 31
Talking About the Plot ............................................................... 32
Music ........................................................................................ 33
Famous People .......................................................................... 34
New Technology ........................................................................ 35
Shopping ................................................................................... 37
Fashion and Trends .................................................................... 41
Inviting People Out .................................................................... 42
Going Out .................................................................................. 43
Revision Summary ..................................................................... 45

## SECTION 5 — HOLIDAYS

Holiday Destinations .................................................................. 46
Catching the Train ..................................................................... 47
All Kinds of Transport ................................................................ 49
Planning Your Holiday ................................................................ 50
Holiday Accommodation ............................................................ 51
Booking a Room / Pitch ............................................................. 52
Where / When is...? ................................................................... 53
At a Restaurant .......................................................................... 54
Talking About Your Holiday ........................................................ 56
The Weather .............................................................................. 60
Revision Summary ..................................................................... 61

## SECTION 6 — HOME AND ENVIRONMENT

Names of Buildings ............................................................................... 62
Asking Directions ................................................................................. 63
Talking About Where You Live ............................................................. 64
Inside Your Home ................................................................................ 66
Daily Routine ....................................................................................... 67
Festivals and Special Occasions ........................................................... 68
The Environment .................................................................................. 69
Revision Summary ............................................................................... 71

## SECTION 7 — WORK AND EDUCATION

School Subjects .................................................................................... 72
The School Routine .............................................................................. 73
More School Stuff ................................................................................ 74
Classroom Language ........................................................................... 75
Problems at School .............................................................................. 76
Work Experience ................................................................................. 78
Plans for the Future ............................................................................. 79
Types of Job ........................................................................................ 80
Jobs: Advantages and Disadvantages .................................................. 81
Getting a Job ....................................................................................... 82
Telephones .......................................................................................... 84
Revision Summary ............................................................................... 85

## SECTION 8 — GRAMMAR

Words for People and Objects (Nouns) ................................................ 86
'The' and 'A' (Articles) ......................................................................... 87
Words to Describe Things (Adjectives) ................................................. 88
Words to Describe Actions (Adverbs) ................................................... 91
Comparing Things (Comparatives and Superlatives) ............................. 92
Sneaky Wee Words (Prepositions and Relative Pronouns) ..................... 94
I, You, Him, Them and En & Y (Pronouns) .......................................... 96
Me, You, Him, Them, Mine, Yours... (Pronouns) ................................. 97
This & That and Which (Demonstratives and Relative Pronouns) ........... 98
Joining Words — Longer Sentences (Conjunctions) .............................. 99
The Lowdown on Verbs (Verbs, Tenses and the Infinitive) .................. 100
Verbs in the Present Tense ................................................................. 101
Talking About the Future (Future Tense) ............................................ 103
Talking About the Past (Perfect Tense) ............................................... 104
'Was Doing' or 'Used to Do' (Imperfect Tense) .................................. 107
Myself, Yourself, etc. (Reflexive Verbs) ............................................. 109
Saying 'Not', 'Never' and 'Nobody' (Negatives) ................................. 110
Would, Could & Should (Conditional) ................................................ 111
Ordering People Around (Imperative) ................................................ 112
Know and Can (Savoir, Connaître and Pouvoir) ................................. 113
Had Done and '-ing' (Pluperfect Tense and Present Participles) ........... 114
The Passive ........................................................................................ 115
Impersonal Verbs & the Subjunctive .................................................. 116
Revision Summary ............................................................................. 117

Do Well in Your Exam ....................................................................... 118
French–English Dictionary ................................................................. 125
Index ................................................................................................. 131

Published by Coordination Group Publications Ltd.

*Contributors*:
Angela Billington
Chris Dennett
Lindsay Jordan
Hannah-Louise Nash
Sam Norman
Rachael Powers
Katherine Stewart
Claire Thompson
Jennifer Underwood
Tim Wakeling
James Paul Wallis

With thanks to Sam Norman & Cheryl Robinson for the proofreading.

No corny clichés about French people were harmed in the making of this book.

ISBN: 978 1 84762 285 3

Groovy website: www.cgpbooks.co.uk
Jolly bits of clipart from CorelDRAW®
Printed by Elanders Hindson Ltd, Newcastle upon Tyne.

Based on the classic CGP style created by Richard Parsons.

## Numbers

Welcome to page one. On the count of three — get cracking.

### Un, deux, trois — One, two, three...

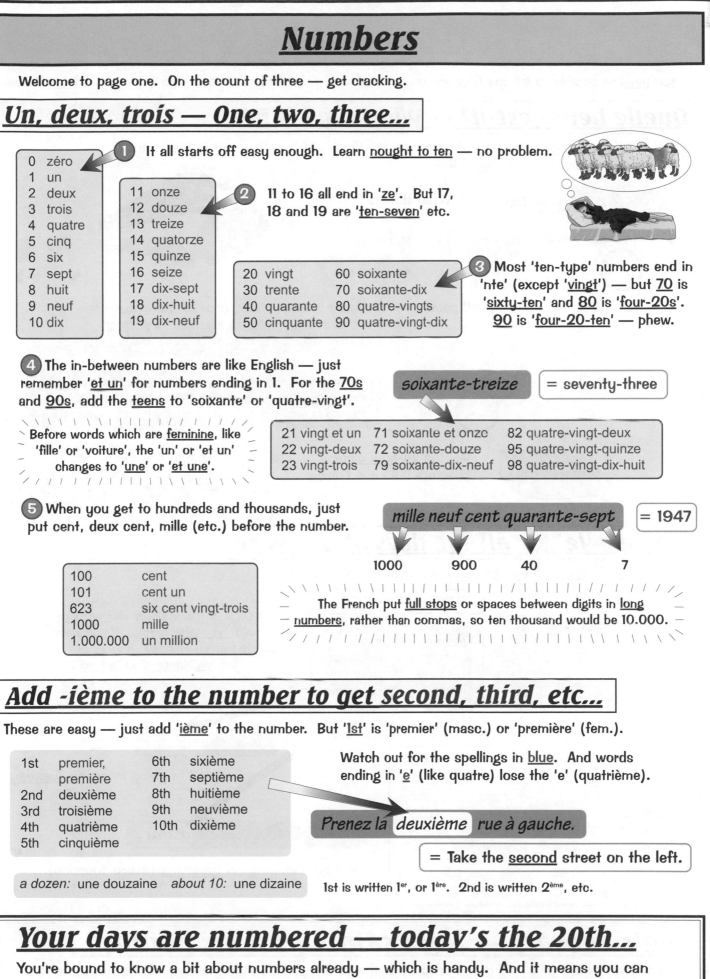

**1** It all starts off easy enough. Learn <u>nought to ten</u> — no problem.

| | |
|---|---|
| 0 | zéro |
| 1 | un |
| 2 | deux |
| 3 | trois |
| 4 | quatre |
| 5 | cinq |
| 6 | six |
| 7 | sept |
| 8 | huit |
| 9 | neuf |
| 10 | dix |

| | |
|---|---|
| 11 | onze |
| 12 | douze |
| 13 | treize |
| 14 | quatorze |
| 15 | quinze |
| 16 | seize |
| 17 | dix-sept |
| 18 | dix-huit |
| 19 | dix-neuf |

**2** 11 to 16 all end in '<u>ze</u>'. But 17, 18 and 19 are '<u>ten-seven</u>' etc.

| | | | |
|---|---|---|---|
| 20 | vingt | 60 | soixante |
| 30 | trente | 70 | soixante-dix |
| 40 | quarante | 80 | quatre-vingts |
| 50 | cinquante | 90 | quatre-vingt-dix |

**3** Most 'ten-type' numbers end in 'nte' (except '<u>vingt</u>') — but <u>70</u> is '<u>sixty-ten</u>' and <u>80</u> is '<u>four-20s</u>'. <u>90</u> is '<u>four-20-ten</u>' — phew.

**4** The in-between numbers are like English — just remember '<u>et un</u>' for numbers ending in 1. For the <u>70s</u> and <u>90s</u>, add the <u>teens</u> to 'soixante' or 'quatre-vingt'.

Before words which are <u>feminine</u>, like 'fille' or 'voiture', the 'un' or 'et un' changes to '<u>une</u>' or '<u>et une</u>'.

| **soixante-treize** | = seventy-three |
|---|---|

| | | |
|---|---|---|
| 21 vingt et un | 71 soixante et onze | 82 quatre-vingt-deux |
| 22 vingt-deux | 72 soixante-douze | 95 quatre-vingt-quinze |
| 23 vingt-trois | 79 soixante-dix-neuf | 98 quatre-vingt-dix-huit |

**5** When you get to hundreds and thousands, just put cent, deux cent, mille (etc.) before the number.

| 100 | cent |
|---|---|
| 101 | cent un |
| 623 | six cent vingt-trois |
| 1000 | mille |
| 1.000.000 | un million |

| **mille neuf cent quarante-sept** | = 1947 |
|---|---|

| 1000 | 900 | 40 | 7 |

The French put <u>full stops</u> or spaces between digits in <u>long numbers</u>, rather than commas, so ten thousand would be 10.000.

### Add -ième to the number to get second, third, etc...

These are easy — just add '<u>ième</u>' to the number. But '<u>1st</u>' is 'premier' (masc.) or 'première' (fem.).

| 1st | premier, première | 6th | sixième |
|---|---|---|---|
| 2nd | deuxième | 7th | septième |
| 3rd | troisième | 8th | huitième |
| 4th | quatrième | 9th | neuvième |
| 5th | cinquième | 10th | dixième |

Watch out for the spellings in <u>blue</u>. And words ending in '<u>e</u>' (like quatre) lose the 'e' (quatrième).

Prenez la deuxième rue à gauche.

= Take the <u>second</u> street on the left.

*a dozen:* une douzaine   *about 10:* une dizaine

1st is written 1<sup>er</sup>, or 1<sup>ère</sup>. 2nd is written 2<sup>ème</sup>, etc.

### Your days are numbered — today's the 20th...

You're bound to know a bit about numbers already — which is handy. And it means you can spend more time checking that you know the rest of the page. Learn <u>all</u> of these words about numbers. The <u>best</u> way to check is to cover up the page and then try to write them down.

# Times and Dates

You **need** to be able to tell the <u>time</u> and understand what time things happen — so if you can't, <u>learn</u> it now.

## Quelle heure est-il? — What time is it?

Just like there are <u>loads</u> of ways of saying the time in English, so there are in French too.
Of course, you have to <u>learn all</u> of them.

| Quelle heure est-il? | = What time is it? |

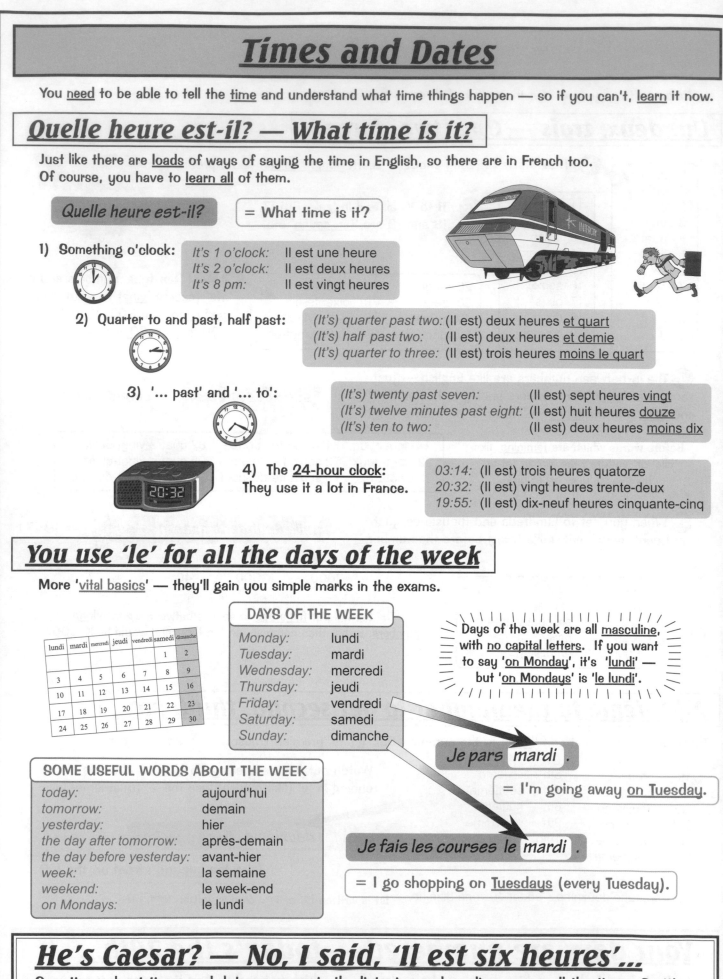

1) **Something o'clock:**

It's 1 o'clock: Il est une heure
It's 2 o'clock: Il est deux heures
It's 8 pm: Il est vingt heures

2) **Quarter to and past, half past:**

(It's) quarter past two: (Il est) deux heures <u>et quart</u>
(It's) half past two: (Il est) deux heures <u>et demie</u>
(It's) quarter to three: (Il est) trois heures <u>moins le quart</u>

3) **'... past' and '... to':**

(It's) twenty past seven: (Il est) sept heures <u>vingt</u>
(It's) twelve minutes past eight: (Il est) huit heures <u>douze</u>
(It's) ten to two: (Il est) deux heures <u>moins dix</u>

4) **The <u>24-hour clock</u>:**
They use it a lot in France.

03:14: (Il est) trois heures quatorze
20:32: (Il est) vingt heures trente-deux
19:55: (Il est) dix-neuf heures cinquante-cinq

## You use 'le' for all the days of the week

More '<u>vital basics</u>' — they'll gain you simple marks in the exams.

| lundi | mardi | mercredi | jeudi | vendredi | samedi | dimanche |
|-------|-------|----------|-------|----------|--------|----------|
|       |       |          |       |          | 1      | 2        |
| 3     | 4     | 5        | 6     | 7        | 8      | 9        |
| 10    | 11    | 12       | 13    | 14       | 15     | 16       |
| 17    | 18    | 19       | 20    | 21       | 22     | 23       |
| 24    | 25    | 26       | 27    | 28       | 29     | 30       |

**DAYS OF THE WEEK**

| Monday: | lundi |
| Tuesday: | mardi |
| Wednesday: | mercredi |
| Thursday: | jeudi |
| Friday: | vendredi |
| Saturday: | samedi |
| Sunday: | dimanche |

Days of the week are all <u>masculine</u>, with <u>no capital letters</u>. If you want to say '<u>on Monday</u>', it's '<u>lundi</u>' — but '<u>on Mondays</u>' is '<u>le lundi</u>'.

Je pars mardi .

= I'm going away <u>on Tuesday</u>.

Je fais les courses le mardi .

= I go shopping on <u>Tuesdays</u> (every Tuesday).

**SOME USEFUL WORDS ABOUT THE WEEK**

| today: | aujourd'hui |
| tomorrow: | demain |
| yesterday: | hier |
| the day after tomorrow: | après-demain |
| the day before yesterday: | avant-hier |
| week: | la semaine |
| weekend: | le week-end |
| on Mondays: | le lundi |

## He's Caesar? — No, I said, 'Il est six heures'...

Questions about times and dates crop up in the listening and reading exams all the time. So it's <u>megatastically important</u> to be able to understand all things <u>clock-</u> and <u>calendar-related</u>. You must know the <u>days of the week</u> and things like '<u>tomorrow</u>' or '<u>weekend</u>' inside out. So find the time...

# Times and Dates

You can <u>bet</u> your bottom dollar you'll find this stuff on dates and times really useful.
These essentials will make your sentences sound a whole lot more interesting. It's <u>guaranteed</u>.

## Janvier, février, mars, avril...

French months bear a striking resemblance to the
English ones — make sure you <u>learn</u> what's <u>different</u>.

*Il part* en juillet .    = He's leaving <u>in July</u>.

Months and seasons are <u>masculine</u>, with no capital letters.

| | | | |
|---|---|---|---|
| *January:* | janvier | *July:* | juillet |
| *February:* | février | *August:* | août |
| *March:* | mars | *September:* | septembre |
| *April:* | avril | *October:* | octobre |
| *May:* | mai | *November:* | novembre |
| *June:* | juin | *December:* | décembre |

| | |
|---|---|
| *winter:* | hiver |
| *spring:* | printemps |
| *summer:* | été |
| *autumn:* | automne |

You say '<u>au printemps</u>' for <u>in spring</u>. But you use '<u>en</u>' in front of all the other seasons.

## You say "the 3 May" instead of "the 3rd of May"

Here's how to say <u>the date</u> in French. This is <u>bound to come up</u> somewhere in your <u>exam</u> — and the examiners won't be impressed if you can't understand what the date is.

Check out p.1 for help with the numbers.

1) In French, they don't say "the <u>third of</u> May" — they say "the <u>three</u> May". Weird, huh?

*J'arrive le trois octobre.*    = I am coming on the 3rd of October.

2) The <u>first</u> is the odd one out, because it's more like English. They say "<u>the first May</u>" ("<u>le premier mai</u>").

*Je suis né(e) le premier mars mille neuf cent quatre-vingt-treize.*

= I was born on the first of March 1993.

3) And this is how you <u>write the date</u> in a letter:

*Londres, le 5 mars 2009*

See p.10-11 for letters.

= London, 5th March 2009

4) And here are some other useful bits:

| | |
|---|---|
| *in the year 2000:* | en l'an deux mille |
| *in 2009:* | en deux mille neuf |

NOT 'deux mille <u>et</u> neuf'

## Ce matin — This morning... Ce soir — This evening

You'll use these phrases <u>all the time</u> — they're <u>great</u> for making loads of <u>arrangements</u>.

*Je fais* souvent *du ski.*    = I <u>often</u> go skiing.

| | |
|---|---|
| *always:* | toujours |
| *sometimes:* | quelquefois |
| *(quite) often:* | (assez) souvent |
| *(quite) rarely:* | (assez) rarement |

See p.110 for how to say you <u>never</u> do something.

| | |
|---|---|
| *this morning:* | ce matin |
| *this afternoon:* | cet après-midi |
| *this evening/tonight:* | ce soir |
| *tomorrow morning:* | demain matin |
| *this week:* | cette semaine |
| *next week:* | la semaine prochaine |
| *last week:* | la semaine dernière |
| *this weekend:* | ce week-end |

*Qu'est-ce que tu fais* ce soir *?*    = What are you doing <u>tonight</u>?

## Dates — better at the cinema than in French...

It doesn't come much more <u>crucial</u> than this. This is fairly basic stuff, but it <u>will</u> get you more marks, so don't forget to learn it. It's not that hard, either. Just learn the phrase '<u>Qu'est-ce que tu fais ce soir?</u>', and then learn all the different words you can slot in instead of 'ce soir'.

# Asking Questions

Curiosity may have killed the cat, but you've <u>got</u> to be able to <u>understand</u> and <u>ask questions</u> — so <u>learn this</u>.

## Quand — When... Pourquoi — Why... Où — Where

| | |
|---|---|
| *when?* | *quand?* |
| *why?* | *pourquoi?* |
| *where?* | *où?* |
| *how?* | *comment?* |
| *how much/many?* | *combien de...?* |
| *at what time...?* | *à quelle heure...?* |
| *who/whom?* | *qui?* |
| *which...?* | *quel(le)...?* |

Learn these question words — they're pretty important.

*Quand est-ce que tu rentres?*

= <u>When</u> are you coming back?

Grammar fans: These are interrogative adverbs.

*Qui a cassé la fenêtre?*  = <u>Who</u> broke the window?

*Quelle est la date?*  = <u>What</u> is the date?

'Quel' is a tricky question word. It can mean 'which' or 'what' <u>and</u> it has to agree with the object it's talking about. It has masc., fem., singular and plural forms.

which...? what...?:
quel...?  quels...?
quelle...?  quelles...?

*Quels vêtements allez-vous porter?*

= <u>Which</u> clothes are you going to wear?

## 1) Use Est-ce que to start questions

To turn a statement into a <u>yes-no question</u>, put '<u>Est-ce que</u>' onto the beginning of the sentence.

*Est-ce que tes bananes sont jaunes?*  = Are your bananas yellow?

To answer <u>yes</u> to a question containing a <u>negative</u>, use '<u>si</u>'.

*Est-ce que tu n'as pas soif?*  = Aren't you thirsty?  *Si, j'ai soif.*  = Yes, I'm thirsty.

If your question starts with '<u>What...</u>', use '<u>Qu'est-ce que</u>'.

*Qu'est-ce que tu manges le soir?*  = What do you eat in the evening?

OR...  *Que manges-tu le soir?*

You can start the question with '<u>Que</u>' — but the verb (manges) and the subject (tu) <u>switch places</u> in the question and you add a <u>hyphen</u>.

## 2) Ask a question by putting the verb first

In English, you change '<u>I can go</u>' to '<u>Can I go?</u>' to make it a <u>question</u> (swapping the subject and verb round) — it's exactly the same in French except you need to add a hyphen between the subject and the verb.

*Est-elle partie?*  = Has she gone?  *Peux-tu m'aider?*  = Can you help me?

## 3) Ask a question by changing your tone of voice

You can say a <u>normal sentence</u> but just raise your voice at the end to show it's a question.

*Tu as des frères ou des sœurs?*  = Do you have any brothers or sisters?  (<u>Literally</u>: You have brothers or sisters?)

## *If you have a question for her — why not 'est-ce que'...*

This page is full of question words — start by <u>learning them all</u>. Shut the book and <u>write down all the question words</u> at the top of the page. <u>Look back</u> for the ones you missed and <u>try again</u> till you get them <u>all</u>. Then, all you need to do is <u>remember</u> the <u>three</u> main ways to <u>ask a question</u>.

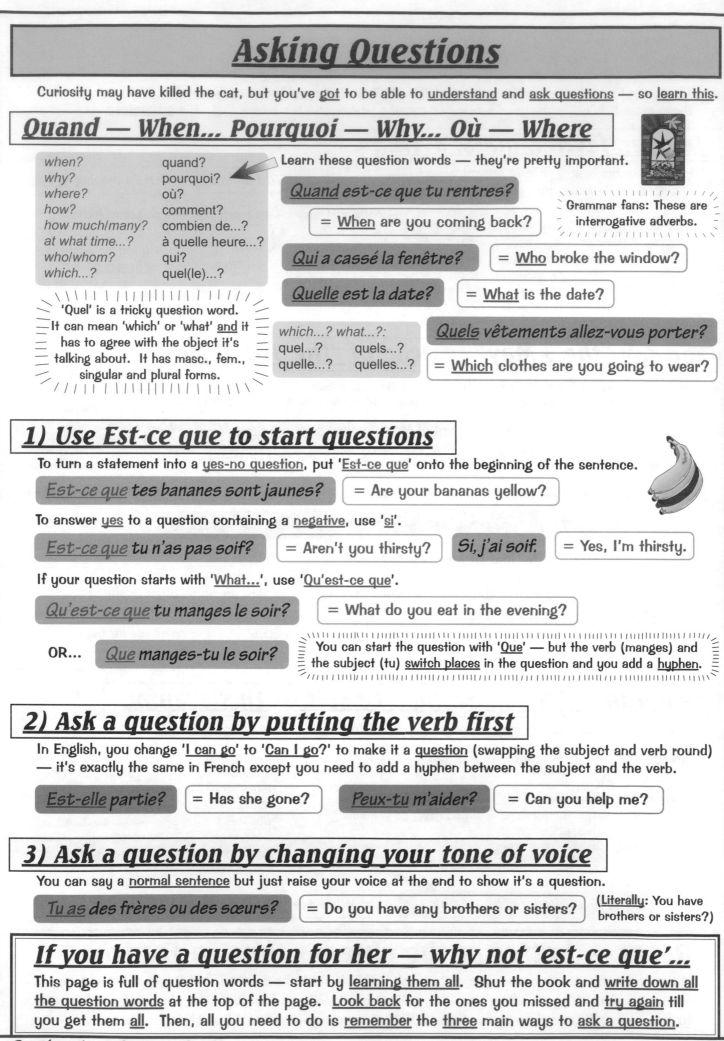

# Being Polite

OK, you may know all of the French covered so far, but it won't look good if the first thing you say to an actual French speaker is "Hello Bogface" — try opening with these <u>superb gems</u> of <u>politeness</u> instead.

## Bonjour — Hello

Learn these phrases — they're <u>crucial</u>. Nuff said.

| | |
|---|---|
| *Bonjour:* | Hello |
| *Salut:* | Hi |
| *Bienvenue:* | Welcome |
| *Bonsoir:* | Good evening |
| *Bonne nuit:* | Good night |
| *Au revoir:* | Goodbye |

| | |
|---|---|
| *Bon voyage:* | Have a good trip |
| *Bon anniversaire:* | Happy birthday |
| *Bonne année:* | Happy New Year |
| *Bonne chance:* | Good luck |

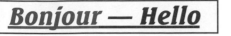

## Comment ça va? — How are you?

Keeping a <u>conversation</u> going is <u>easy</u> if you use a few of these <u>lil' sparklers</u>.

**Comment ça va?** = How are you?

**Comment allez-vous?** = How are you? (Polite)

**Et toi?** = And you? (Informal)

**Et vous?** = And you? (Polite)

'<u>Tu</u>' and '<u>vous</u>' both mean '<u>you</u>' in French. If you're talking to <u>someone older</u> than you, or to a <u>stranger</u>, you <u>usually</u> use '<u>vous</u>'. <u>Only</u> use '<u>tu</u>' if you're talking to <u>friends</u>, <u>family</u> or <u>other young people</u>.

**Other possible answers**

| | |
|---|---|
| *Not good:* | Ça ne va pas bien. |
| *Not bad:* | Pas mal. |
| *I don't know:* | Je ne sais pas. |
| *Great!:* | Super! |
| *I feel fantastic:* | Je me sens fantastique. |
| *I feel good:* | Je me sens bien. |
| *I feel awful:* | Je me sens affreux / affreuse. |
| *OK:* | Comme ci comme ça. |

**Ça va bien, merci.** = (I am) fine, thanks.

You <u>can</u> just say 'Bien, merci' (you might get more <u>marks</u> for the whole thing, though).

See p.16 if you're not well and you need to explain why.

## Puis-je vous présenter Gertrude?

### — May I introduce Gertrude?

Other <u>useful stuff</u> you should know...

**Voici Gertrude .** = This is <u>Gertrude</u>.

**Enchanté(e).** = Pleased to meet you. (Literally 'enchanted')

**Entre. Assieds-toi.** = Come in. Sit down. (Familiar, singular)

**Entrez. Asseyez-vous.** = Come in. Sit down. (Formal or plural)

**Merci bien. C'est très gentil.** = Thank you. That's very kind.

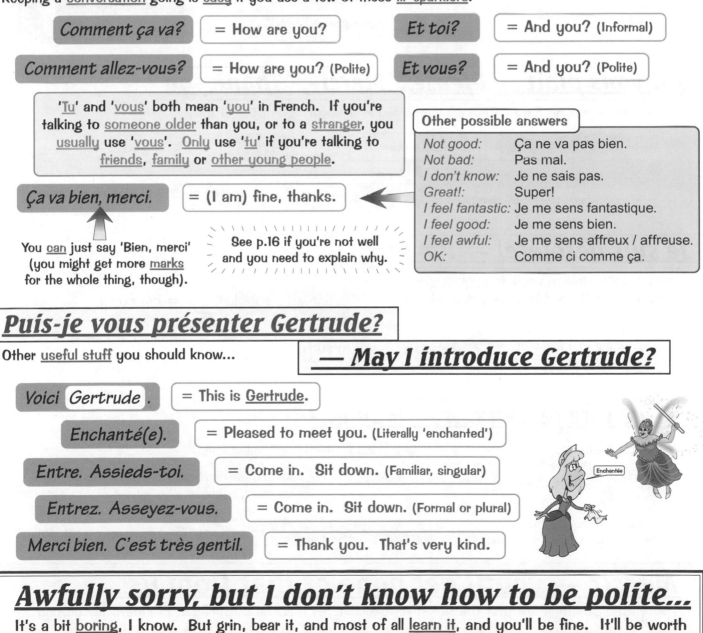

# Awfully sorry, but I don't know how to be polite...

It's a bit <u>boring</u>, I know. But grin, bear it, and most of all <u>learn it</u>, and you'll be fine. It'll be worth it when you can sit there wafting your A* in the air — this is all guaranteed to improve your marks.

# Being Polite

Minding your Ps and Qs (whatever that means). You'll be expected to use appropriate language, so if I can't get away with saying, 'Oh just get on and learn this, Hairy-toes', then you can't get away with rude-isms either.

## Je voudrais — I would like

It's more polite to say 'je voudrais' (I would like) than 'je veux' (I want).

Here's how to say you would like a thing:

| Je voudrais du pain. | = I would like some bread. |

Here's how to say you would like to do something:

| Je voudrais voyager en Europe. |

*She would like:* Elle voudrait

= I would like to travel in Europe.

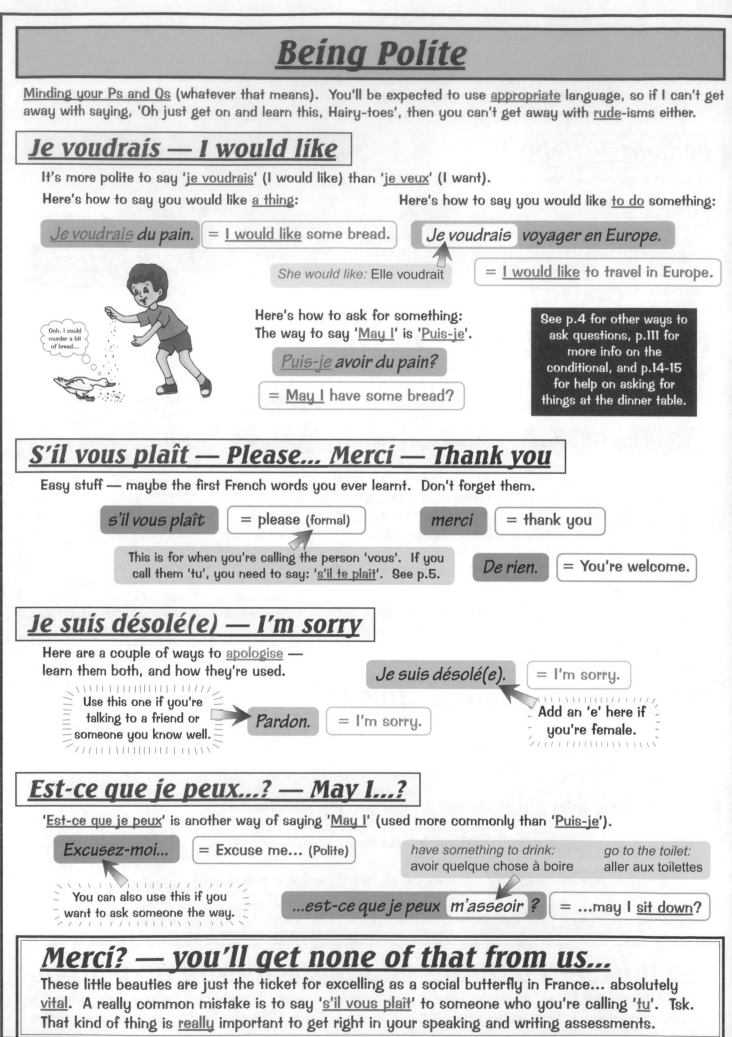

Ooh, I could murder a bit of bread...

Here's how to ask for something:
The way to say 'May I' is 'Puis-je'.

*Puis-je avoir du pain?*

= May I have some bread?

See p.4 for other ways to ask questions, p.111 for more info on the conditional, and p.14-15 for help on asking for things at the dinner table.

## S'il vous plaît — Please... Merci — Thank you

Easy stuff — maybe the first French words you ever learnt. Don't forget them.

| s'il vous plaît | = please (formal) |

| merci | = thank you |

This is for when you're calling the person 'vous'. If you call them 'tu', you need to say: 's'il te plaît'. See p.5.

| De rien. | = You're welcome. |

## Je suis désolé(e) — I'm sorry

Here are a couple of ways to apologise — learn them both, and how they're used.

| Je suis désolé(e). | = I'm sorry. |

Use this one if you're talking to a friend or someone you know well.

| Pardon. | = I'm sorry. |

Add an 'e' here if you're female.

## Est-ce que je peux...? — May I...?

'Est-ce que je peux' is another way of saying 'May I' (used more commonly than 'Puis-je').

| Excusez-moi... | = Excuse me... (Polite) |

You can also use this if you want to ask someone the way.

*have something to drink:*
avoir quelque chose à boire

*go to the toilet:*
aller aux toilettes

| ...est-ce que je peux m'asseoir ? | = ...may I sit down? |

## Merci? — you'll get none of that from us...

These little beauties are just the ticket for excelling as a social butterfly in France... absolutely vital. A really common mistake is to say 's'il vous plaît' to someone who you're calling 'tu'. Tsk. That kind of thing is really important to get right in your speaking and writing assessments.

# Opinions

It pays to have an opinion. <u>Learn how</u> to say what you think... in many different ways. Genius.

## Say what you think — it'll sound impressive...

You'll often be asked what <u>you think</u> of stuff. So get learning these handy phrases.

> Sport? It's great. Just great.

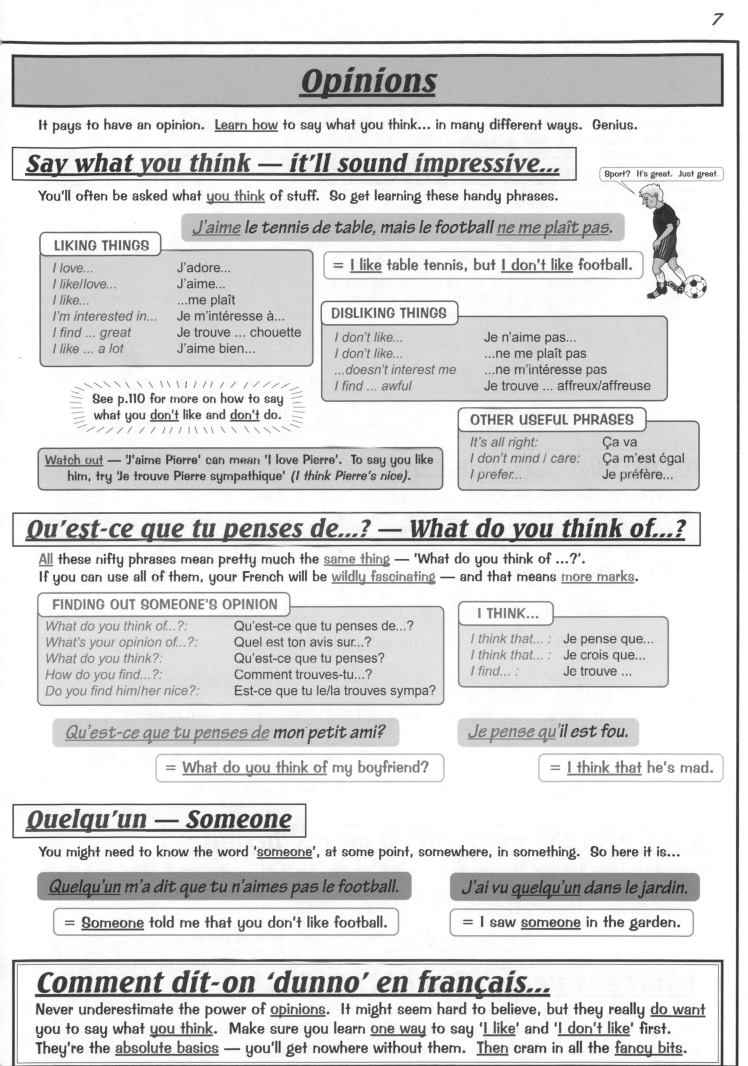

*J'aime le tennis de table, mais le football ne me plaît pas.*

= <u>I like</u> table tennis, but <u>I don't like</u> football.

**LIKING THINGS**

| | |
|---|---|
| *I love...* | J'adore... |
| *I like/love...* | J'aime... |
| *I like...* | ...me plaît |
| *I'm interested in...* | Je m'intéresse à... |
| *I find ... great* | Je trouve ... chouette |
| *I like ... a lot* | J'aime bien... |

*See p.110 for more on how to say what you <u>don't</u> like and <u>don't</u> do.*

<u>Watch out</u> — 'J'aime Pierre' can mean 'I love Pierre'. To say you like him, try 'Je trouve Pierre sympathique' *(I think Pierre's nice).*

**DISLIKING THINGS**

| | |
|---|---|
| *I don't like...* | Je n'aime pas... |
| *I don't like...* | ...ne me plaît pas |
| *...doesn't interest me* | ...ne m'intéresse pas |
| *I find ... awful* | Je trouve ... affreux/affreuse |

**OTHER USEFUL PHRASES**

| | |
|---|---|
| *It's all right:* | Ça va |
| *I don't mind / care:* | Ça m'est égal |
| *I prefer...* | Je préfère... |

## Qu'est-ce que tu penses de...? — What do you think of...?

<u>All</u> these nifty phrases mean pretty much the <u>same thing</u> — 'What do you think of ...?'.
If you can use all of them, your French will be <u>wildly fascinating</u> — and that means <u>more marks</u>.

**FINDING OUT SOMEONE'S OPINION**

| | |
|---|---|
| *What do you think of...?:* | Qu'est-ce que tu penses de...? |
| *What's your opinion of...?:* | Quel est ton avis sur...? |
| *What do you think?:* | Qu'est-ce que tu penses? |
| *How do you find...?:* | Comment trouves-tu...? |
| *Do you find him/her nice?:* | Est-ce que tu le/la trouves sympa? |

**I THINK...**

| | |
|---|---|
| *I think that... :* | Je pense que... |
| *I think that... :* | Je crois que... |
| *I find... :* | Je trouve ... |

*Qu'est-ce que tu penses de mon petit ami?*

= <u>What do you think of</u> my boyfriend?

*Je pense qu'il est fou.*

= <u>I think that</u> he's mad.

## Quelqu'un — Someone

You might need to know the word '<u>someone</u>', at some point, somewhere, in something. So here it is...

*Quelqu'un m'a dit que tu n'aimes pas le football.*

= <u>Someone</u> told me that you don't like football.

*J'ai vu quelqu'un dans le jardin.*

= I saw <u>someone</u> in the garden.

## Comment dit-on 'dunno' en français...

Never underestimate the power of <u>opinions</u>. It might seem hard to believe, but they really <u>do want</u> you to say what <u>you think</u>. Make sure you learn <u>one way</u> to say '<u>I like</u>' and '<u>I don't like</u>' first. They're the <u>absolute basics</u> — you'll get nowhere without them. <u>Then</u> cram in all the <u>fancy bits</u>.

# Opinions

Don't just say that you like or hate something — really blow your teacher away by explaining why.
Go for it — and knock their socks clean off.

## Use these words to describe things

Here's a whole load of words to describe things you like or don't like.
They're dead easy to use, so it really is worth learning them.

> Describing words are adjectives.
> See p.88-90 for more on this.

| | | | | | |
|---|---|---|---|---|---|
| *good:* | bon(ne) | *fantastic:* | formidable / fantastique | *marvellous:* | merveilleux / merveilleuse |
| *great:* | super / chouette | *interesting:* | intéressant(e) | *bad:* | mauvais(e) |
| *beautiful:* | beau / belle | *brilliant:* | génial(e) / super | *awful:* | affreux / affreuse |
| *friendly:* | amical(e) | *nice (person):* | sympa / sympathique | *boring:* | ennuyeux/ennuyeuse |
| *splendid:* | magnifique | *nice / kind:* | gentil(le) | | |

**Bob** est **super** .

= Bob is great.

**Les filles** sont **affreuses** .

= The girls are awful.

## For 'because' say 'parce que'

To make your opinion more convincing, give a reason for it. The best way
to do that is to use the handy phrase 'parce que' — 'because'.

*J'aime bien ce film, parce que les acteurs sont formidables.*

= I like this film a lot, because the actors are fantastic.

*Je trouve ce film affreux, parce que l'histoire est ennuyeuse.*

= I think this film is awful, because the story is boring.

*J'adore jouer du violon, parce que je trouve la musique classique très belle.*

= I love playing the violin, because I find classical music very beautiful.

*Le rugby me plaît beaucoup, parce que l'ambiance dans mon équipe est très amicale.*

= I really like rugby, because the atmosphere in my team is very friendly.

Extra marks
for style

## If you hear the word 'car', it means 'because'

It's handy to know that 'car', like 'parce que', means 'because' (or 'for'). Nothing to do with cars at all.

*Elle est très fatiguée, car elle travaille tout le temps.*

= She is very tired, because she works all the time.

## What's your opinion of French, then...

It's not much cop only knowing how to ask someone else's opinion, or how to say 'I think', without
being able to say what and why you think. All these phrases are easy — just stick them together
to get a sentence. Just make sure you don't say something daft like 'I hate it because it's lovely'.

# What Do You Think of...?

To boost your grade, you need to give your opinions. 'Boost' is such a fun word, I think — it never gets enough coverage, so I'll use it again... learn this, do well and boost away.

## Use 'je trouve...' to give your opinion

Giving opinions is really important in French. It shows that you can be creative with the language.

I think it's safe...

Je trouve **ce groupe** **magnifique**. = I think this group is splendid.

this team: cette équipe
this magazine: ce magazine
this music: cette musique

bad: mauvais(e)
boring: ennuyeux/ennuyeuse
quite good: assez bon(ne)

Use these adjectives and the others on page 8 to give your opinion.

## Est-ce que tu aimes...? — Do you like...?

You'll also need to be able to understand other people's opinions.

Est-ce que tu aimes **ce groupe** ?

this film: ce film      this book: ce livre
this newspaper: ce journal      this programme: cette émission

= Do you like this group?

it: le/la    For more on object pronouns, see p.96.

Je n'aime pas ce groupe. Je **le** trouve **mauvais**.

= I don't like this group. I think they're bad.

These are linked. If the first bit is masculine, then the second bit must be masculine too. If the thing was feminine, it would be 'la' and mauvaise.

Je trouve ce journal **ennuyeux**. Et toi?

= I think this newspaper is boring. What do you think?

We need a rethink, Liam.

Use any of the adjectives at the top of p.8.

This is a good way of asking informally whether somebody agrees with what you've just said.

Moi aussi, je le trouve ennuyeux. = I think it's boring, too.

## But no one says "splendid" any more...

Giving your opinion about things gets you big marks in the assessments. It's quite easy to say why you like something, so you've got no excuses — you've just got to learn these phrases.

# Writing Informal Letters

I just know you're gonna be <u>chuffed</u> to bits when I tell you that you'll probably have to write a letter in French at some point — it could very easily be in your written assessment.

## Start a letter with 'Cher Bob' — 'Dear Bob'

Learn the <u>layout</u> of letters, and how to say 'Dear Blank...' and all that stuff. It's essential. This letter's short on content, but it shows you how to <u>start</u> and <u>end</u> it properly, and where to put the <u>date</u>.

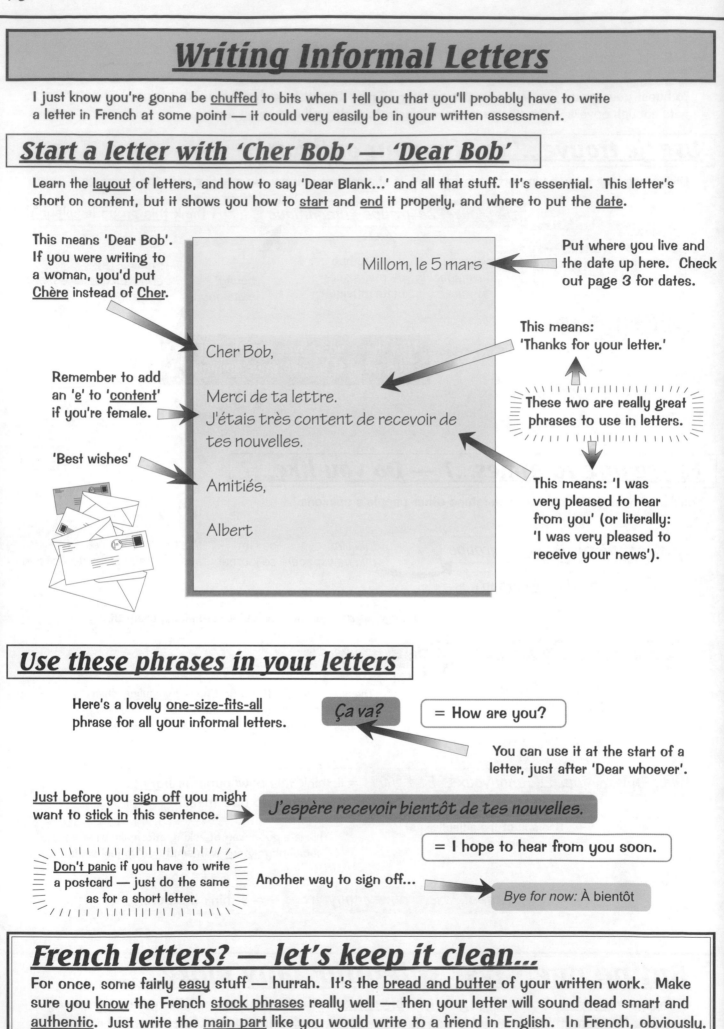

This means 'Dear Bob'. If you were writing to a woman, you'd put <u>Chère</u> instead of <u>Cher</u>.

Remember to add an '<u>e</u>' to '<u>content</u>' if you're female.

'Best wishes'

Millom, le 5 mars

Cher Bob,

Merci de ta lettre.
J'étais très content de recevoir de tes nouvelles.

Amitiés,

Albert

Put where you live and the date up here. Check out page 3 for dates.

This means: 'Thanks for your letter.'

These two are really great phrases to use in letters.

This means: 'I was very pleased to hear from you' (or literally: 'I was very pleased to receive your news').

## Use these phrases in your letters

Here's a lovely <u>one-size-fits-all</u> phrase for all your informal letters.

Ça va?

= How are you?

You can use it at the start of a letter, just after 'Dear whoever'.

<u>Just before</u> you <u>sign off</u> you might want to <u>stick in</u> this sentence.

J'espère recevoir bientôt de tes nouvelles.

= I hope to hear from you soon.

<u>Don't panic</u> if you have to write a postcard — just do the same as for a short letter.

Another way to sign off...

Bye for now: À bientôt

## French letters? — let's keep it clean...

For once, some fairly <u>easy</u> stuff — hurrah. It's the <u>bread and butter</u> of your written work. Make sure you <u>know</u> the French <u>stock phrases</u> really well — then your letter will sound dead smart and <u>authentic</u>. Just write the <u>main part</u> like you would write to a friend in English. In French, obviously.

# Writing Formal Letters

You may be asked to write a <u>formal</u> letter as well — it's a bit mean, but sadly you've <u>no choice</u>. On the plus side, you might have to write a <u>letter of complaint</u> — who doesn't love a rant in a foreign language... Study the basic format below and practise creating some formal correspondence of your own.

## Put your name and address at the top left

The <u>name and address</u> of who you're writing to goes here.

Letters — they really are just as <u>simple</u> as this...

It looks impressive if you put <u>your</u> name and address at the top. (In French, the addresses go the <u>opposite</u> way round to in English — <u>sender</u> on the <u>left</u>, <u>recipient</u> on the <u>right</u>.)

Put this if you <u>don't know</u> the person's name or gender. If you know it's Monsieur Claude Terrier, put that above his address and write 'Monsieur' here.

This <u>little lot</u> simply <u>means</u>: I spent two nights at the Saint Michel Hotel between the 12th and the 14th of April. The employees were great, very kind and welcoming and the room was clean.

Unfortunately, I'm not at all satisfied with my stay because the shower didn't work, the TV was broken and there was too much noise everywhere, so I didn't sleep very well.

> Aleesha Thompson
> 16 Rusland Drive
> Manchester
> M14 7ZN
> Grande-Bretagne
>
>                                               Hôtel Saint Michel
>                                            16, rue des Papillons
>                                                       Paris
>                                                       France
>
>                                   le 20 avril, 2009
>
> Monsieur / Madame,
>
> J'ai passé deux nuits à l'Hôtel Saint Michel entre le 12 ct le 14 avril. Les employés étaient super, très agréables et accueillants, et la chambre était propre.
>
> Malheureusement, je ne suis pas du tout satisfaite de mon séjour parce que la douche n'a pas fonctionné, la télévision était cassée et il y avait trop de bruit partout, donc je n'ai pas très bien dormi.
>
> Veuillez agréer, Monsieur/Madame, l'expression de mes sentiments distingués.
>
> *A. Thompson*
> Aleesha Thompson

Put the date here.

Yours faithfully / sincerely

> *Check out page 58 for <u>problems vocab</u> and page 83 for help writing a <u>job application letter</u>.*

## Learn these ways to end a letter

This <u>set ending</u> is quite long, I'm afraid — just <u>learn it</u> and churn it out.

*to a woman:* Madame

> *Je vous prie d'agréer,* | Monsieur | *, l'expression de mes sentiments distingués.*

= Yours faithfully / sincerely

Another <u>useful</u> phrase:     *Je vous remercie d'avance.*     = Many thanks in advance.

## How to end a letter — just stop writing...

I know, I know — <u>letter structure</u> needs a lot of <u>effort</u> to get it firmly lodged in your brain. And then there are <u>set polite phrases</u> for formal French letters just like there are in English — it's <u>essential</u> to know the right ones for the <u>start</u> and <u>end</u>. Have a go at writing some practice letters.

# Revision Summary

This section includes all the <u>absolute</u> basics... with a few lessons in <u>letter writing</u> thrown in for good measure. All the bits on your <u>opinions</u>, and on <u>dates</u> and <u>times</u> (including today, tomorrow, every week, on Mondays etc.) can make a huge <u>difference</u> to your marks. Go back over and <u>over the section</u> again until you can answer every single one of the questions here first time — sans hésitation.

1) Count out loud from 1 to 20 in French.

2) How do you say these numbers in French?  a) 22  b) 35  c) 58  d) 71  e) 112

3) What are these in French?  a) 1st  b) 4th  c) 7th  d) 19th  e) 25th  f) 52nd

4) Ask 'What time is it?' in French.
   How would you say these times in French?  a) 5:00  b) 10:30  c) 13:22  d) 16:45

5) Say all the days of the week in French, from Monday to Sunday.

6) How do you say these in French?  a) yesterday  b) today  c) tomorrow

7) Say all of the months of the year in French, from January to December.

8) How do you say the <u>date</u> of your birthday in French?

9) 'Qu'est-ce que tu fais <u>ce soir</u>?' means 'What are you doing <u>this evening</u>?'
   Say in French, 'What are you doing: a) this afternoon?'  b) this morning?'  c) next week?'

10) 'Tu chantes' means 'You sing' or 'You are singing'. What do these questions mean?
    a) Pourquoi tu chantes?  b) Où est-ce que tu chantes?  c) Qu'est-ce que tu chantes?
    d) Chantes-tu bien?  e) Quand est-ce que tu chantes?  f) Est-ce que tu chantes?

11) Give the French for:  a) Please  b) Thank you  c) How are you?  d) I'm sorry  e) May I...

12) How would you ask someone what they think of Elvis Presley?  (In French.)
    Give as many ways of asking it as you can.

13) How would you say these things in French?  Give at least one way to say each of them.
    a) I like Elvis Presley.  b) I don't like Elvis Presley.  c) I find Elvis Presley interesting.
    d) I love Elvis Presley.  e) I find Elvis Presley awful.  f) I think that Elvis Presley is fantastic.

14) To win this week's star prize, complete the following sentence in
    10 words or fewer (in French):  'I like Elvis Presley because...'

15) You like the group 'The Sheep Shearers', but you think 'James and the Infinite Monkeys'
    are brilliant. How would you tell someone that in French? (Leave the band names in English.)

16) Write a letter to your friend Marie-Claire. Write your address, say hello and tell her something
    you've done. You would like to hear from her soon — how would you say that in your letter?

17) Which side of the page does your address go on in a formal French letter?

18) How would you end a formal letter in French?

19) What does this phrase mean: 'Je vous remercie d'avance'? Is it for a formal or informal letter?

# Food

You need to learn the vocab for all the basic food, especially the things you like and eat often. There's a lot of information to digest here, but the more you know, the better.

## L'épicerie et la boucherie — Greengrocer's and Butcher's

This is basic, meat and two veg vocab. You really do need to know it.

**VEGETABLES: les légumes (masc.)**

| potato: | la pomme de terre |
|---|---|
| carrot: | la carotte |
| tomato: | la tomate |
| cucumber: | le concombre |
| onion: | l'oignon (masc.) |
| cauliflower: | le chou-fleur |
| French beans: | les haricots verts |
| lettuce: | la salade / la laitue |
| mushroom: | le champignon |
| cabbage: | le chou |
| peas: | les petits pois |

**MEATS: les viandes (fem.)**

| pork: | le porc | lamb: | l'agneau (masc.) |
|---|---|---|---|
| sausage: | la saucisse | chicken: | le poulet |
| salami: | le saucisson | veal: | le veau |
| ham: | le jambon | duck: | le canard |

| beef: | le bœuf |
|---|---|
| steak: | le bifteck |
| rare: | saignant |
| medium: | à point |
| bien cuit: | well done |

**SEA FOOD: les fruits de mer (masc.)**

| fish: | le poisson | trout: | la truite |
|---|---|---|---|
| salmon: | le saumon | prawn / shrimp: | la crevette |
| oyster: | l'huître (fem.) | | |

## Les boissons et les desserts — Drinks and Desserts

Every decent meal needs a dessert and a drink.

**DRINKS: les boissons (fem.)**

| tea: | le thé |
|---|---|
| coffee: | le café |
| beer: | la bière |
| cider: | le cidre |
| wine: | le vin |
| cola: | le coca |
| fruit juice: | le jus de fruit |
| lemonade: | la limonade |
| mineral water: | l'eau minérale (fem.) |

**DESSERTS: les desserts (masc.)**

| cake: | le gâteau |
|---|---|
| biscuit: | le biscuit |
| ice cream: | la glace |
| pancake: | la crêpe |
| yogurt: | le yaourt |
| jam: | la confiture |
| chocolate: | le chocolat |
| sweets: | les bonbons |

**FRUITS: les fruits (masc.)**

| apple: | la pomme |
|---|---|
| banana: | la banane |
| strawberry: | la fraise |
| raspberry: | la framboise |
| grapefruit: | le pamplemousse |
| cherry: | la cerise |
| pineapple: | l'ananas (masc.) |
| apricot: | l'abricot (masc.) |
| plum: | la prune |
| peach: | la pêche |
| pear: | la poire |
| lemon: | le citron |

## D'autres aliments — Other foods

Here are some more basic foods and some French specialities you might want to try — learn them really well.

**OTHER FOODS: d'autres aliments (masc.)**

| bread: | le pain | sugar: | le sucre | soup: | la soupe |
|---|---|---|---|---|---|
| milk: | le lait | salt: | le sel | pasta: | les pâtes (fem.) |
| cream: | la crème | pepper: | le poivre | cereals: | les céréales (fem.) |
| butter: | le beurre | vinegar: | le vinaigre | chips: | les frites (fem.) |
| cheese: | le fromage | flour: | la farine | crisps: | les chips (fem.) |
| egg: | l'œuf (masc.) | rice: | le riz | nuts: | les noix (fem.) |

**SPECIALITIES: les spécialités (fem.)**

| croissant: | le croissant | potatoes with cheese topping: | le gratin dauphinois |
|---|---|---|---|
| snails: | les escargots (masc.) | roast leg of lamb: | le gigot d'agneau rôti |
| salad starter: | les crudités (fem.) | chop, cutlet: | la côtelette |

## Learn the crêpe out of this page...

A lot of foods are easy to remember in French — like le biscuit, la crème, le café... But some aren't — you just have to learn the tricky ones. Have a good look at the French specialities too. Always order the gratin dauphinois (sliced potato baked with cream — mmm). Snails though — geesh...

# Mealtimes

You can use the vocab on this page to behave <u>appropriately</u> at the dinner table. Or just grunt, grab the food and slurp it down in front of an episode of "When dishwashers attack". That's what I do.

## Voudriez-vous...? — Would you like...?

This is another form of that useful verb '<u>vouloir</u>'.

> 'Voudriez' is in the conditional — see p. 111.

**Voudriez-vous** le sel **?** = Would you like <u>the salt</u>?

*the pepper:* le poivre   *the wine:* le vin   *the butter:* le beurre

**Est-ce que je peux vous passer** une serviette **?** = Can I pass you <u>a napkin</u>?

*to drink:* boire

**Voudriez-vous** manger **?** = Would you like <u>to eat</u>?

Either '<u>Oui, je veux bien</u>' or '<u>Oui, merci</u>' sound more French than '<u>Oui, s'il vous plaît</u>'.

**Oui, je veux bien.** = Yes please.   **Non, merci.** = No thanks.

## Est-ce que tu as faim ou soif? — Are you hungry or thirsty?

Questions like these are <u>important</u>. Make <u>sure</u> you understand them, or you may go hungry... or lose marks.

**Est-ce que tu as** faim **?** = Are you <u>hungry</u>?

*thirsty:* soif

**J'ai** faim **.** = I'm <u>hungry</u>.

*thirsty:* soif

**Non, je n'ai pas** faim **.** = No, I'm not hungry.

## Pourriez-vous...? — Could you...?

Here are two <u>dead nifty</u> phrases to <u>learn</u>. Use them <u>properly</u> and you'll be the soul of politeness.

**Est-ce que je peux avoir** le sel **, s'il vous plaît?** = May I have <u>the salt</u>, please?

*a napkin:* une serviette   *the sugar:* le sucre

**Pourriez-vous me passer** le poivre **, s'il vous plaît?** = Could you pass me <u>the pepper</u>, please?

## You'd like the salt? Just help your sel...

Make sure you remain polite in French at <u>all</u> times... You never know who might be listening. This stuff is likely to crop up in your <u>listening exam</u>, so make sure that you've got the hang of it and that you can recognise it when you hear it. It'll earn you brownie points in France, too — bonus.

# Mealtimes

For top marks this stuff can be really useful. And it's useful in tons of different situations too. Bonus.

## Je ne mange pas de... — I don't eat...

Je suis désolé(e). Je ne mange pas de petits pois . = I'm sorry. I don't eat peas.

always: toujours

no longer: plus
never: jamais

meat: viande (fem.)

See p.13 for more foods.

Je mange souvent des fruits. J'adore les fruits. = I often eat fruit. I love fruit.

Je suis végétarien(ne) / végétalien(ne) . = I'm a vegetarian / vegan.

## Vous dînez en famille? — Do you eat with your family?

Now show that you can link the family and food topics.

See p.22 for more family members.

On mange toujours en famille . = We always eat as a family.

at the same time: en même temps     separately: séparémont

Mon père travaille tard , donc il n'est pas possible de manger ensemble.

My mother: Ma mère
My sister: Ma sœur
My brother: Mon frère

goes to the gym: va au gymnase
has a football match: a un match de foot
is going ice skating: va à la patinoire

= My dad works late, so it's not possible to eat together.

## If you only want a little, ask for 'un peu'

These amount words are dead useful.

a bit: un peu

Je voudrais beaucoup de sucre, s'il vous plaît. = I would like lots of sugar, please.

Je voudrais un grand morceau de gâteau. = I would like a big piece of cake.

J'ai assez mangé, merci. = I've eaten enough, thanks.

a lot: beaucoup     trop: too much

Ça suffit. = That's enough.

For more quantities look at page 38.

## Est-ce que ça vous a plu? — Did you like it?

You'd get asked this question in most restaurants and it might pop up in your listening exam.

Le repas était bon . 

very good: très bon
bad: mauvais
very bad: très mauvais
delicious: délicieux

Le repas n'était pas bon.

= The meal was good.

= The meal wasn't good.

## Que c'est bon, que c'est bon...

I for one seriously love French food. They're really big on high-quality, fresh produce. You can see that just by going round a French market. The fruit stalls look like a beautiful Renoir painting.

# Feeling Ill

Pain, illness and suffering — more fun and frolics from those full-of-glee examiners. I suppose if setting the exams every year is as mind-numbing as taking them, it's not surprising they aren't too chirpy.

## Comment ça va? — How are you?

Je suis malade.   = I feel ill.

Je ne me sens pas bien.   = I don't feel well.

*to the hospital:* à l'hôpital (masc.)
*to the chemist's:* à la pharmacie

Je dois aller voir le médecin .   = I need to go to see the doctor.

## Où as-tu mal? — Where does it hurt?

Here's how you say what bit hurts...

J'ai mal à l'estomac .   = I have stomach ache.

You can use 'j'ai mal à' with any part of your body that's hurting...

*a headache:* mal à la tête   *a sore throat:* mal à la gorge
*backache:* mal au dos   *earache:* mal à l'oreille

Use 'au' for 'le' words, 'à la' for 'la' words, 'à l'' for words starting with a vowel or a silent 'h', and 'aux' for plurals.

*My arms:* Mes bras (masc.)
*My ears:* Mes oreilles (fem.)
*My head:* Ma tête

Mon doigt me fait mal .   = My finger hurts / has been hurting.

*hurt (plural):* font mal

Je me suis cassé le bras.   = I've broken my arm.

J'ai le mal de mer.   = I'm seasick.

Je tousse beaucoup.   = I'm coughing a lot.

## Pouvez-vous me donner quelque chose?
## — Can you give me something?

Pouvez-vous me donner un médicament ?   = Can you give me some medicine?

*some tablets:* des comprimés (masc.)
*some aspirin:* de l'aspirine (fem.)
*an injection:* une piqûre

Ça va mieux.   = I feel better.

Ça va bien .   = I feel well.

# Not the most upbeat page in the book...

This feeling ill vocab might come up in the exam or one of the tasks. Or then again, it might not. Much in the same way that Daniel Craig may or may not propose to me this year. There's no way of knowing — so you'd best keep learning this stuff and I'll keep hoping. Best learn it just in case.

# Health and Health Issues

These next three pages are a bit like PSHE in French — you lucky, lucky people. You probably have an <u>opinion</u> on this stuff already. Some of the French vocab and expressions are a bit tricky though.

## Qu'est-ce que tu fais pour rester en bonne santé?

**Pour rester en bonne santé ...**

= To stay healthy ...

### What do you do to stay healthy?

**Je fais beaucoup de sport pour ...**

= I play a lot of sport to ...

| | |
|---|---|
| *I eat lots of vegetables:* | je mange beaucoup de légumes. |
| *I rarely eat chocolate:* | je mange rarement du chocolat. |
| *I drink water often:* | je bois souvent de l'eau. |

| | |
|---|---|
| *keep fit:* | rester en forme. |
| *have fun:* | m'amuser. |

**Je ne fais rien parce que ...**

= I do nothing because ...

| | |
|---|---|
| *exercising is boring:* | faire de l'exercice, c'est ennuyeux. |
| *I don't have time:* | je n'ai pas le temps. |
| *I'm already perfect:* | je suis déjà parfait(e). |

**Je suis au régime. Je ne mange que de l'alimentation saine.**

= I'm on a diet. I only eat healthy food.

## L'obésité est devenue un grand problème

Here's how to give your opinion on <u>expanding waistlines</u>...

### Obesity has become a big problem

**Il est  triste  de voir des enfants  très  gros.**

= It's <u>sad</u> to see <u>very</u> fat children.

*awful:* affreux   *depressing:* déprimant   *extremely:* extrèmement   *really:* vraiment

**Ils mangent trop de matières grasses.**

= They eat too much fat.

**À mon avis, c'est la faute  de la publicité .**

In my opinion, it's the fault <u>of advertising</u>.

*of society:* de la société   *of the parents:* des parents

## Il y a des gens qui ne mangent pas suffisamment

### Some people don't eat enough

**Beaucoup de gens pensent qu'il faut être maigre comme les mannequins.**

= Many people think it's necessary to be thin like models.

**Il y a des filles qui pensent à leur taille tout le temps, mais ce n'est pas sain.**

= There are girls who think about their size all the time, but it's not healthy.

**Il faut bien manger, et mener une vie active.**

= You have to eat well and lead an active life.

## Get your 5 a day — no, not 5 doughnuts...

Seriously, there's loads of stuff on this page that could easily come up somewhere in the <u>assessments</u>. Some of the 'opinions' stuff is quite tricky, but you need to be <u>ready for anything</u>.

# Health and Health Issues

Drugs, booze and fags. Enjoy.

## Qu'est-ce que tu penses du tabagisme?

This stuff's relevant for <u>drugs</u> and <u>alcohol</u> — so learn the <u>vocab</u> in the pale boxes too.

## What do you think of smoking?

Je ne fume pas.    = I don't smoke.

*Alcohol:* L'alcool (masc.)    *drink:* boivent

Le tabagisme , c'est dégoûtant. Je déteste quand les autres fument , c'est vraiment impoli. Je ne sortirais jamais avec un fumeur / une fumeuse .

*alcoholic:*   un/une alcoolique

= <u>Smoking</u> is disgusting. I hate it when others <u>smoke</u>, it's really impolite. I'd never go out with <u>a smoker</u>.

Il est interdit de fumer dans les lieux publics.

J'aime fumer.    = I like smoking.

Quand je fume, je me détends. Je sais que ce n'est pas sain, mais je pense que c'est cool.

= When I smoke, I relax. I know it's unhealthy, but I think it's cool.

*drink:* bois

Je fume mais je ne deviendrais jamais toxicomane . C'est trop dangereux.

= I <u>smoke</u> but <u>I would never become a drug addict</u>. It's too dangerous.

*I would never drink:* je ne boirais jamais
*I would never smoke:* je ne fumerais jamais

= It's forbidden to smoke in public places.

## J'ai arrêté de fumer il y a un an — I stopped smoking a year ago

Pourquoi avez-vous décidé d'arrêter ?    = Why did you decide to stop?

*to give up:* de renoncer

Je commençais à avoir des problèmes de santé.    = <u>I was starting to have health problems.</u>

| | |
|---|---|
| *I had trouble breathing, especially when doing sport:* | J'avais du mal à respirer, surtout en faisant du sport. |
| *I was always out of breath:* | J'étais toujours hors d'haleine. |
| *I couldn't afford it. There's too much tax on tobacco:* | Ça me coûtait trop cher. Il y a trop de taxe sur le tabac. |
| *My boyfriend/girlfriend doesn't like it when I smoke/drink:* | Mon copain/Ma copine n'aime pas quand je fume/bois. |

Mon grand-père a eu une crise cardiaque à cause du tabagisme.    = My grandfather had a heart attack due to smoking.

*lung cancer:* un cancer du poumon

## What a cheerful page...

When I was learning French, I always used to get <u>confused</u> between '<u>haleine</u>', which means '<u>breath</u>' and '<u>baleine</u>', which means '<u>whale</u>'. Luckily 'baleine' isn't on your vocab list so you'll be just fine...

# Health and Health Issues

More of the <u>same</u>. Just slightly trickier (and therefore <u>more sophisticated</u>) things to say...

## L'alcoolisme est un grand problème pour les jeunes
## Alcoholism is a big problem for young people

Beaucoup de jeunes britanniques boivent trop d'alcool.

= Lots of young British people drink too much alcohol.

Les gens ivres font des choses dangereuses.

= Drunk people do dangerous things.

L'alcool provoque des maladies du foie.

= Alcohol causes liver disease.

Il est interdit d'acheter des boissons alcoolisées, si on a moins de 18 ans.

= It's against the law to buy alcoholic drinks if you're under 18.

## La drogue est dangereuse — Drugs are dangerous

Je n'aime pas quand mes ami(e)s se droguent.

= I don't like it when my friends take drugs.

Certains jeunes se droguent parce qu'ils veulent se détendre.

= Some young people take drugs because they want to relax.

Quelquefois les drogués volent pour acheter de la drogue.

Don't forget — "la drogue" in French means "drugs" in English — it's <u>singular</u>.

= Sometimes drug addicts steal to buy drugs.

Les revendeurs sont souvent violents.

= The dealers are often violent.

## La drogue dans le sport — Drugs in sport

Often a big talking-point for the French, this. Especially when the <u>Tour de France</u> is on.

La drogue est un problème dans le cyclisme.

= Drugs are a problem in <u>cycling</u>.

athletics: l'athlétisme (masc.)

athletes: athlètes  players: joueurs

= It's not fair for the majority of <u>cyclists</u> who don't cheat.

Ce n'est pas juste pour la majorité des cyclistes qui ne trichent pas.

## Performance-enhancing revision guides are OK...

There's loads you might want to say about these <u>exciting</u> topics, but learning the stuff on this page is a <u>good</u> start. <u>Think</u> about what else you might want to say, write it down, and <u>practise</u> it.

*Section 2 — Lifestyle (Food and Health)*

# Revision Summary

So that's the end of AQA's take on 'health', then. Phew. By now you should be able to deal with most food situations that come up in the reading and listening, as well as talk for hours about how you run five miles before breakfast and eat fourteen bags of chips a day. Test yourself with these handy little questions just to make sure, though.

1) You're making fruit salad for a party. Think of as many different fruits as you can to put into it — and write down at least 5 in French. Make a list (in French) of 5 drinks for the party, too.

2) Your hosts are offering you more chocolate cake. Decline politely and say the meal was delicious. Offer to pass your hostess the milk for her coffee.

3) Write down how you'd say that you like vegetables but you don't like sausages. You don't eat meat any more and you're hungry.

4) How would you say in French that your mother works late so you eat separately?

5) Sophie says "Je suis malade. J'ai mal à la tête." What is she saying?

6) Write down in French "Can you give me some aspirin?"

7) Est-ce que tu es en bonne santé? Pourquoi? Pourquoi pas?

8) Write down 3 sentences in French about obesity and healthy eating.

9) Write down the French words or phrases for:

    a) fat (in food)    b) to keep fit    c) an active life

10) How would you say in French "I eat lots of sausages and I rarely eat vegetables".

11) Jean-Luc says "Je ne bois pas. Mes amis boivent beaucoup, et ils pensent que c'est cool." What is he saying?

12) You stopped smoking a year ago. Say this in French, and give a reason why you gave up.

13) What do the following French words and phrases mean?

    a) une crise cardiaque    b) le cancer du poumon    c) hors d'haleine

14) How would you say in French that it's against the law to buy cigarettes if you're under 18?

15) What is the French for the following words or phrases?

    a) drug addict    b) drugs    c) drunk    d) alcohol

16) Translate this conversation between Marie and Christophe about drugs into English:

    M:    Je pense que la drogue est un grand problème dans l'athlétisme.

    C:    Je suis d'accord. Et ce n'est pas juste pour la majorité des athlètes.

    M:    Tu as raison, parce que la majorité des athlètes ne trichent pas.

    C:    Si j'étais un athlète, je ne me droguerais jamais.

# About Yourself

You might already know some of this stuff, but it's <u>ultra-important</u>, so make sure you know it back to front. Talking about yourself in your speaking or writing assessment — it's pretty much a dead cert.

## Parle-moi de toi-même — Tell me about yourself

These are the <u>basics</u>. <u>Learn</u> them <u>all</u>.

*What are you called?:* Comment tu t'appelles?

Je m'appelle Angela . = I'm called <u>Angela</u>.

*How old are you?:* Quel âge as-tu?

J'ai quinze ans . = I'm <u>15 years old</u>.

*When is your birthday?:* Quand est ton anniversaire?

Mon anniversaire est le douze décembre . = My birthday is the <u>12th of December</u>.

> See pages 64-65 for where you live, page 1 for more numbers and page 3 for more dates.

*Where do you live?:* Où habites-tu?

J'habite à Lancaster . = I live in <u>Lancaster</u>.

*What do you like?:* Qu'est-ce que tu aimes?

J'aime le football . = I like <u>football</u>.

> You can use this to say you like anything, but be careful: 'Je t'aime' means 'I love you'.

## Comment es-tu? — What are you like?

You have to <u>describe</u> how gorgeous you are as well.

Je suis grand(e) . = I am <u>tall</u>.

J'ai les yeux marron . = I have <u>brown</u> eyes.

short: petit(e)
fat: gros(se)
thin: maigre
slim: mince

*medium height:* de taille moyenne

> For more colours, see page 39.

blue: bleus
green: verts

> 'Marron' is a strange adjective — it doesn't need an 's' on the end even though 'yeux' is plural.

J'ai les cheveux longs . = I have <u>long</u> hair.

short: courts
quite long: assez longs
curly: bouclés

dark: foncés    red: roux
light: clairs    black: noirs
blond: blonds    brown: bruns

> England
> Dear Simon,
> I am a sixteen-year-old-girl with blackish hair, fair skin and brown eyes.

## Comment ça s'écrit? — How do you spell that?

You may have to <u>spell</u> your name and home town letter by letter in your <u>speaking assessments</u>. Here's how to <u>pronounce</u> the letters of the French <u>alphabet</u>. Practise going through it <u>out loud</u> — yes, you'll sound daft, but you'd sound dafter getting it wrong.

| | | |
|---|---|---|
| A — ah (like in 'car') | J — jee ('j' like 'g' in 'beige') | S — ess |
| B — bay | K — kah | T — tay |
| C — say | L — ell | U — ue (as in 'tu') |
| D — day | M — em | V — vay |
| E — eu (like in 'peu') | N — en | W — doob-le-vay |
| F — eff | O — oh | X — eex |
| G — jay ('j' like 'g' in 'beige') | P — pay | Y — ee-grek |
| H — ash | Q — kue ('ue' like in 'tu') | Z — zed |
| I — ee (like in 'me') | R — air | |

é — aigu       ç — cédille
è — grave      ï — tréma
ê — circonflexe

> For letters with accents, you just say the letter followed by the accent, so 'â' would be 'ah circonflexe'.

## I'm tall, handsome, witty, a compulsive liar...

<u>Learn</u> the ins and outs of describing yourself, and make <u>darn sure</u> you know the French alphabet. It's the kind of thing that could crop up in the <u>listening</u> exam — e.g. there'll be someone saying they're from a <u>random French town</u> you won't have heard of, and then they'll <u>spell it out</u>.

# Family and Pets

You might have to talk or write about your <u>family</u> situation and your <u>pets</u> — it's best to be prepared...

## J'ai une sœur — I have one sister

To <u>describe</u> your family structure, use these sentences:

J'ai <u>deux</u> frère<u>s</u> et une sœur . = I have two <u>brothers</u> and one <u>sister</u>.

Ils s'appellent Jack, Henry et Charlotte. = They are called Jack, Henry and Charlotte.

'Ils' is used for a group of <u>males</u> or a <u>mixture</u> of males and females.

*a girlfriend:* une petite amie

J'ai <u>un petit ami</u> . = I have <u>a boyfriend</u>.

Je suis célibataire. = I am single.

*The average family*

## Ma sœur / Mon frère est... — My sister / brother is...

Remember, <u>detail</u> is key in the assessments. Use these phrases to <u>describe</u> your family in more <u>detail</u>:

Il a douze ans. = <u>He</u>'s 12 years old.

Elle a les yeux <u>bleus</u> . = <u>She</u> has <u>blue</u> eyes.

| | | | | | |
|---|---|---|---|---|---|
| My father: | Mon père | My male cousin: | Mon cousin | My girlfriend: | Ma petite amie/ma copine |
| My brother: | Mon frère | My female cousin: | Ma cousine | My boyfriend: | Mon petit ami/mon copain |
| My sister: | Ma sœur | My stepmother: | Ma belle-mère | | |
| My mother: | Ma mère | My stepfather: | Mon beau-père | | |
| My aunt: | Ma tante | My grandmother: | Ma grand-mère | | |
| My uncle: | Mon oncle | My grandfather: | Mon grand-père | | |
| My niece: | Ma nièce | My wife: | Ma femme | | |
| My nephew: | Mon neveu | My husband: | Mon mari | | |

Il est <u>marié</u> . = He's <u>married</u>.

| | |
|---|---|
| single: | célibataire |
| separated: | séparé(e) |
| divorced: | divorcé(e) |
| widowed: | veuf / veuve |

Je viens d'une famille monoparentale. = I come from a single-parent family.

## Est-ce que tu as des animaux domestiques?

### — Do you have any pets?

| | | | |
|---|---|---|---|
| *a cat:* | un chat | *a guinea pig:* | un cochon d'Inde |
| *a bird:* | un oiseau | *a rabbit:* | un lapin |
| *a fish:* | un poisson | *a mouse:* | une souris |
| *a horse:* | un cheval | *a hamster:* | un hamster |

<u>Animals</u>. Always <u>useful vocab</u> to know. And oh so cute...

Non, je <u>n'</u>ai <u>pas</u> d'animaux . = No, I don't have <u>any animals</u>.

Oui, j'ai <u>un chien</u> . = Yes, I have <u>a dog</u>.

Mon chien s'appelle Cannelle. = My dog is called Cannelle.

Il est <u>marron</u> . = He is <u>brown</u>.

Swap in <u>any</u> descriptive word here.

See page 39 for colours, page 21 for things like fat and thin, and page 110 for more info on <u>negatives</u>.

## No pets — why not just make some up...

This stuff is pretty straightforward. You learn the sentence, learn the words, and just <u>slot in</u> whichever words you need. There's no excuse for not being able to do this stuff — learn it.

# Personality

It helps you <u>connect</u> to other people, makes or breaks that job interview, could win you a spot on X Factor or in the hearts of the nation, and it's <u>who you are</u>. It's <u>personality</u>, and it's <u>important</u>.

## Comment es-tu? — What are you like?

You might be asked to <u>talk about your personality</u> in the speaking tasks, so here goes...

*He is:* Il est  *She is:* Elle est

Je suis **magnifique** .

= <u>I am</u> <u>amazing</u>.

| | |
|---|---|
| *nice:* | agréable / sympa |
| *funny:* | amusant(e) / drôle/ rigolo(te) |
| *lively:* | plein(e) de vie / animé(e) |
| *chatty:* | bavard(e) |

| | |
|---|---|
| *friendly:* | amical(e) |
| *kind:* | aimable / gentil(le) |
| *generous:* | généreux / généreuse |
| *hard-working:* | travailleur / travailleuse |
| *honest:* | honnête |

*quite:* assez

Je suis **un peu** **idiot(e)** .

= I am <u>a bit</u> <u>stupid</u>.

| | |
|---|---|
| *impatient:* | impatient(e) |
| *impolite:* | impoli(e) |
| *mean:* | méchant(e) |
| *boring:* | ennuyeux / ennuyeuse |
| *lazy:* | paresseux / paresseuse |

| | |
|---|---|
| *jealous:* | jaloux / jalouse |
| *selfish:* | égoïste |
| *proud:* | fier / fière |
| *shy:* | timide |
| *sad:* | triste |

## J'ai une attitude positive — I have a positive attitude

J'ai toujours une attitude **positive** .  = <u>I</u> always <u>have</u> a <u>positive</u> attitude.

*He has:* Il a...  *She has:* Elle a...  *negative:* négative

Oh we do, do we? Go on then, amuse us...

Je sais faire **rire** les gens.  = <u>I know how</u> to make people <u>laugh</u>.

*He knows how:* Il sait...  *She knows how:* Elle sait...  *cry:* pleurer

*in a bad mood:* de mauvaise humeur

Je suis souvent **de bonne humeur** .  = I'm often <u>in a good mood</u>.

## La personalité des autres — Other people's personalities

Talking about other people's <u>personalities</u> is simple — just use these celeb <u>examples</u> as <u>guidelines</u>...

J'ai beaucoup de respect pour Reese Witherspoon. Elle a le sens de l'humour. Elle est **travailleuse** , **optimiste** et **pleine de vie** . Elle est aussi une bonne mère.

= I have lots of respect for Reese Witherspoon. She has a sense of humour. She is <u>hard-working</u>, <u>optimistic</u> and <u>lively</u>. She is also a good mother.

You can put any of the personality traits above in these white boxes.

= I have lots of respect for Lewis Hamilton. He always has a positive attitude. He is <u>hard-working</u>, <u>chatty</u> and <u>kind</u>. He drives well, too.

J'ai beaucoup de respect pour Lewis Hamilton. Il a toujours une attitude positive . Il est **travailleur** , **bavard** et **aimable** . Il conduit bien, aussi.

## Am I decisive? Well, yes and no...

This <u>personality</u> vocab isn't just useful for GCSE French — it could also come in handy to describe the man or woman of your dreams if you're ever a contestant on Blind Date in France...

# Relationships

This page is <u>particularly useful</u> if you want to send a letter to a French <u>agony aunt</u>.

## *Un bon ami doit être... — A good friend must be...*

It's good to know the <u>qualities</u> you're looking for...

*a good partner:* un(e) bon(ne) partenaire

*À mon avis,* un(e) bon(ne) ami(e) *doit* ... = In my opinion, <u>a good friend</u> must...

| | | | |
|---|---|---|---|
| *be honest:* | être honnête | *be chatty:* | être bavard(e) |
| *be trustworthy:* | être fidèle | *be fun:* | être amusant(e) |
| *be kind:* | être sympa | *be like me:* | être comme moi |
| *be understanding:* | être compréhensif / compréhensive | *be there for me:* | être là pour moi |

*Il est important de pouvoir* compter sur *ses amis.*

*to respect:* respecter

= It's important to be able <u>to count on</u> your friends.

## *On s'entend bien... — We get on well...*

<u>Friendship</u> isn't always plain sailing. Painful, but here's <u>how to tell</u> a French person all about it:

*Je m'entends bien avec* mon ami(e) . = I get on well with <u>my friend</u>.

*my mother:* ma mère    *my sister:* ma sœur    *my brother:* mon frère

*Nous sommes meilleur(e)s ami(e)s.*

= We are best friends.

*Il me plaît.*  = I fancy him.

*Nous nous connaissons depuis* l'école primaire .

*we were seven:* l'âge de sept ans

= We've known each other since <u>primary school</u>.

*On ne se comprend pas.*  = We don't understand each other.

*Il ne m'écoute pas* .

*Elle est trop égoïste.*  = She's too selfish.

*She doesn't listen to me:* Elle ne m'écoute pas
*They don't listen to me:* Ils ne m'écoutent pas

= <u>He doesn't listen to me.</u>

*On se dispute toujours.*  = We argue all the time.

*a girlfriend:* une petite amie

*Mon ami(e) vient de trouver* un petit ami *et on ne se voit presque plus.*

= My friend has just got <u>a boyfriend</u> and we barely see each other any more.

## *My mate's an abacus — I can really count on him...*

Ah, friendship — it's a topic you've been <u>talking about</u> in French for <u>years</u>, so it shouldn't be too tough to get to grips with. If you can, <u>spice up</u> what you say with some of the <u>longer sentences</u>.

# Marriage

Not sure what it's got to do with GCSE French but you need to be able to talk about your <u>future marriage plans</u>. Here's everything you need to know about giving your <u>views</u> on <u>white dresses</u> and saying '<u>I do</u>'.

## *Je voudrais me marier...* — *I'd like to get married...*

If you've already met <u>the one</u> and you're keen to <u>tie the knot</u> as soon as possible, then learn how to say so:

*À l'avenir, je voudrais* **...**

| | |
|---|---|
| *to fall in love:* | tomber amoureux(euse) |
| *to get engaged:* | me fiancer |
| *to get married:* | me marier |
| *to have children:* | avoir des enfants |

= In the future, I'd like **...**

*J'ai trouvé un(e) partenaire idéal(e).* = I've found an ideal partner.

*Je sors avec* **mon copain** *depuis* **trois** *ans.*

*my girlfriend:* ma copine

More numbers on page 1.

= I've been going out with <u>my boyfriend</u> for <u>three</u> years.

*Nous allons bientôt fêter nos fiançailles.* = We're going to celebrate our engagement soon.

## *Je vais attendre quelques années...* — *I'm going to wait a few years...*

What to say if you're <u>happy</u> to <u>hang on</u>...

*Je peux très bien me débrouiller seul(e) — je n'ai pas l'intention de me marier tout de suite.*

= I can get along fine on my own — I don't intend to get married right away.

*Je ne suis pas prêt(e) à y penser.* = I'm not ready to think about it.

*Mon copain n'a pas suffisamment d'argent pour m'acheter* **une bague** *.*

*a wedding ring:* une alliance

= My boyfriend doesn't have enough money to buy me <u>a ring</u>.

## *Je ne veux pas me marier* — *I don't want to get married*

*Je préfère rester célibataire.* = I prefer to stay single.

*Je n'ai pas envie d'une grande noce.* = I don't want a big wedding.

*On peut vivre ensemble sans se marier.* = You can live together without getting married.

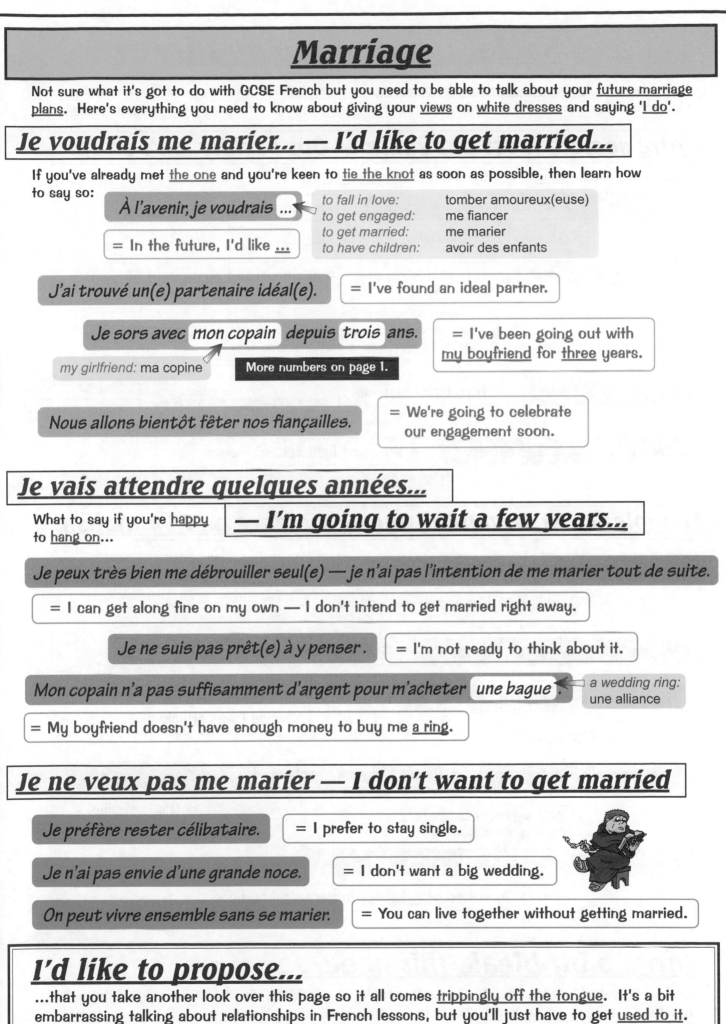

## *I'd like to propose...*

...that you take another look over this page so it all comes <u>trippingly off the tongue</u>. It's a bit embarrassing talking about relationships in French lessons, but you'll just have to get <u>used to it</u>.

# Social Issues and Equality

Unemployment, equal ops, gender and race issues — it's enough to make you want to wave around a big banner. Try a verse of 'We shall not, we shall not be moved' — simply superb for revision morale.

## Notre société n'est pas égale — Our society isn't equal

How to talk about racism and other forms of discrimination...

Parfois les gens **sont méchants** avec moi. = Sometimes people are mean to me.

*are violent:* sont violents      *are racist:* sont racistes

C'est parce que **je viens d'Afrique**. = It's because I come from Africa.

*I am a girl / a guy:*    je suis une fille / un garçon
*I am younger / older:*    je suis plus jeune / plus âgé(e)
*I am Jewish / Muslim / Christian*   je suis juif / juive / musulman(e) / chrétien(ne)

Ça me gêne beaucoup. = It really bothers me.

*humiliated:* humilié(e)

Je me sens **exclu(e)**. = I feel excluded.

Il faut lutter contre le racisme. = We must fight against racism.

## La violence et le vandalisme — Violence and vandalism

Il y a beaucoup de **violence** dans ma ville. = There is lots of violence in my town.

*poverty:* pauvreté      *vandalism:* vandalisme

Il y a des endroits où j'évite d'aller. = There are some places I avoid going to.

En rentrant à la maison une fois j'ai été **agressé(e)**. = On the way home once I was attacked.

*hit:* battu(e)

*threaten:* menace

On me **brutalise** au collège. = People bully me at school.

C'est effrayant.

= It's terrifying.

*of the low-lifes:* de la racaille
*of the thugs:*    des voyous

J'ai vraiment peur **des bandes** dans mon quartier.

= I'm really scared of the gangs in my neighbourhood.

It wasn't like this in my day

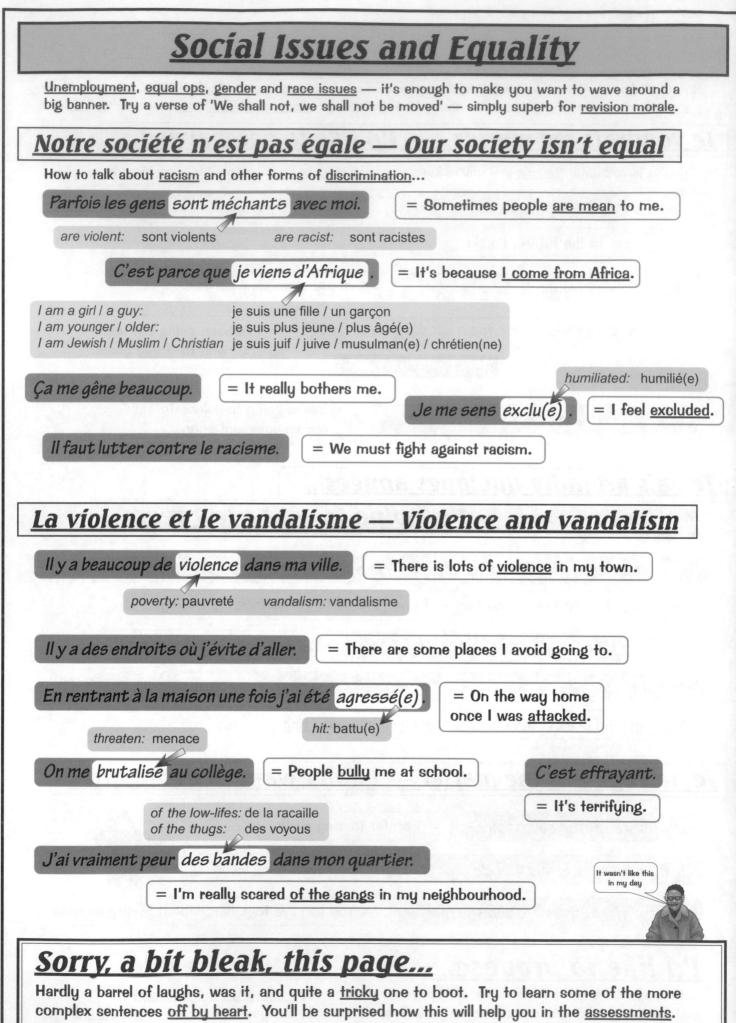

## Sorry, a bit bleak, this page...

Hardly a barrel of laughs, was it, and quite a tricky one to boot. Try to learn some of the more complex sentences off by heart. You'll be surprised how this will help you in the assessments.

# Social Issues and Equality

Yup, another page on <u>big global issues</u>. This stuff's tough, but <u>learn it well</u> and you'll simply <u>glide through</u> those <u>reading</u> and <u>listening</u> exams.

## Je viens d'un autre pays — I come from another country

This is the kind of thing you might expect to <u>read</u> or <u>hear</u> about someone who <u>wasn't born</u> in <u>France</u>.

Je suis arrivé(e) en France comme immigré(e). = I arrived <u>in France</u> as an immigrant.

*in England:* en Angleterre   *in Canada:* au Canada   For other countries, see page 46.

Je suis réfugié(e) à cause d'une guerre. = I am a refugee because of a war.

Avant, je n'avais pas de libertés civiques. = Before, I didn't have any civil liberties.

On ne respecte pas toujours les droits de l'homme. = People don't always respect human rights.

## Je ne peux pas trouver un boulot — I can't find a job

Not having a job isn't as good as it sounds. Here's how to give your <u>views</u> on <u>unemployment</u>.

Il y a beaucoup de chômeurs dans ma ville. = There are lots of <u>unemployed people</u> in my town.

*homeless people:*   sans abri / SDF
*disadvantaged people:*   personnes défavorisées

Mon père est au chômage depuis deux ans.

= My father has been out of work for two years.

On commence à se sentir déprimé.

= You start to feel depressed.   Sans argent, il est difficile de trouver un logement.

= Without money, it's difficult to find housing.

J'ai peur de faire des dettes.

= I'm afraid of getting into debt.   J'habite une HLM. = I live in a council house.

## Qu'est-ce qu'on peut faire pour aider?

## — What can we do to help?

*give money:* donner de l'argent

On peut faire du travail bénévole pour aider les organisations caritatives.

= You can <u>do voluntary work</u> to help charities.

On doit respecter tout le monde. = We should respect everybody.

## Civil liberty — feeling free to be nice...

Lots of tricky stuff in this section and we're not even halfway through the book yet. Still, if you've really <u>got to grips</u> with the topics you've covered so far, you should be well <u>on track</u> for that <u>A*</u>.

# Revision Summary

These questions are here to make sure you know your stuff. Work through them and look up the answers to any tough ones you're struggling with. Keep practising them all again and again. Do I sound like a broken record yet... Hope so. I've always wondered what that might be like.

1) How would you tell your name, age and birthday to a French person you've just met?

2) Now spell your name and surname out loud three times using the French alphabet.

3) Describe three of your friends and say how old they are. Comment on the colour of their eyes and their marital status, and spell their names out loud, in French.

4) Tell your French penfriend what relations you have — including how many aunts, cousins etc.

5) Your animal-loving friend has six rabbits, a bird, a guinea pig and two cats. How could she say what these are in French?

6) Imagine that you are a boring, impolite, chatty, funny, lively person who has a sense of humour and knows how to make people laugh. How would you say all this in French?

7) Write three sentences about the personalities of two of your favourite celebrities.

8) In your opinion, what three qualities should a good friend have? Finish the following sentence: À mon avis, un bon ami / une bonne amie doit...

9) Say that you get on well with your friend Émilie and that you've known each other since you were five. Then say that you argue all the time with David because he's selfish and he doesn't listen to you.

10) Isabelle dit: "J'ai un petit ami qui s'appelle François. On s'entend bien. Nous sommes meilleurs amis. On ne se dispute jamais. François est honnête, fidèle et compréhensif, et il est toujours là pour moi. Je pense que je suis tombée amoureuse." (Sickening.) What did she say in English?

11) You've been dreaming of your wedding day for years and now you think you've found the boy/girl of your dreams. In French, describe your plans for the future together in as much detail as you can.

12) This time imagine you're your super-independent best friend who's planning to stay single for ever. Explain why in French, giving at least two reasons.

13) You've just got a letter from your French penpal Xavier which says "Au collège en ce moment, des élèves sont méchants avec moi parce que je viens d'Afrique. Je me sens humilié et ça me gêne beaucoup." Translate what he said into English.

14) You're worried about problems in your local area. Write a short email to the mayor of your town saying that there's lots of violence in your neighbourhood and that there are some places you avoid going because you're scared of the gangs.

15) Imagine you've been looking for a job for six months but you still haven't found one. Write a short paragraph in French explaining your thoughts on unemployment.

16) Give one way that you could help people who are socially disadvantaged (e.g. homeless or poor).

## Free time Activities

Examiners don't believe in couch potatoes — there's always loads in the exams about <u>sports</u> and <u>hobbies</u>.

## Est-ce que tu fais du sport? — Do you do any sport?

<u>Sports</u> and <u>hobbies</u> are a popular choice for speaking and writing assessments. Even if you're no demon on the pitch, you <u>need</u> to be good at talking about all things sport 'en français'.

**NAMES OF SPORTS**

| | |
|---|---|
| *basketball:* | le basket |
| *football:* | le foot(ball) |
| *climbing:* | l'alpinisme (masc.) |
| *tennis:* | le tennis |
| *table tennis:* | le ping pong |
| *skateboarding:* | le skate |
| *horse riding:* | l'équitation |
| *swimming:* | la natation |
| *ice skating:* | le patinage |
| *snowboarding:* | le surf des neiges |
| *water sports:* | les sports nautiques |
| *winter sports:* | les sports d'hiver |

**VERBS FOR SPORTS**

| | |
|---|---|
| *to go fishing:* | aller à la pêche |
| *to run:* | courir |
| *to cycle:* | faire du cyclisme |
| *to swim:* | nager |
| *to ski:* | faire du ski |
| *to play:* | jouer |
| *to walk, hike:* | faire une randonnée |
| *to ice skate:* | patiner |

**PLACES YOU CAN DO SPORTS**

| | |
|---|---|
| *sports centre:* | le centre sportif |
| *leisure centre:* | le centre de loisirs |
| *swimming pool:* | la piscine |
| *sports field:* | le terrain de sport |
| *gymnasium:* | le gymnase |
| *park:* | le parc |
| *ice rink:* | la patinoire |
| *mountains:* | les montagnes (fem.) |

## Tu aimes regarder le sport? — Do you like watching sport?

Je préfère participer parce que **...**

= I prefer to take part because <u>...</u>

| | |
|---|---|
| *I love training:* | j'adore m'entraîner. |
| *I like working in a team:* | j'aime travailler en équipe. |
| *it's good for your health:* | c'est bon pour la santé. |

Je préfère regarder le jeu parce que **...**

= I prefer to watch the game because <u>...</u>

| | |
|---|---|
| *I'm injured and I can't play any more:* | |
| je suis blessé(e) et je ne peux plus jouer. | |
| *it's expensive to play:* | ça coûte cher de jouer. |

## Est-ce que tu as un passe-temps? — Do you have a hobby?

There are <u>other things</u> to do apart from sports — that's where these <u>tasty selections</u> come into play.

**GENERAL BUT VITAL**

| | |
|---|---|
| *hobby:* | le passe-temps |
| *interest:* | l'intérêt (masc.) |
| *club:* | le club (de...) |
| *member:* | le membre |

**VERBS FOR INDOOR ACTIVITIES**

| | |
|---|---|
| *to dance:* | danser |
| *to sing:* | chanter |
| *to collect:* | collectionner |
| *to read:* | lire |

To see how to use verbs with different people, see pages 101-102.

**OTHER IMPORTANT WORDS**

| | |
|---|---|
| *chess:* | les échecs (masc.) |
| *darts:* | les fléchettes (fem.) |
| *film:* | le film |
| *performance:* | le spectacle |
| *play:* | la pièce de théâtre |
| *reading:* | la lecture |

**MUSICAL WORDS**

| | |
|---|---|
| *band, group:* | le groupe |
| *CD:* | le CD, le disque compact |
| *concert:* | le concert |

If music's what you're into, see page 33 for loads more detail.

## Get on your hobby-horse...

Blummin' great. Not only do you have to do sport in PE, you have to talk about it in French. Even if you hate sport and music, you'll have to <u>pretend</u> you do something. And you'll need to know the others when you hear them. Luckily most of them sound more or less like the English. Phew.

# Free time Activities

What you do in your <u>free time</u> comes up somewhere in the assessments <u>every year</u>. You have to be able to write about what <u>you</u> get up to, and give <u>opinions</u> of other hobbies. It's <u>must-learn</u> stuff. Yeah it is.

## <u>Qu'est-ce que tu fais pendant ton temps libre?</u>
### — What do you do in your free time?

<u>Sport</u> and <u>music</u> are really big topics in the assessments.

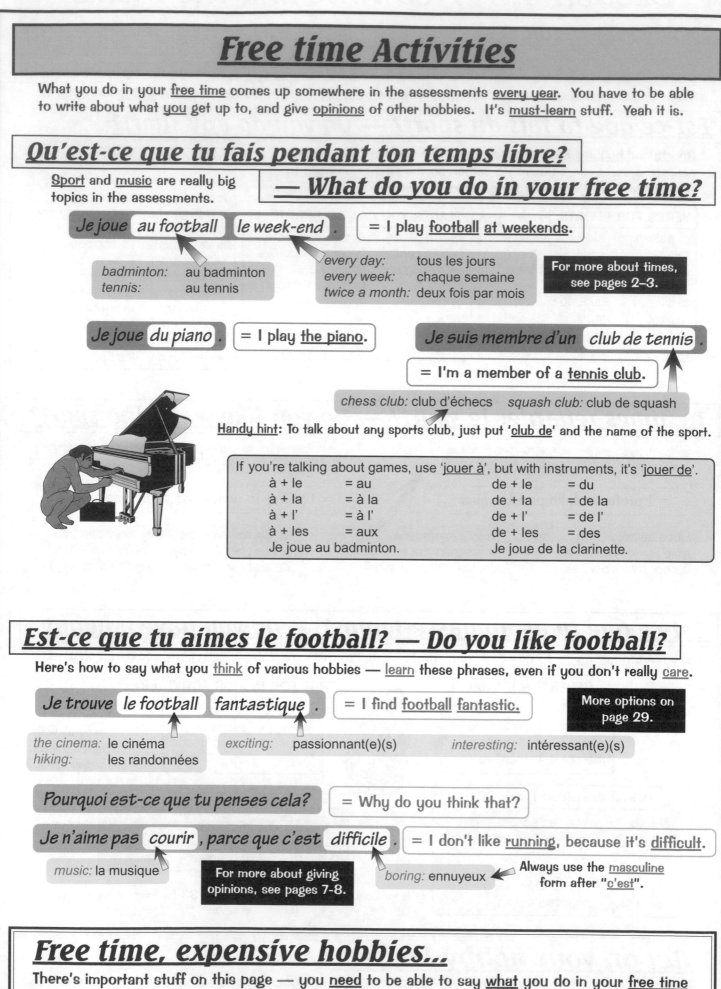

Je joue **au football** **le week-end** .  = I play <u>football</u> <u>at weekends</u>.

*badminton:* au badminton
*tennis:* au tennis

*every day:*      tous les jours
*every week:*    chaque semaine
*twice a month:* deux fois par mois

For more about times, see pages 2–3.

Je joue **du piano** .  = I play <u>the piano</u>.

Je suis membre d'un **club de tennis** .

= I'm a member of a <u>tennis club</u>.

*chess club:* club d'échecs    *squash club:* club de squash

<u>Handy hint</u>: To talk about any sports club, just put '<u>club de</u>' and the name of the sport.

If you're talking about games, use '<u>jouer à</u>', but with instruments, it's '<u>jouer de</u>'.

| à + le | = au | de + le | = du |
| à + la | = à la | de + la | = de la |
| à + l' | = à l' | de + l' | = de l' |
| à + les | = aux | de + les | = des |
| Je joue au badminton. | | Je joue de la clarinette. | |

## <u>Est-ce que tu aimes le football? — Do you like football?</u>

Here's how to say what you <u>think</u> of various hobbies — <u>learn</u> these phrases, even if you don't really <u>care</u>.

Je trouve **le football** **fantastique** .  = I find <u>football</u> <u>fantastic.</u>

More options on page 29.

*the cinema:* le cinéma
*hiking:*     les randonnées

*exciting:*   passionnant(e)(s)     *interesting:* intéressant(e)(s)

Pourquoi est-ce que tu penses cela?  = Why do you think that?

Je n'aime pas **courir** , parce que c'est **difficile** .  = I don't like <u>running</u>, because it's <u>difficult</u>.

*music:* la musique

For more about giving opinions, see pages 7-8.

*boring:* ennuyeux

Always use the <u>masculine</u> form after "<u>c'est</u>".

## Free time, expensive hobbies...

There's important stuff on this page — you <u>need</u> to be able to say <u>what</u> you do in your <u>free time</u> and <u>why</u>. Make sure you remember when it's 'jouer <u>à</u>' and when it's 'jouer <u>de</u>'. While you're at it, learn all this <u>opinion</u> stuff for saying what you think about sports and hobbies. Fu-un...

# Television

Ah, the <u>telly</u>. You might have to listen to people talk about television in the exam, or you may need to talk about it in the speaking assessment. You never know, so make sure this is part of your <u>repertoire</u>.

## Qu'est-ce que tu aimes regarder à la télé?
## — What do you like to watch on TV?

Basically, this stuff's all really handy.

Quelles émissions est-ce que tu aimes regarder ?

*Which books:* Quels livres

*to read:* lire

= <u>Which programmes</u> do you like <u>to watch</u>?

*to listen to:* écouter    *to read:* lire

Put what you like to watch, listen to or read here.

J'aime regarder Westenders .

= I like <u>to watch</u> <u>Westenders</u>.

| | |
|---|---|
| *a documentary:* | un documentaire |
| *a soap:* | un feuilleton |
| *a film:* | un film |
| *a play:* | une pièce de théâtre |
| *a show:* | un spectacle |
| *an advertisement:* | une publicité |

| | |
|---|---|
| *documentaries:* | des documentaires |
| *soaps:* | des feuilletons |
| *films:* | des films |
| *plays:* | des pièces de théâtre |
| *shows:* | des spectacles |
| *advertisements:* | des publicités |
| *the news:* | les actualités (fem.) |

For more about giving opinions, see pages 7-8.

This one's always plural, like in English.

Je voudrais regarder ...

= I would like to watch ...

L'émission commence à vingt heures et finit à vingt et une heures trente .

For more info. about telling the time, see page 2.

= The programme starts at <u>8pm</u> and finishes at <u>9:30pm</u>.

## Qu'est-ce que tu as fait récemment?
## — What have you done recently?

This bit of <u>past tense</u> looks really impressive — and it's always good for a little bit o' <u>French banter</u>...

For more about times and dates, see pages 2–3.

J'ai vu Amélie récemment .

= I <u>saw</u> <u>Amélie</u> <u>recently</u>.

| | |
|---|---|
| *heard:* | écouté |
| *read:* | lu |

| | |
|---|---|
| *the radio:* | la radio |
| *the new song by Take This:* | |
| la nouvelle chanson de Take This | |

| | |
|---|---|
| *last week:* | la semaine dernière |
| *two weeks ago:* | il y a deux semaines |
| *a month ago:* | il y a un mois |

## A soap set in a pâtisserie — Millefeuilleton...

The French often call TV '<u>le petit écran</u>' (= 'the small screen'), even if it's one of those 48" monster screens. So it's no surprise that sometimes they call the cinema '<u>le grand écran</u>'. Now try to say exactly what sort of programmes you like to watch, and explain <u>why</u> you like them.

# Talking About the Plot

Books, films, telly programmes — you may have to discuss things you've read, seen or heard recently. It sounds quite daunting, even in English, but it's really simple if you learn these easy phrases...

## J'ai lu, J'ai vu, J'ai entendu... — I read, I saw, I heard...

Je viens de lire un livre impressionnant. = I've just read an impressive book.

| | |
|---|---|
| listened to: | d'écouter |
| watched: | de regarder |
| seen: | de voir |

| | |
|---|---|
| interesting: | intéressant(e) |
| superb: | superbe |
| funny: | drôle |

| | |
|---|---|
| a play: | une pièce de théâtre |
| a show: | un spectacle |
| a film: | un film |
| a cartoon: | une bande dessinée |

It: Elle

Yes, Emperor.

Il s'appelait 'Pride and Prejudice'. = It was called 'Pride and Prejudice'.

## Parle-moi de ce qui s'est passé...
## — Tell me about what happened...

You can make up anything you like here. (Maybe don't mention robots if you're talking about a classic novel...) Just stick to the present tense (see pages 101-102).

Il y a un homme qui porte des lunettes et un manteau invisible. = There's a man who wears glasses and an invisible coat.

| | | | |
|---|---|---|---|
| woman: | une femme | boy: | un garçon |
| girl: | une fille | actor: | un acteur |
| actress: | une actrice | star: | une vedette |
| singer: | un chanteur / une chanteuse | | |

has lots of money: a beaucoup d'argent
loves to travel: adore voyager
is very handsome but a bit stupid: est très beau mais un peu stupide.

Ça finit bien. = It has a happy ending.

## Qu'est-ce que tu en pensais? — What did you think of it?

Opinions go down really well at GCSE French — so you need to learn this stuff... and get an opinion.

Je l'ai trouvé(e) génial(e). = I thought it was great.

This is quite tricky — remember to add an 'e' to the past participle and the adjective (if necessary) if the thing you are referring to is feminine, e.g. une émission, une publicité, une pièce de théâtre.

For more about giving opinions, see pages 7-8.

| | |
|---|---|
| informative: | instructif / instructive |
| entertaining: | amusant(e) |
| interesting: | intéressant(e) |
| boring: | ennuyeux / ennuyeuse |
| fantastic: | fantastique |

## Lu, vu and entendu — that's a lot of ooos...

I really should be writing song lyrics for Kylie or Take That, but I'm far too busy writing a French book. Once again, it's all about me. They'll be making a film of my life soon, called... um...

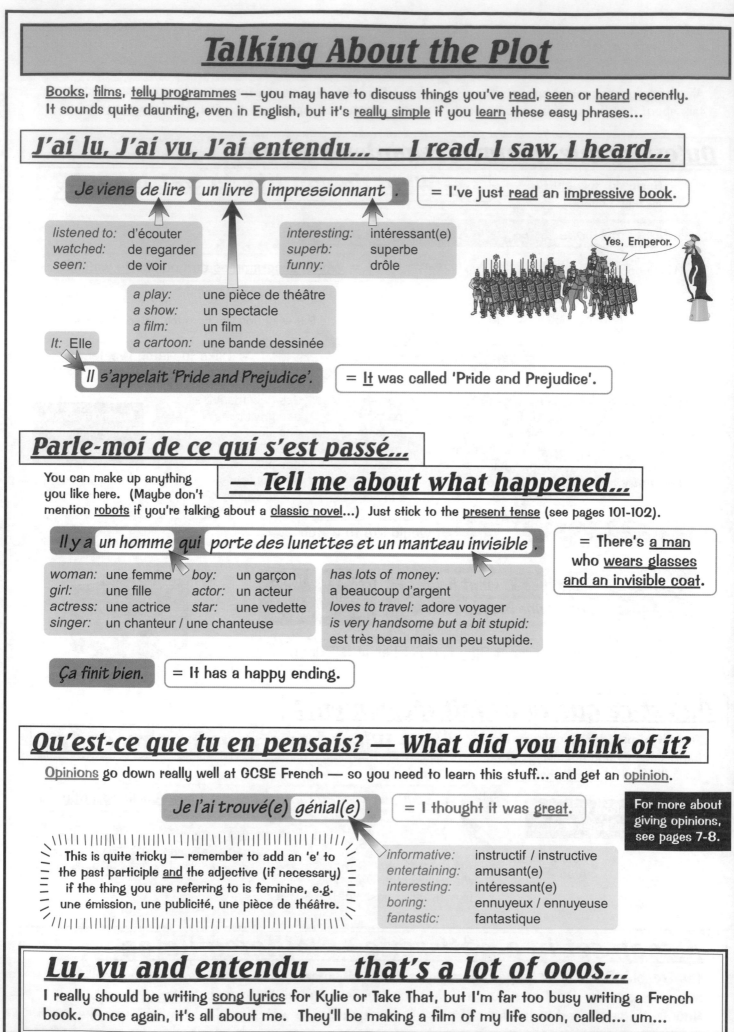

# Music

Treasons, strategems and spoils. That's what Shakespeare said you're fit for if you don't like music. Learn how to say what music you're into. If you are fit for those things, there's no harm in making it up.

## Qu'est-ce que tu aimes comme musique?
## — What kind of music do you like?

All fairly basic stuff this. You need to find interesting ways of talking about your musical tastes though.

*Mon genre musical préféré, c'est la musique jazz.*  = My favourite type of music is jazz.

pop   rock   danse   classique   rap

It's really good if you can explain exactly what you like.
(And remember, it doesn't have to be true.)

*J'aime toutes les chansons qu'on entend en boîte.*  = I like all the songs you hear in clubs.

*Je trouve les symphonies de Beethoven incroyables.*  = I find Beethoven's symphonies incredible.

*songs by Take This:* les chansons de Take This
*pieces by Schumann:* les pièces de Schumann

*very good:* très bons / bonnes
*really great:* vraiment chouettes
*interesting:* intéressants / intéressantes

It's good to talk about any foreign music you've heard, too — you can bet your French teacher loves Europop.

## Où est-ce que tu aimes écouter de la musique?
## — Where do you like listening to music?

This bit's how to say where and how you listen to music.

*J'écoute de la musique en voiture sur mon lecteur mp3.*  = I listen to music in the car on my mp3 player.

*on the bus:* en autobus
*at home:* à la maison
*while I'm walking:* en marchant

*on the radio:* à la radio
*on my mobile phone:* sur mon portable

## To play an instrument is 'jouer d'un instrument'

*Je joue du piano. Je m'entraîne tous les jours.*  = I play the piano. I practise every day.

*the guitar:* de la guitare
*the keyboard:* du clavier
*the drums:* de la batterie
*the violin:* du violon

*once a week:* une fois par semaine    *at weekends:* le week-end

*Je fais partie d'un groupe de rock.*  = I play in a rock band.

## Never say never...

If music comes up in one of the assessments, and you haven't got much to say, you could try: 'J'aimerais jouer du piano' (= 'I'd like to...'), and then give a reason. Gotta be better than nothing.

# Famous People

Now this choice of topic seems a tad weird to me, but apparently you are supposed to be <u>fascinated</u> by celebs. So much so that you want to <u>talk</u> about them in French...

## Quelles vedettes aimes-tu? — Which celebrities do you like?

This is the same <u>straightforward</u> stuff that you use to talk about you and your family.

| WHO | Je trouve Beyoncé Knowles fantastique. | = I think Beyoncé Knowles is fantastic. |
| WHAT | C'est une chanteuse américaine célèbre. | = She is a famous American singer. |
| WHY | Elle chante très bien. J'aimerais pouvoir chanter comme elle. | = She sings very well. I'd like to be able to sing like her. |

## La vie de vedette... — Celebrity life...

You may be asked to put yourself in someone else's French-speaking shoes — when you're <u>imagining</u> you're a <u>celebrity</u>, these phrases may come in useful...

My dad:     Mon père
Elvis:       Elvis

he's always been proud of me: il a toujours été fier de moi
I love his style of music:      j'adore son style de musique.

... m'a beaucoup influencé(e) parce que ... = ... has influenced me a lot because ...

Mon plus grand succès est ...

the work that I've done for charity: le travail que j'ai fait pour les organisations caritatives.
having sold a million albums: d'avoir vendu un million de disques.

= My greatest success is ...

J'ai l'ambition de ...   = My ambition is to ...   Je voudrais ...   = I would like to ...

travel: voyager.     donate money: donner de l'argent.     win an Oscar: gagner un Oscar.

## Vous aimez être célèbre? — Do you like being famous?

If they ask you to write an <u>interview</u> with a celeb, here are some useful phrases:

Oui, j'aime la vie de vedette parce que ...

I am successful:        j'ai du succès.
I have lots of money:   j'ai beaucoup d'argent.
I am able to travel:     je peux voyager.

= Yes, I love life as a celebrity because ...

Non, je déteste la vie de vedette car ...

I don't have a private life:    je n'ai pas de vie privée.
people follow me everywhere:  les gens me suivent partout.

= No, I hate life as a celebrity because ...

Est-ce que vous avez beaucoup de fanas ?   = Do you <u>have</u> lots <u>of fans</u>?

like having: aimez avoir     of well-known songs: de chansons bien connues     of money: d'argent

## I'm your number one fan...

This page gives <u>you</u> the freedom to give <u>your opinion</u> on <u>celebrities</u> and their <u>influence in society</u> — all in a <u>foreign language</u>. It's tricky stuff, but master this and your French will be fabulous.

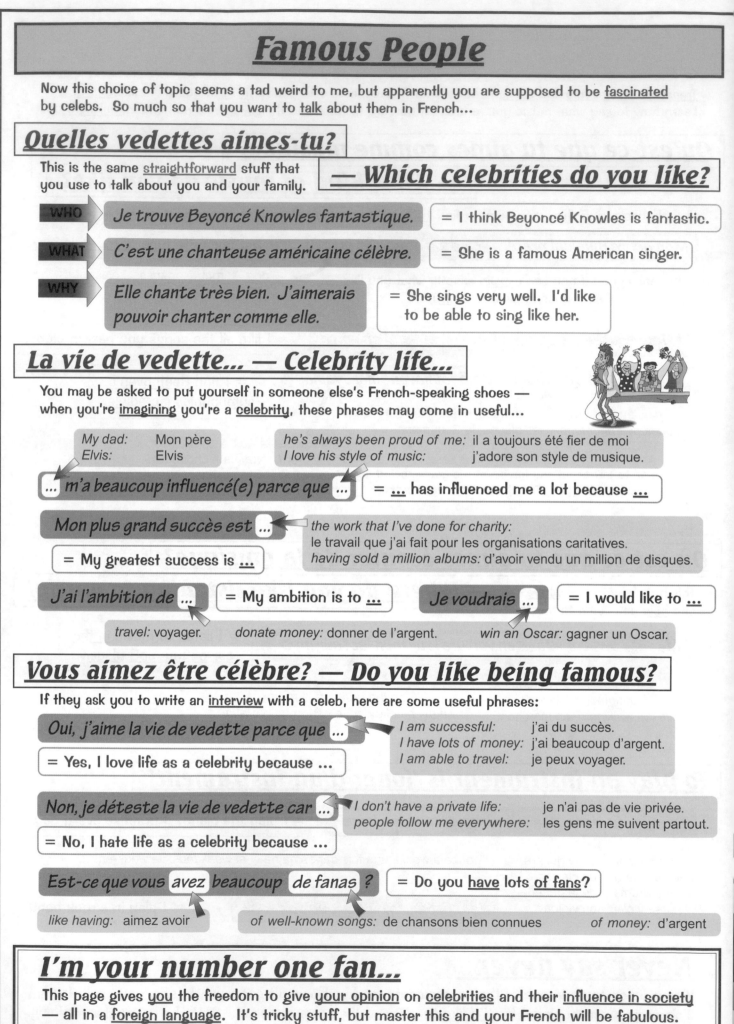

# New Technology

Ah, <u>computers</u>. They've even found their way into GCSE French.

## Je suis toujours sur l'ordinateur
## — I'm always on the computer

It's good to be able to give details about what you <u>use</u> computers for.

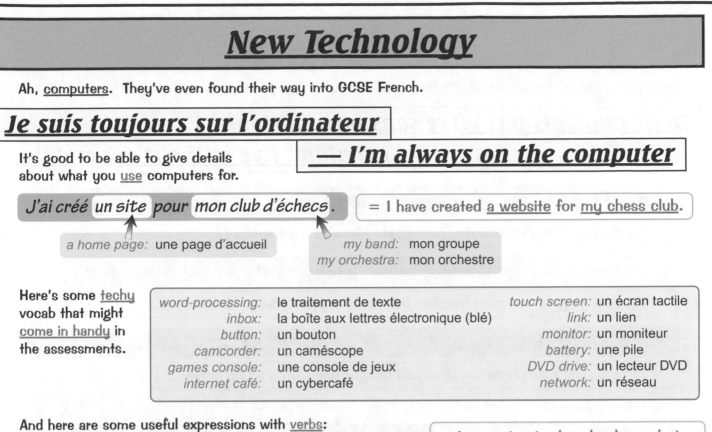

**J'ai créé** *un site* **pour** *mon club d'échecs*. = I have created <u>a website</u> for <u>my chess club</u>.

a home page: une page d'accueil

my band: mon groupe
my orchestra: mon orchestre

Here's some <u>techy</u> vocab that might <u>come in handy</u> in the assessments.

| | | | |
|---|---|---|---|
| *word-processing:* | le traitement de texte | *touch screen:* | un écran tactile |
| *inbox:* | la boîte aux lettres électronique (blé) | *link:* | un lien |
| *button:* | un bouton | *monitor:* | un moniteur |
| *camcorder:* | un caméscope | *battery:* | une pile |
| *games console:* | une console de jeux | *DVD drive:* | un lecteur DVD |
| *internet café:* | un cybercafé | *network:* | un réseau |

And here are some useful expressions with <u>verbs</u>:

*Je vais <u>télécharger</u> mes photos sur mon ordinateur. Avant de les <u>mettre en ligne</u>, je vais les <u>imprimer</u>.*

= I am going to <u>download</u> my photos onto my computer. Before <u>putting</u> them <u>online</u>, I am going to <u>print</u> them.

## Un bloggeur — A blogger

If you have a <u>particularly interesting</u> life, you might want to share your experiences on your <u>blog</u>. Also, they might ask you to imagine you're writing a blog for your <u>written assessment</u>.

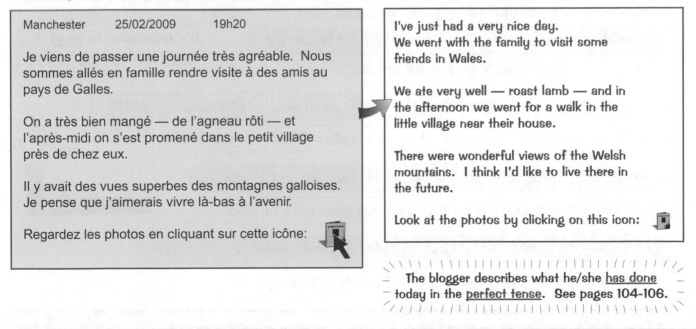

Manchester     25/02/2009     19h20

Je viens de passer une journée très agréable. Nous sommes allés en famille rendre visite à des amis au pays de Galles.

On a très bien mangé — de l'agneau rôti — et l'après-midi on s'est promené dans le petit village près de chez eux.

Il y avait des vues superbes des montagnes galloises. Je pense que j'aimerais vivre là-bas à l'avenir.

Regardez les photos en cliquant sur cette icône:

I've just had a very nice day. We went with the family to visit some friends in Wales.

We ate very well — roast lamb — and in the afternoon we went for a walk in the little village near their house.

There were wonderful views of the Welsh mountains. I think I'd like to live there in the future.

Look at the photos by clicking on this icon:

The blogger describes what he/she <u>has done</u> today in the <u>perfect tense</u>. See pages 104-106.

## Bloggity blog blog...

Everyone's blogging nowadays. Even if you think it's the <u>scourge of the digital age</u>, and a medium for unadulterated <u>drivel</u>, for the sake of your French GCSE, get the contents of this page <u>learnt</u>.

# New Technology

Now you've got the vocab sorted, it's time to talk about the pros and cons...

## Je ne pourrais pas vivre sans mon portable
## — I couldn't live without my mobile

Reasons why you love your mobile...

*J'envoie environ dix textos par jour pour suggérer des projets à mes ami(e)s.*

= I send around ten texts a day to suggest plans to my friends.

*Mes parents me donnent plus de liberté car ils peuvent toujours me contacter.*

= My parents give me more freedom because they can always contact me.

*J'aime acheter de nouveaux portables — je viens d'en acheter un avec un écran tactile.*

= I like buying new phones — I've just bought one with a touch screen.

...and your PC...

*On peut faire des choses pédagogiques sur internet — ça aide avec les études.*

= You can do educational things on the internet — it helps with your studies.

*Je reçois beaucoup de courriers électroniques de ma famille à l'étranger.*

= I receive lots of emails from my family abroad.

## J'utilise rarement mon portable — I rarely use my mobile

If you don't think much of emails and texting, say so.

*Ça coûte cher d'envoyer des textos toute la journée.*

to make calls: faire des appels

= It's expensive to send texts all day long.

*Je crois que les portables pourraient avoir de mauvais effets sur la santé.*

= I believe that mobile phones could have negative effects on your health.

*Passer trop de temps sur l'ordinateur me donne mal à la tête.*

= Spending too much time on the computer gives me a headache.

*Les emails ne sont pas très personnels. Je préfère écrire une lettre.*

= Emails aren't very personal. I prefer to write a letter.

## The internet can be very educational...

Sometimes it can be hard to think of the downsides of new technology — after all, nobody would rather trawl round a town centre looking for a phone box when they could just pull a dinky mobile out of their bag. You'll be expected to understand both sides of the debate though, so get learning.

# Shopping

This section gives you all the bog-standard stuff you need to know when you're out and about shopping.

## Où est...? — Where is...?

A dead handy question, this one.

Où est la boulangerie , s'il vous plaît?

the till: la caisse

= Where is the baker's, please?

### D'autres magasins — Other shops

| | | | |
|---|---|---|---|
| grocer's: | l'épicerie (fem.) | cake shop: | la pâtisserie |
| hypermarket: | l'hypermarché (masc.) | sweet shop: | la confiserie |
| perfume shop: | la parfumerie | fishmonger's: | la poissonnerie |
| jeweller's: | la bijouterie | delicatessen: | la charcuterie |
| bookshop: | la librairie | butcher's: | la boucherie |

## À quelle heure...? — What time...?

You need these useful sentences to talk about when shops are open or closed.

À quelle heure est-ce que le magasin ouvre ?

= What time does the shop open?

close: ferme

For times, see page 2.

Le supermarché ouvre à neuf heures .

= The supermarket opens at nine o'clock.

Tous les magasins ferment à six heures .

= All the shops shut at six o'clock.

## Allons faire les magasins! — Let's go shopping!

Whether you prefer to shop online or fight it out in the shops for a bargain, this vocab'll be useful...

Il y a des soldes au centre commercial .

= There are sales at the shopping centre.

discounts: des réductions (fem.)

at my favourite shop: à ma boutique préférée

in town: en ville

Je préfère faire des courses sur internet .

= I prefer to shop on the internet.

| | | | |
|---|---|---|---|
| easier: | plus facile | cheaper: | moins cher |
| more difficult: | plus difficile | less fun: | moins drôle |

Faire des achats sur internet, c'est plus rapide que dans les magasins .

= Buying things on the internet is quicker than in the shops.

try on: essayer

Je préfère voir les choses avant de les acheter.

= I prefer to see things before buying them.

## Hypermarché — an excited market...

You might have to talk about where things are and when they open in your speaking assessment — you'd be daft not to learn it. If this stuff doesn't come up, then I'm a wombat. Get these sentences learnt, along with the names of as many shops as you can possibly squeeze up there...

# *Shopping*

So you reckon you'll get through your exam <u>without</u> ever having to mention (or recognise someone else mentioning) <u>buying stuff</u> — better wake yourself up, then. It's all here because you need it. Trust me.

## *Est-ce que je peux vous aider? — Can I help you?*

Say what you'd like using '<u>Je voudrais...</u>'

*1kg:* un kilo    *a litre:* un litre    *a packet:* un paquet

**Je voudrais** cinq cents grammes **de sucre, s'il vous plaît.** = I'd like <u>500g</u> of sugar, please.

The <u>shop assistant</u> might say:

**Autre chose?** = Anything else?

**C'est tout?** = Is that everything?

See page 1 for more on numbers.

*two apples:* deux pommes (fem.)
*three pears:* trois poires (fem.)

<u>You</u> could reply:

**Non, merci.** = No, thank you.

**Non, je voudrais aussi** des pommes de terre **, s'il vous plaît.** = No, I'd also like <u>some potatoes</u>, please.

## *Avez-vous...? — Do you have...?*

It's useful to know this vocab in case it pops up in your listening or speaking assessments...

**Excusez-moi, avez-vous** du pain **?** = Excuse me, do you have <u>any bread</u>?

*milk:* du lait    *cheese:* du fromage    *eggs:* des œufs (masc.)    *bananas:* des bananes (fem.)

**Oui,** le **voilà.** = Yes, there <u>it</u> is.    **Non, nous n'en avons pas.** = No, we don't have any.

*it:* le / la

**Je voudrais** un peu de **fromage.** = I'd like <u>a little bit of</u> cheese.

*lots of:* beaucoup de    *a slice of:* une tranche de    *several:* plusieurs

See page 13 for more on food.

**Je voudrais** quelques **pommes.** = I'd like <u>some</u> apples.

## *Ça fait combien? — How much is that?*

French money's easy. There are <u>100 cents</u> in a <u>euro</u>, like there are 100 pence in a pound.

This is what you'd <u>see</u> on a French <u>price tag</u>: € 5,50

**Ça fait** cinq euros cinquante **.** = That'll be <u>5 euros 50</u>.

This is how you <u>say</u> the price.

*by bank card:* par carte bancaire

**Est-ce que je peux payer** par carte de crédit **?** = Can I pay <u>by credit card</u>?

## *Splash out, buy a boat...*

<u>Money</u> and <u>shop talk</u> are pretty important, especially for those nasty (and often embarrassing) speaking assessment thingies. Don't worry. Simply revise. And be happy. (Oh, and just in case it comes up in the listening exam — the French don't pronounce the 'f' in '<u>des œufs</u>'.)

# Shopping

Shopping for a bunch of bananas is all well and good, but shopping for clothes could pop up in your exams too — when someone in the listening exam is banging on about the fab pair of socks they just bought online.

## Je fais des économies... — I'm saving up...

Knowing this useful vocab about pocket money will make your shop talk more interesting...

Je reçois **dix euros** d'argent de poche par **mois** .

£5: cinq livres          week: semaine          = I get ten euros pocket money a month.

*I'd like to buy:*
Je voudrais acheter → **J'achète** **des vêtements de sport** avec mon argent de poche.

make-up:          du maquillage
video games:     des jeux vidéos (masc.)

= I buy sports clothes
with my pocket money.

## Les vêtements — Clothes

Most of these clothes are everyday items — so you need to know them.

J'aime **cette chemise** .     = I like this shirt.

Je n'aime pas **ce manteau** .     = I don't like this coat.

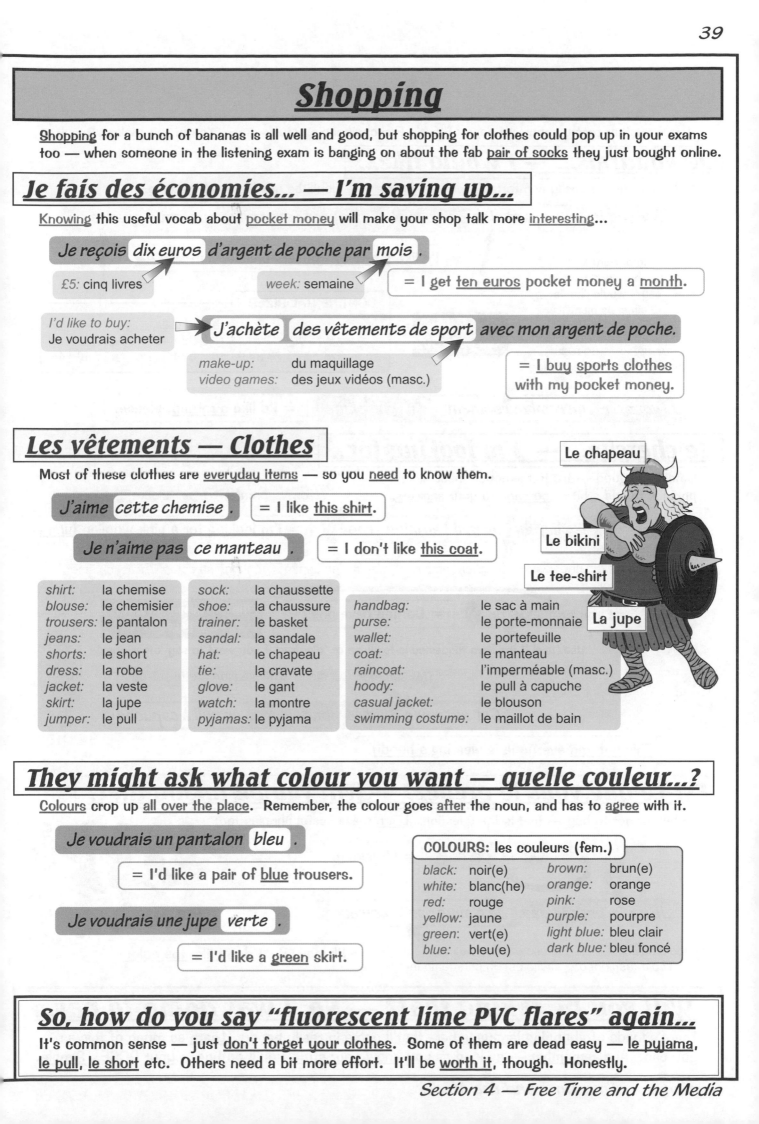

Le chapeau

Le bikini

Le tee-shirt

La jupe

| | | | |
|---|---|---|---|
| *shirt:* | la chemise | *sock:* | la chaussette |
| *blouse:* | le chemisier | *shoe:* | la chaussure |
| *trousers:* | le pantalon | *trainer:* | le basket |
| *jeans:* | le jean | *sandal:* | la sandale |
| *shorts:* | le short | *hat:* | le chapeau |
| *dress:* | la robe | *tie:* | la cravate |
| *jacket:* | la veste | *glove:* | le gant |
| *skirt:* | la jupe | *watch:* | la montre |
| *jumper:* | le pull | *pyjamas:* | le pyjama |

| | |
|---|---|
| *handbag:* | le sac à main |
| *purse:* | le porte-monnaie |
| *wallet:* | le portefeuille |
| *coat:* | le manteau |
| *raincoat:* | l'imperméable (masc.) |
| *hoody:* | le pull à capuche |
| *casual jacket:* | le blouson |
| *swimming costume:* | le maillot de bain |

## They might ask what colour you want — quelle couleur...?

Colours crop up all over the place. Remember, the colour goes after the noun, and has to agree with it.

Je voudrais un pantalon **bleu** .

= I'd like a pair of blue trousers.

Je voudrais une jupe **verte** .

= I'd like a green skirt.

| COLOURS: les couleurs (fem.) | | | |
|---|---|---|---|
| *black:* | noir(e) | *brown:* | brun(e) |
| *white:* | blanc(he) | *orange:* | orange |
| *red:* | rouge | *pink:* | rose |
| *yellow:* | jaune | *purple:* | pourpre |
| *green:* | vert(e) | *light blue:* | bleu clair |
| *blue:* | bleu(e) | *dark blue:* | bleu foncé |

## So, how do you say "fluorescent lime PVC flares" again...

It's common sense — just don't forget your clothes. Some of them are dead easy — le pyjama, le pull, le short etc. Others need a bit more effort. It'll be worth it, though. Honestly.

# *Shopping*

Here's another <u>pretty important</u> page of lovely French shopping stuff — and it's not too tricky. <u>Result</u>...

## *Je voudrais... — I would like...*

Make sure you're really comfortable with '<u>Je voudrais</u>' — you'll be needing it <u>all the time</u>.

*Je voudrais* un pantalon *s'il vous plaît. Je prends la taille* quarante-quatre .

= I'd like <u>a pair of trousers</u> please. I'm size <u>44</u>.

**Important Bit:**
Another good way to say 'I would like' is 'J'aimerais bien...'

For clothing, see page 39.

**CONTINENTAL SIZES**

| | |
|---|---|
| *size:* | la taille |
| *dress size 10 / 12 / 14 / 16:* | 38 / 40 / 42 / 44 |
| *shoe size 5 / 6 / 7 / 8 / 9 / 10:* | 38 / 39 / 41 / 42 / 43 / 44 |

*a receipt:* un reçu
*an exchange:* un échange

*Je voudrais* un remboursement *, s'il vous plaît.*

= I'd like <u>a refund</u>, please.

## *Je cherche... — I'm looking for...*

Details are good — try to memorise these easy phrases to add a bit of <u>ooomph</u> to your <u>answers</u>.

*brown:* brun(e)    *blue:* bleu(e)

*Je cherche* un pull en laine rose .

= I'm looking for a <u>pink</u> <u>woollen</u> <u>jumper</u>.

*a jacket:* une veste    *leather:* en cuir    *denim:* en denim    *cotton:* en coton    *silk:* en soie

*Est-ce que vous en avez* un ?

= Do you have <u>one</u>?

The 'en' means 'of them'.
See page 97.

Use '*une*' if the item requested is feminine or '*d'autres*' if you want to say 'other ones'.

*This summer:* Cet été    *This season:* Cette saison

Cet automne *tout le monde porte* un pull à capuche .

= <u>This autumn</u> everyone is wearing <u>a hoody</u>.

## *Est-ce que vous le prenez? — Will you be taking that?*

To buy or not to buy — that is the question. <u>Learn</u> these useful phrases too:

*it:* le / la    *Je* le *prends.*    = I'll take <u>it</u>.

*Je ne* le *prends pas. Je n'aime pas la couleur* .

*It's too small:*    Il/elle est trop petit(e).
*It's a bit old-fashioned:*    Il/elle est un peu démodé(e).

= I'll leave <u>it</u>. <u>I don't like the colour</u>.

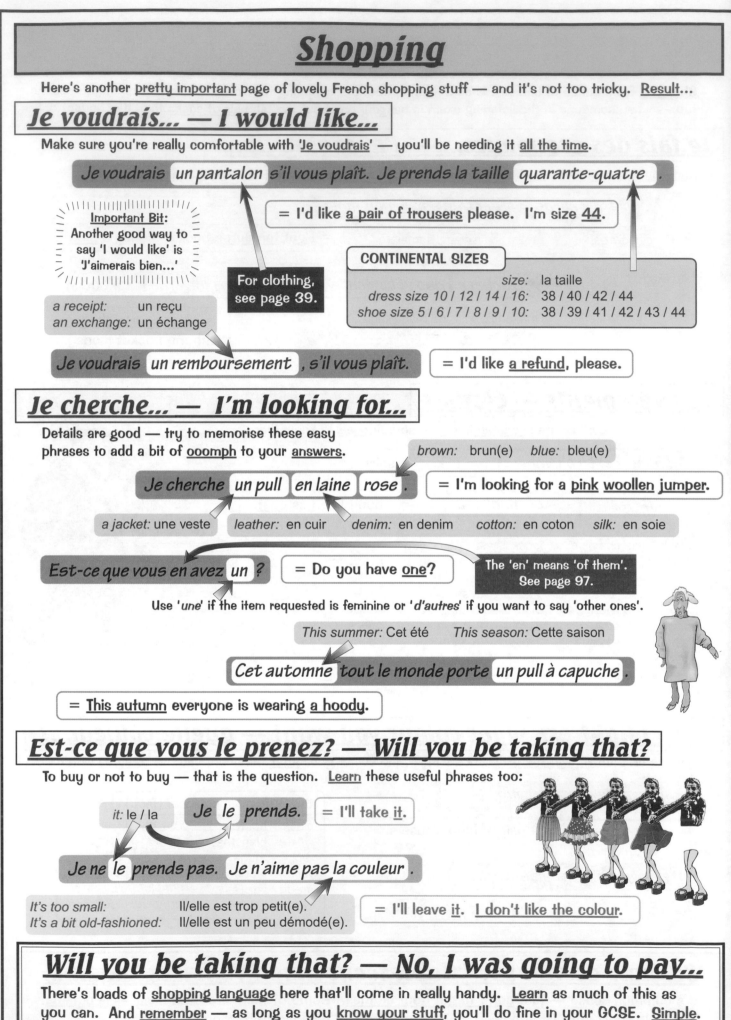

## *Will you be taking that? — No, I was going to pay...*

There's loads of <u>shopping language</u> here that'll come in really handy. <u>Learn</u> as much of this as you can. And <u>remember</u> — as long as you <u>know your stuff</u>, you'll do fine in your GCSE. <u>Simple</u>.

# Fashion and Trends

A whole page on how to talk about your <u>passion</u> for <u>skinny jeans</u>...

## Cette saison toutes les filles portent une jupe — This season all the girls are wearing skirts

Talking about fashion <u>in general</u>...

En ce moment les cardigans sont très à la mode pour les garçons.

*jumpers:* les pulls    *ties:* les cravates

= At the moment, <u>cardigans</u> are very in fashion for boys.

Les vedettes ont lancé la mode des sacs à main chers.

*fifties:* années cinquante

= Celebrities have set the trend for expensive handbags.

Les vêtements des années soixante sont à la mode cette année.

= The clothes of the <u>sixties</u> are fashionable this year.

## Je mets toujours les vêtements à la mode — I always wear fashionable clothes

For <u>followers</u> of the latest trends...

J'achète les vêtements que je vois dans les magazines.

= I buy the clothes that I see in magazines.

J'ai plus de confiance quand je porte les vêtements à la mode.

= I have more confidence when I wear fashionable clothes.

## Je porte des choses qui me vont bien — I wear things that suit me well

...and <u>trend-setters</u>...

J'ai un style personnel.

= I have an individual style.

*cheap:* bon marchés

La mode ne m'intéresse pas. Je préfère les vêtements pratiques.

For more adjectives, see pages 88-90.

= Fashion doesn't interest me. I prefer <u>practical</u> clothes.

Je ne choisis pas mes vêtements parce que ma mère les achète.

*shoes:* chaussures

= I don't choose my <u>clothes</u> because my mum buys them.

Il y a des choses plus importantes dans la vie.

= There are more important things in life.

## I don't choose my clothes — my nan still knits them...

Talking fashion is pretty tricky, so it's good for scoring <u>high marks</u> in the <u>speaking assessment</u>. Again, it doesn't matter if you give your actual opinion, as long as you give <u>an opinion</u>.

# Inviting People Out

A brief guide to having fun in French: 1) get someone to <u>agree</u> to do some fun stuff 2) come to a mutual <u>agreement</u> about what you're going to do 3) <u>organise a party</u> to celebrate all the fun...

## Sortons — Let's go out

These are all really <u>useful</u> phrases for the assessments, so get them <u>learnt</u>.

Using the 'nous' form here means 'let's' — see page 112.

**Allons** *à la piscine* .    = Let's go <u>to the swimming pool</u>.

*to the theatre:* au théâtre    *to the park:* au parc

*Oui, je veux bien* .    = <u>Yes, I'd love to.</u>

*Non, merci* .    = <u>No, thank you.</u>

*Good idea!:* Bonne idée!
*Great!:* Super!

*I'm sorry, I can't:* Je suis désolé(e), je ne peux pas.
*I don't have enough money:* Je n'ai pas assez d'argent.

## Je préférerais faire une randonnée — I'd prefer to go for a walk

To suggest an alternative activity or to talk about your dream hobby, use the <u>conditional</u>.

*Si j'étais riche,* *je ferais du ski* *tous les week-ends.*

For more on the conditional, see page 111.

*I'd buy clothes:* j'achèterais des vêtements
*I'd go clubbing:* j'irais en boîte (de nuit)

= If I were rich, <u>I would go skiing</u> every weekend.

If you learn this and use it in the right way you'll score loads more marks — worth it, even though it's a bit tricky.

## J'organise une surprise-partie...
## — I'm organising a surprise party...

<u>Party planning</u>. In French. Could be <u>useful</u>...

*On va* *écouter de la musique* *et manger* *une pizza* .    = We're going <u>to listen to music</u> and eat a <u>pizza</u>.

*to watch films:* regarder des films
*to dance:* danser

*sweets:* des bonbons
*popcorn:* du pop-corn

*C'est pour fêter l'anniversaire de Sophie.*    = It's to celebrate Sophie's Birthday.

*Veux-tu venir?*    = Do you want to come?

*On aura besoin* *du chocolat* .    = We'll need <u>some chocolate</u>.

*some films:* des films    *some CDs:* des CD

For more foods, see page 13.

## Désolé, je me lave les cheveux...

Great. Now you can invite Thierry Henry or Juliette Binoche to your <u>soirée</u> — or at least understand when they say they're washing their hair. If you <u>can't</u>, then <u>go back</u> over it until you can.

# Going Out

This stuff about <u>buying tickets</u>, <u>opening times</u> and <u>where things are</u> is essential — you need to be able to <u>talk</u> about it for your speaking assessments, or <u>understand</u> it in the listening exam.

## ...près d'ici? — ...near here?

Est-ce qu'il y a **un théâtre** près d'ici?　　= Is there <u>a theatre</u> near here?

*a sports field:* un terrain de sport
*a bowling alley:* un bowling
*a cinema:* un cinéma

*play tennis:* jouer au tennis　　*go for walks:* se promener

Peut-on **nager** près d'ici?　　= Can we <u>swim</u> near here?

## Qu'est-ce qu'il y a à l'affiche? — What's on?

À quelle heure **commence** **le spectacle** ?　　= What time does <u>the performance start</u>?

*finish:* finit　　*the film:* le film　　*the match:* le match

Il commence à **huit heures** et finit à **dix heures** .　　= <u>It</u> starts at **8.00** and finishes at **10.00**.

## Ask how much it costs — 'combien ça coûte?'

Combien coûte l'entrée **à la piscine** ?　　= How much does it cost to go <u>swimming</u>?

*bowling:* au bowling
*to the cinema:* au cinéma

Ça coûte **deux euros** l'heure.　　= It costs <u>2 euros</u> per hour.

Combien coûte **un billet** ?　　= How much does <u>one ticket</u> cost?

*How much do two tickets cost?:*
Combien coût**ent** deux billet**s** ?

**Plural endings.**

Un billet coûte cinq euros.　　= One ticket costs 5 euros.

*two tickets:* deux billets

Je voudrais **un billet** , s'il vous plaît.　　= I'd like <u>one ticket</u>, please.

## Quelles sont les heures d'ouverture?
## — What are the opening times?

À quelle heure est-ce que **la piscine** est **ouverte** ?　　= What time is <u>the swimming pool open</u>?

*the sports centre:* le centre sportif　　*closed:* fermé(e)

For other places, see page 62.

**Elle** ouvre à **neuf heures et demie** et ferme à **cinq heures** .

'Il' for a masculine place.　　= <u>It</u> opens at <u>half past nine</u> and closes at <u>five o'clock</u>.

## French makes my head spin — I feel "d'ici"...

This stuff could come up in your <u>speaking assessment</u> or <u>listening exam</u> — you need to be able to <u>understand</u> it all... So don't just sit there, let's get to it — <u>get into gear</u> and get down to it.

# Going Out

Finally... something fun to stick on the French revision schedule — <u>films</u> and <u>major sporting events</u>.

## Je suis allé(e) au cinéma — I went to the cinema

There's a chance you'll have to mention what you did last weekend. Make sure you have a plausible answer.

*my parents:* mes parents    *some friends:* des ami(e)s    *in the evening:* le soir    *later:* plus tard

J'ai regardé un film avec un ami et après nous avons mangé au restaurant.

= <u>I watched a film</u> with <u>a friend</u> and <u>afterwards</u> we ate in a restaurant.

*I went shopping:* J'ai fait des courses    *I went clubbing:* Je suis allé(e) en boîte (de nuit)

For more on talking about the past, see pages 104-106.

## Est-ce que le film était bon? — Was the film good?

You've got to be able to say whether <u>you thought</u> the film was any good — it's dead easy.

Qu'est-ce que tu penses du film ?

= What do you think <u>of the film</u>?

*of the performance:*    du spectacle
*of the play:*    de la pièce (de théâtre)
*of the concert:*    du concert

To find out more about giving opinions, see pages 7-8.

Est-ce que c'était un film d'horreur ?

= Was it a <u>horror</u> film?

*romantic:*    romantique
*adventure:*    d'aventures
*sci-fi:*    de science-fiction
*comedy:*    comique
*war:*    de guerre

Il était assez bon .

= <u>It</u> was <u>quite good</u>.

If you're asked about something <u>feminine</u>, you need '<u>Elle</u>' here.
But '<u>le film</u>' is masculine — so this is '<u>Il</u>'.

*very good:*    très bon(ne)
*bad:*    mauvais(e)

Le film était bon, mais on était trop près de l'écran.

= The film was good, but we were <u>too close to</u> the screen.

*too far from:*    trop loin de

## Qui a gagné le match? — Who won the match?

It looks <u>really good</u> if you can give some <u>details</u> in the <u>past tense</u> about what you've seen...

J'étais très content(e) du résultat.

= <u>I was</u> really pleased with the result.

*I wasn't:*    Je n'étais pas

*passed the ball:*    a passé le ballon

Mon équipe a gagné .

= My team <u>won</u>.

*lost:*    a perdu

Mon joueur préféré a marqué deux buts .

= My favourite player <u>scored two goals</u>.

## Et qui a gagné l'allumette?

<u>Tough</u> page — lots to learn. As long as you can give your <u>opinion</u> on whatever you've <u>seen</u> or <u>done</u>, it's a big piece of gâteau... That's all I have to say. There's no more advice at this point.

# Revision Summary

These questions are here to make sure you <u>know your stuff</u>. Work through them <u>all</u> and check the ones you couldn't do. <u>Look back</u> through the section to find the answers, then have another go at knocking those pesky troublesome ones right out of the parking lot. And (eventually) <u>voilà</u>.

1) What is the French for each of these sports? What's the French for the place where you would do them? a) football b) swimming c) snowboarding d) ice skating

2) Write down as many French words as you can to do with playing or listening to music.

3) Say that you go swimming at the weekend and that you're a member of a badminton club.

4) You like watching films and soaps on TV. Tonight you'd like to watch a documentary that starts at nine o'clock. How would you say all this in French?

5) Think of a film you saw recently and one you saw a month ago, and say this in French. (You don't have to translate the film titles into French.)

6) You have just watched an interesting and funny show. Say this in French. Remember to tell me its title and tell me what happened.

7) Your friend Paul is music mad. Ask him in French whether he listens to music on the radio, or on his MP3 player. Now pretend to be Paul and answer the question, giving a reason.

8) Nadine thinks she's fallen in love with Robbie Williams. Write a paragraph in French to her saying what you think of him.

9) Would you like to be famous? Give <u>two reasons</u> why or why not.

10) Your French uncle wants to find out the UK weather forecast on the web, but he's not very internet savvy. Tell him there's a link on the homepage of the BBC website.

11) You send twenty text messages every day. Tell the French-speaking world.

12) What are the French names for: a) a cake shop b) a butcher's c) a bookshop d) a sweet shop e) a supermarket f) a delicatessen?

13) Do you like shopping online? Why or why not?

14) A shop assistant asks you 'Est-ce que je peux vous aider?' and later 'Voulez-vous autre chose?' What do these two questions mean in English? How would you answer them?

15) You want to buy a brown jumper, size 38, and some cotton pyjamas. How do you say this to the shop assistant?

16) In perfect French, summarise your views on fashion in 3 sentences.

17) Describe your perfectly planned surprise party in no more than 3 French sentences.

18) Tu veux aller au concert. Le concert commence à vingt et une heures et finit à vingt-deux heures trente. Un billet coûte cinq euros. How would you say that in English?

19) In three sentences, describe a film, show or match that you've seen recently.

# Holiday Destinations

You need to know about <u>countries</u> and <u>nationalities</u> for describing yourself or your <u>holiday</u> plans in your <u>speaking</u> and <u>writing</u> tasks, or for <u>understanding descriptions</u> of people in the <u>reading</u> and <u>listening</u> papers.

## D'où viens-tu? — Where do you come from?

Learn this phrase <u>off by heart</u> — if the country you're from isn't here, check in a dictionary...

**Je viens** d'Angleterre **. Je suis** anglais(e) **.**   = I come <u>from England</u>.  I am <u>English</u>.

| | |
|---|---|
| *Wales:* | du pays de Galles |
| *Northern Ireland:* | d'Irlande du Nord |
| *Scotland:* | d'Écosse |

| | |
|---|---|
| *Welsh:* | gallois(e) |
| *Northern Irish:* | nord-irlandais(e) |
| *Scottish:* | écossais(e) |

**IMPORTANT BIT:**
You must add '<u>e</u>' on the end for <u>women and girls</u> (see page 88).
*Je suis anglaise.*

**Je suis** anglophone **.**   *French-speaking:* francophone

= I am <u>English-speaking</u>.

**J'habite en** Angleterre **.**   = I live in <u>England</u>.

**Où habites-tu?**   = Where do you live?

or 'Où est-ce que tu habites?'

Use 'en' for feminine countries and masculine ones beginning with a vowel, and 'au' for all other masculine countries.  For plural countries, it's 'aux'.

## Learn these foreign countries

You also need to <u>understand</u> where <u>other people</u> come from.

| | |
|---|---|
| *Algeria:* | l'Algérie (fem.) |
| *America:* | l'Amérique (fem.) / les États-Unis (masc.) |
| *Australia:* | l'Australie (fem.) |
| *Belgium:* | la Belgique |
| *Canada:* | le Canada |
| *China:* | la Chine |
| *France:* | la France |
| *Germany:* | l'Allemagne (fem.) |
| *Greece:* | la Grèce |
| *India:* | l'Inde (fem.) |
| *Italy:* | l'Italie (fem.) |
| *Japan:* | le Japon |
| *Morocco:* | le Maroc |
| *Poland:* | la Pologne |
| *Portugal:* | le Portugal |
| *Spain:* | l'Espagne (fem.) |
| *Switzerland:* | la Suisse |

| | |
|---|---|
| *African:* | africain(e) |
| *Algerian:* | algérien(ne) |
| *American:* | américain(e) |
| *Australian:* | australien(ne) |
| *Belgian:* | belge |
| *Canadian:* | canadien(ne) |
| *Chinese:* | chinois(e) |
| *French:* | français(e) |
| *German:* | allemand(e) |
| *Greek:* | grec/grecque |
| *Indian:* | indien(ne) |
| *Italian:* | italien(ne) |
| *Japanese:* | japonais(e) |
| *Moroccan:* | marocain(e) |
| *Polish:* | polonais(e) |
| *Portuguese:* | portugais(e) |
| *Spanish:* | espagnol(e) |
| *Swiss:* | suisse |

| | |
|---|---|
| *England:* | l'Angleterre (f.) |
| *(Northern) Ireland:* | l'Irlande (du Nord) (f.) |
| *Scotland:* | l'Écosse (f.) |
| *Wales:* | le pays de Galles |
| *Great Britain:* | la Grande-Bretagne |

**IMPORTANT:** <u>Don't</u> use a capital letter for all these adjectives.

| | |
|---|---|
| *English:* | anglais(e) |
| *Irish:* | irlandais(e) |
| *N.Irish:* | nord-irlandais(e) |
| *Scottish:* | écossais(e) |
| *Welsh:* | gallois(e) |
| *British:* | britannique |

## Hidden a gender...

Most of the countries are <u>feminine</u>, but there are a few sneaky exceptions which are <u>masculine</u>. And with the ones where the French word is <u>a bit like the English</u>, check you've got the <u>spelling</u> right.  Don't just look at them and <u>assume</u> you know them because they look <u>familiar</u>.

# Catching the Train

Trains, planes and automobiles... Well, just <u>trains</u> for now. This page gives you a few of the <u>basics</u> you might come across in the exam. Examiners like this topic — I think they all have shares in train companies.

## Je veux y aller en train — I want to go there by train

Here's how to buy a <u>ticket</u>. You'd be <u>nuts</u> not to learn this.

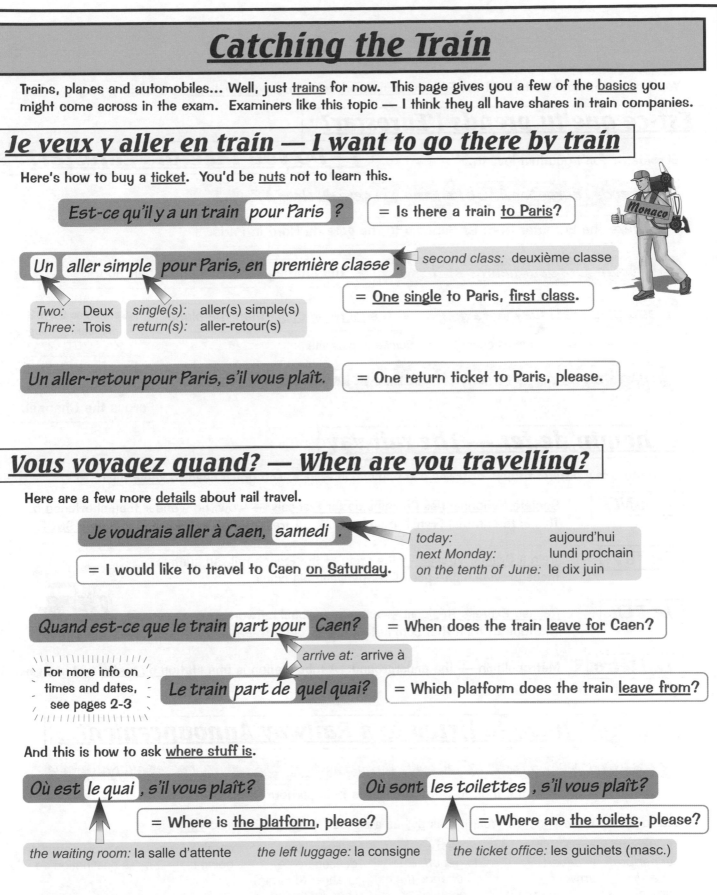

Est-ce qu'il y a un train <u>pour Paris</u> ?   = Is there a train <u>to Paris</u>?

Un <u>aller simple</u> pour Paris, en <u>première classe</u>.   *second class:* deuxième classe

= <u>One single</u> to Paris, <u>first class</u>.

*Two:* Deux   *single(s):* aller(s) simple(s)
*Three:* Trois   *return(s):* aller-retour(s)

Un aller-retour pour Paris, s'il vous plaît.   = One return ticket to Paris, please.

## Vous voyagez quand? — When are you travelling?

Here are a few more <u>details</u> about rail travel.

Je voudrais aller à Caen, <u>samedi</u>.

= I would like to travel to Caen <u>on Saturday</u>.

| | |
|---|---|
| *today:* | aujourd'hui |
| *next Monday:* | lundi prochain |
| *on the tenth of June:* | le dix juin |

Quand est-ce que le train <u>part pour</u> Caen?   = When does the train <u>leave for</u> Caen?

*arrive at:* arrive à

For more info on times and dates, see pages 2-3

Le train <u>part de</u> quel quai?   = Which platform does the train <u>leave from</u>?

And this is how to ask <u>where stuff is</u>.

Où est <u>le quai</u>, s'il vous plaît?   = Where is <u>the platform</u>, please?

Où sont <u>les toilettes</u>, s'il vous plaît?   = Where are <u>the toilets</u>, please?

*the waiting room:* la salle d'attente   *the left luggage:* la consigne   *the ticket office:* les guichets (masc.)

# What's French for 'Not ANOTHER strike'...

Ah yes, the French <u>love</u> their <u>trains</u>, but even more than that they love leaving their trains to rest while they go off and wave a placard in the air. Anyway, assume the trains will be running during your next visit to the continent, and <u>learn</u> all this <u>wonderful vocabulary</u> in anticipation.

# Catching the Train

You'll need to know a bit about the <u>French rail network</u> too. You <u>won't believe</u> how exciting it is.

## Est-ce que tu prends l'Eurostar? — Do you take the Eurostar?

Eurostar... don't you just love it...

> *Je prends l'Eurostar de St Pancras à la gare du Nord à Paris.*

= I take the Eurostar from St Pancras to the gare du Nord in Paris.

> *Le voyage dure deux heures et demie.*

= The journey lasts two and a half hours.

> *C'est plus pratique que l'avion.*

= It's <u>more practical</u> than the plane.

*less expensive:* moins cher  *quicker:* plus vite

> *Je préfère prendre le bateau de Douvres pour traverser la Manche.*

= I prefer to take the ferry from Dover to cross the Channel.

\\\\\|||||||||/////
See pages 92-93 for
comparing things.
///////|||||||\\\\\\

## Le chemin de fer — The railway

There are a few different types of trains and stations in France, and you'll need to <u>know</u> them.

**La SNCF** — <u>S</u>ociété <u>N</u>ationale des <u>C</u>hemins de <u>f</u>er <u>F</u>rançais — wow, no wonder they shortened it. This is the normal French train network. A train station in French is <u>une gare SNCF</u>.

**Le TGV** — <u>T</u>rain à <u>G</u>rande <u>V</u>itesse — the pride of the French railway system, these provide high-speed links between big cities.

**Le RER** — <u>R</u>éseau <u>E</u>xpress <u>R</u>égional — express regional network. The type of train that commuters use to get into Paris.

Not a TGV

**Le Métro** — <u>Métro</u>politain — the underground. A tube station is <u>une station de métro</u> (<u>not</u> une gare...).

## You might have to listen to a Railway Announcement...

> *Le train à destination de Bordeaux part du quai numéro huit à quinze heures quarante-cinq.*

= The train to Bordeaux leaves from platform 8 at 15:45.

And to finish, more <u>vocab</u>... Yes, it's as <u>dull</u> as a big dull thing, but it's also <u>vital</u>.

| | | | | | |
|---|---|---|---|---|---|
| *to depart:* | partir | *to get on:* | monter dans | *coming from:* | en provenance de |
| *departure:* | le départ | *to get off:* | descendre de | *going to:* | à destination de |
| *to arrive:* | arriver | *to change (trains):* | changer (de train) | | |
| *arrival:* | l'arrivée (fem.) | *timetable:* | l'horaire (masc.) | | |

## I would catch the train — but it's a bit heavy...*

Lucky you... examiners <u>love</u> to ask about travelling. So you'd better make sure you can answer <u>all</u> the questions they could throw at you about it. The thing is, even if you find this really boring now, when it gets to the exam, you'll be wishing you'd bothered. <u>No doubt</u> about that.

# All Kinds of Transport

Here's what you need to <u>know</u> about other forms of <u>transport</u>. This is another one of those topics that you'll need to know <u>really well</u> — and you need to know loads of <u>vocab</u> for it, too.

## Comment y vas-tu? — How do you get there?

You might need to say <u>how</u> you <u>get about</u>.

**J'y vais à pied.** = I go there on foot.

**D'habitude, je vais en ville en bus.**
to school: à l'école / au collège
= I normally go <u>into town</u> <u>by bus</u>.

| | |
|---|---|
| by bus: | en bus / en autobus |
| on the underground: | en métro |
| by car: | en voiture |
| by boat: | en bateau |
| by plane: | en avion |
| by Eurostar: | en Eurostar |
| by bike: | à bicyclette / à vélo |
| by motorbike: | à moto |

**J'y suis allé(e) par le train.** = I went there <u>by train</u>.

You could say "en train" instead here.

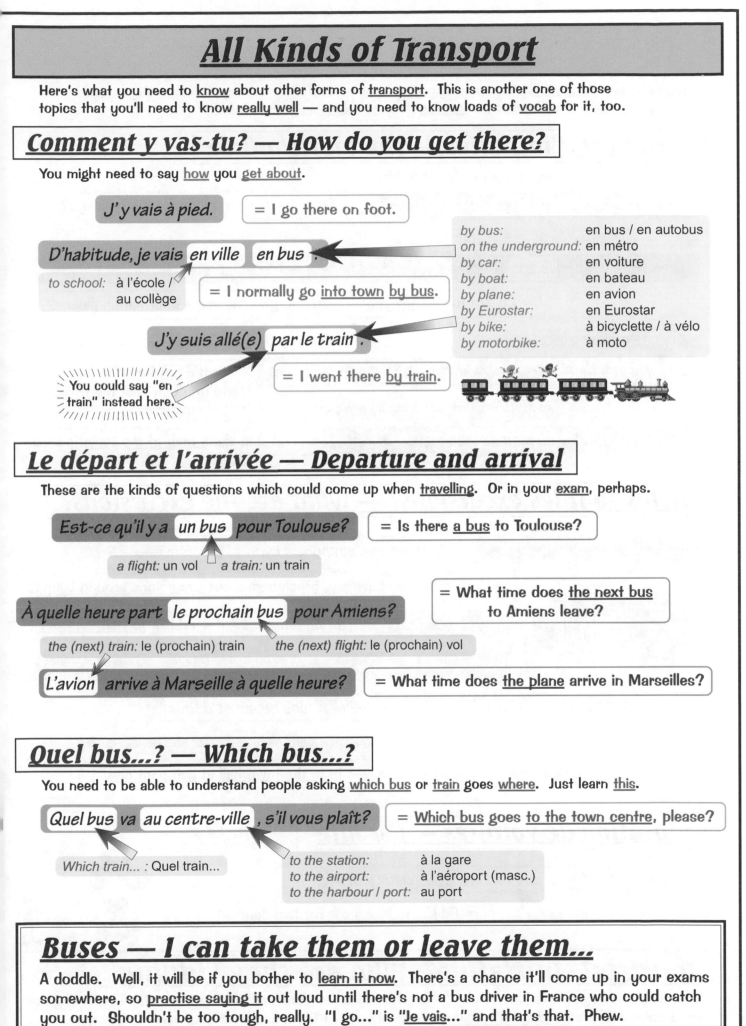

## Le départ et l'arrivée — Departure and arrival

These are the kinds of questions which could come up when <u>travelling</u>. Or in your <u>exam</u>, perhaps.

**Est-ce qu'il y a un bus pour Toulouse?** = Is there <u>a bus</u> to Toulouse?

a flight: un vol    a train: un train

**À quelle heure part le prochain bus pour Amiens?** = What time does <u>the next bus</u> to Amiens leave?

the (next) train: le (prochain) train    the (next) flight: le (prochain) vol

**L'avion arrive à Marseille à quelle heure?** = What time does <u>the plane</u> arrive in Marseilles?

## Quel bus...? — Which bus...?

You need to be able to understand people asking <u>which bus</u> or <u>train</u> goes <u>where</u>. Just learn <u>this</u>.

**Quel bus va au centre-ville, s'il vous plaît?** = <u>Which bus</u> goes <u>to the town centre</u>, please?

Which train... : Quel train...

| | |
|---|---|
| to the station: | à la gare |
| to the airport: | à l'aéroport (masc.) |
| to the harbour / port: | au port |

## Buses — I can take them or leave them...

A doddle. Well, it will be if you bother to <u>learn it now</u>. There's a chance it'll come up in your exams somewhere, so <u>practise saying it</u> out loud until there's not a bus driver in France who could catch you out. Shouldn't be too tough, really. "I go..." is "<u>Je vais</u>..." and that's that. Phew.

# Planning Your Holiday

Excursions and hiring stuff... all really important aspects of effective holiday planning. If you want to get great marks, you'd better get learning these unbelievably useful phrases.

## Le syndicat d'initiative — The tourist office

Where you go to find out what a town's got to offer...

**Avez-vous des projets pour les vacances?** = Do you have any plans for the holidays?

the theme park: la parc d'attractions

**J'aimerais visiter le zoo . Pouvez-vous me donner des renseignements, s'il vous plaît?**
= I'd like to visit the zoo. Could you give me some information please?

It (for a feminine noun): Elle          the bus: l'autobus

**Oui. Il n'est pas loin d'ici et vous pouvez prendre le train .**
= It's not far from here and you can take the train.

a map of the region: une carte de la région

**Je voudrais aussi un plan de ville , s'il vous plaît.** = I'd also like a map of the town, please.

## Quelles sont les excursions? — What are the excursions?

the museums in Metz: les musées à Metz

**Avez-vous des brochures sur les excursions autour de Lyon ?**
= Do you have any brochures about excursions around Lyons?

**Je voudrais visiter Versailles .** = I'd like to visit Versailles.

from the church: de l'église (fem.)          to go to a museum: aller au musée
from the market: du marché          to visit the palace / castle: visiter le château

**Ce car va à Versailles. Il part de l'hôtel de ville à une heure et demie .**

This bus: Ce bus          2 o'clock: deux heures   3:15: trois heures quinze

= This coach goes to Versailles. It leaves from the town hall at half past one.

## La location de voitures — Car hire

**Je voudrais louer une voiture pour deux jours .**

a bike: une bicyclette          = I'd like to hire a car for two days.

Higher...higher...

## Tourists? Initiative? Who are they kidding...

Everyone knows tourists just blindly follow the person at the front holding the umbrella, so why call the tourist office a syndicat d'initiative... I dunno, but I bet it's a word you won't forget now...

# Holiday Accommodation

This page has all the words you need to know about <u>hotels</u>, <u>hostels</u>, <u>camping</u> and <u>foreign exchanges</u>. It's really useful stuff, so you'd better get <u>learning</u>...

## Je cherche un logement — I'm looking for somewhere to stay

Learn these different <u>places to stay</u>...

*hotel:* **l'hôtel (masc.)**

**le camping**

*self-catering cottage:* **le gîte**

*campsite:* **le camping**

*youth hostel:* **l'auberge de jeunesse (fem.)**

*bed and breakfast:* **la chambre d'hôte**

## Learn this vocabulary for Hotels and Hostels

**VERBS USED IN HOTELS:**

| *to recommend:* | recommander | *to stay:* | rester |
| *to reserve:* | réserver | *to leave:* | partir |
| *to confirm:* | confirmer | *to cost:* | coûter |

**THINGS YOU MIGHT WANT TO ASK FOR:**

| *full board (room + all meals):* | la pension complète |
| *half board (room + some meals):* | la demi-pension |

**PARTS OF A HOTEL OR YOUTH HOSTEL:**

| *restaurant:* | le restaurant |
| *dining room:* | la salle à manger |
| *dormitory:* | le dortoir |
| *lift:* | l'ascenseur (masc.) |
| *stairs:* | l'escalier (masc.) |
| *car park:* | le parking |

**THINGS ABOUT YOUR ROOM:**

| *key:* | la clé |
| *balcony:* | le balcon |
| *bath:* | le bain |
| *shower:* | la douche |
| *washbasin:* | le lavabo |

**PAYING FOR YOUR STAY:**

| *bill:* | la note |
| *(set) price:* | le prix (fixe) |

## Je fais un échange — I'm going on a school exchange

If you get a question about exchange visits, <u>don't panic</u>. Chances are the <u>vocab</u> will be very <u>similar</u> to the stuff you've learnt for <u>other types</u> of <u>holiday</u>.

**Je reste** *chez une famille française* . = I'm staying <u>with a French family</u>.

*with my penfriend:* chez mon/ma correspondant(e)

**J'aurai** *l'occasion de voir comment vivre les Français* . = I'll have <u>the chance to see how French people live</u>.

*the chance to speak French every day:*
l'occasion de parler français tous les jours

## Pension — but I'm only sixteen...

If anything on <u>logements</u> comes up, you'll be glad I put this page in. It might just look like another load of vocabulary, but it's your <u>ticket to big marks</u>. If you <u>learn it all</u>, you'll <u>sail through</u> this topic.

# Booking a Room / Pitch

It's crucial when you're <u>planning</u> a holiday to be able to talk about your <u>preference</u> for a suite with a gold-plated bath and a view of the Eiffel Tower. <u>Learn</u> this page and you'll be laughing.

## Avez-vous des chambres libres?

### — Do you have any rooms free?

Je voudrais une chambre pour une personne . = I'd like a <u>single</u> <u>room</u>.

You could be a bit more specific and use these.

room with a bath:    chambre avec bain
room with a balcony:   chambre avec balcon

*double:*
pour deux personnes
*that overlooks the sea:*
qui donne sur la mer

Je voudrais rester ici deux nuits . = I'd like to stay here <u>two nights</u>.

For more numbers, see page 1.

*for one night:* une nuit

If there's more than one person, use deux personne<u>s</u>, trois personne<u>s</u> etc.

C'est combien par nuit pour une personne ? = How much is it per night for <u>one person</u>?

If the 'it' you're talking about is masculine (e.g. l'emplacement) then use 'le'.

Je la prends. = I'll take <u>it</u>.

*it:* le / la

Je ne la prends pas. = I won't take <u>it</u>.

## Est-ce qu'on peut camper ici? — Can I camp here?

Even if you're not the <u>outdoorsy type</u> it's a good idea to get familiar with this camping vocab for your exams.

Je voudrais un emplacement pour une nuit . = I'd like <u>a pitch</u> for <u>one night</u>.

*two weeks:* deux semaines

pitch (place for a tent): un emplacement

*sleeping bag:* un sac de couchage

*holiday camp:* une colonie (de vacances)

*caravan:* une caravane

*tent:* une tente

**YOU MIGHT NEED THESE PHRASES TOO:**

*Is there drinking water here?:*    Est-ce qu'il y a de l'eau potable ici?
*Can I light a fire here?:*    Est-ce que je peux faire du feu ici?
*Where can I find...?:*    Où est-ce que je peux trouver... ?

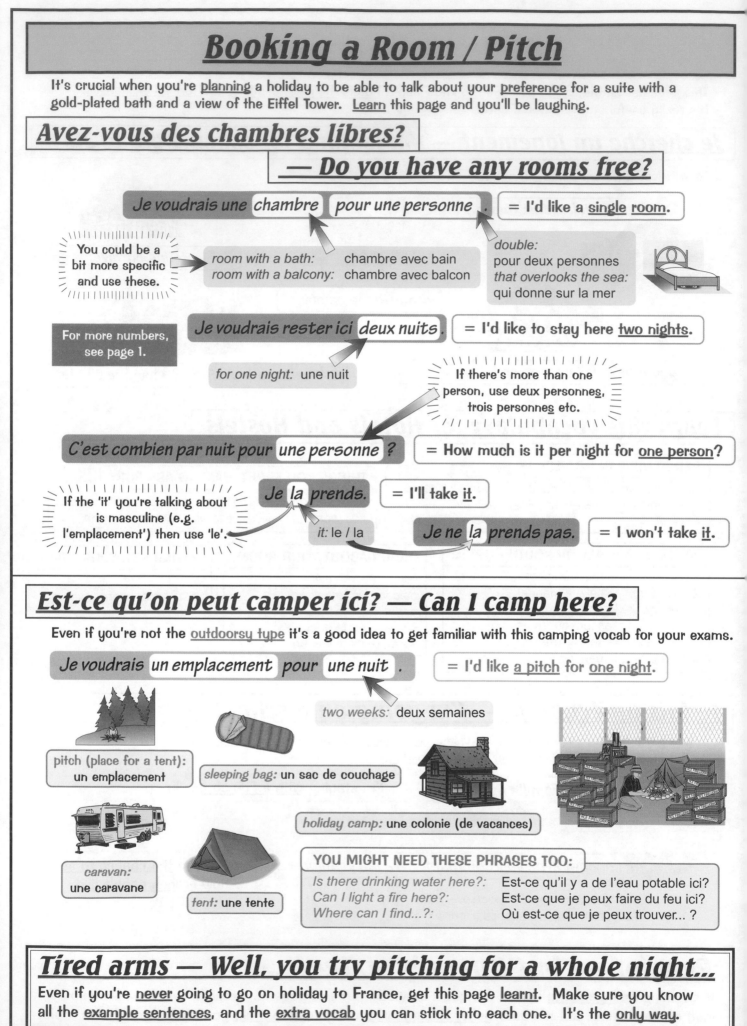

## Tired arms — Well, you try pitching for a whole night...

Even if you're <u>never</u> going to go on holiday to France, get this page <u>learnt</u>. Make sure you know all the <u>example sentences</u>, and the <u>extra vocab</u> you can stick into each one. It's the <u>only way</u>.

# Where / When is...?

Here's how French people ask <u>where</u> and <u>when things are</u>. It's all pretty important stuff for you to know...

## Ask where something is — use 'Où est... ?'

Knowing how the French ask <u>where</u> things are is supremely important — get these <u>learnt</u>.

Où est la salle à manger , s'il vous plaît?  = Where is <u>the dining room</u>, please?

*the car park:* le parking
*the escalator:* l'escalier roulant (masc.)
*the telephone:* le téléphone

See page 51 for more places you might need to find.

Où sont les toilettes ?  = Where are <u>the toilets?</u>

If the place you're looking for is plural, remember to use 'Où sont...' instead of 'Où est...'

Use 'Elle' for 'la' words, 'Elles' and 'Ils' for plural words and 'Il' for 'le' words.

Use 'au' here because 'étage' is masculine. Use 'à la' for feminine words, e.g. 'elle est à la piscine'.

Elle est au troisième étage .  = <u>It</u>'s on the <u>third floor</u>.

*fourth floor:* quatrième étage
*second floor:* deuxième étage
*first floor:* premier étage
*ground floor:* rez-de-chaussée

C'est un "stick-up".
Où est le "money"?

For higher floor numbers, see page 1.

**OTHER WORDS YOU MIGHT NEED:**

| | | | |
|---|---|---|---|
| *straight on:* | tout droit | *outside:* | à l'extérieur |
| *upstairs:* | en haut | *on the left / right:* | à gauche / à droite |
| *downstairs:* | en bas | *at the end of the corridor:* | au bout du couloir |

## À quelle heure... ? — What time... ?

When you've understood <u>where</u> everything is, you'll need to know <u>when</u> things happen, too...

À quelle heure est-ce que le petit déjeuner est servi, s'il vous plaît?

= What time is <u>breakfast</u> served, please?

For more times, see page 2.

*lunch:* le déjeuner
*evening meal:* le dîner

Il est servi entre six heures et huit heures.  = It's served between six and eight o'clock.

## Un petit déjeuner énorme, s'il vous plaît...

The French word '<u>jeûner</u>' means to '<u>fast</u>' (i.e. not to eat anything). When you put '<u>dé-</u>' before a verb, it means 'do the opposite' (e.g. 'défaire' means to 'undo'). So 'dé-jeûner' means to 'un-fast', or to <u>break</u> the <u>fast</u>... or to <u>breakfast</u>. OK, that's enough trivia — make sure you <u>learn</u> this page.

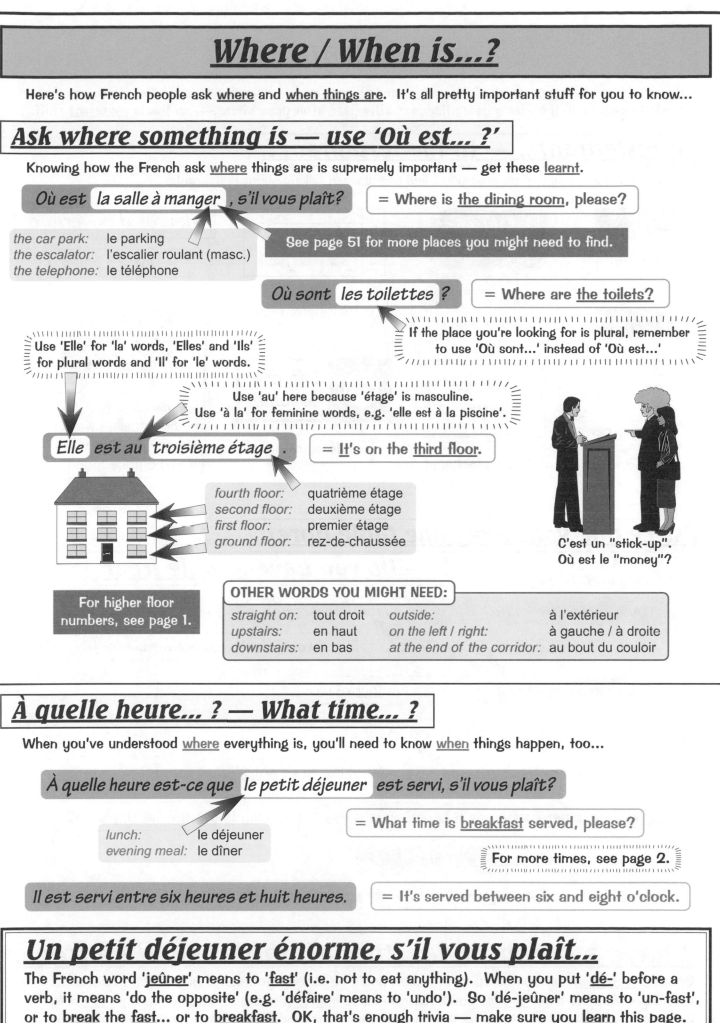

# At a Restaurant

If you've <u>been</u> to <u>France</u>, a lot of these <u>signs</u> and <u>phrases</u> might be <u>familiar</u> to you. The restaurant theme tends to crop up in the exams year after year, after year, after year, after... — so this is <u>important</u> stuff.

## Au restaurant... — In the restaurant...

Here are some <u>words and phrases</u> you'll find useful when talking about <u>restaurants</u>.

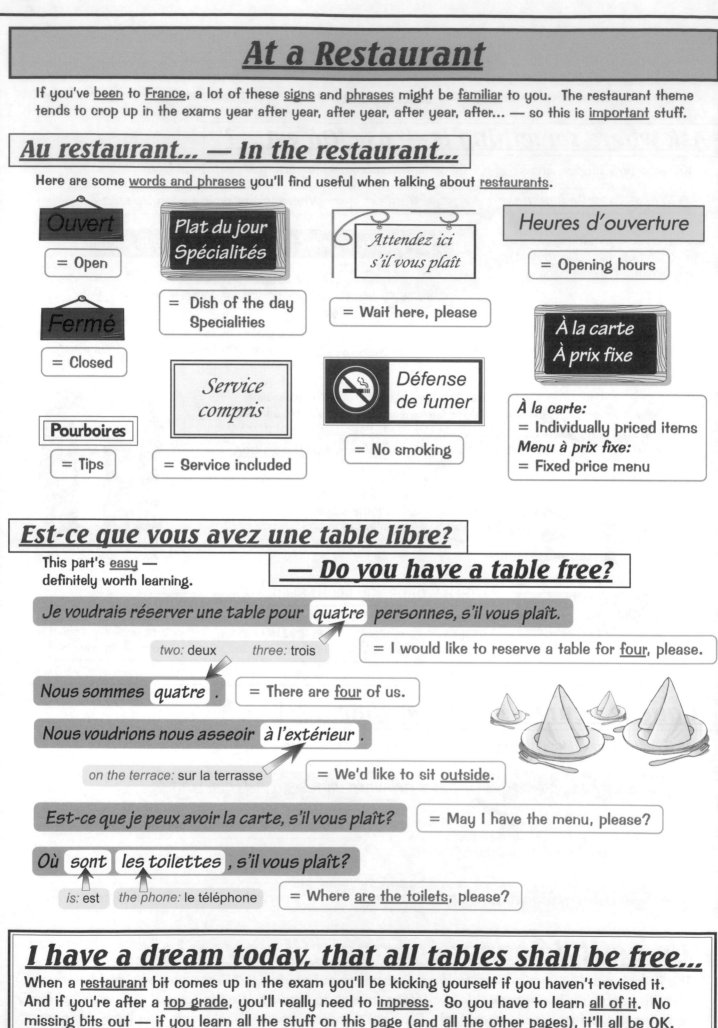

**Ouvert**
= Open

**Fermé**
= Closed

**Pourboires**
= Tips

**Plat du jour Spécialités**
= Dish of the day Specialities

**Service compris**
= Service included

**Attendez ici s'il vous plaît**
= Wait here, please

**Défense de fumer**
= No smoking

**Heures d'ouverture**
= Opening hours

**À la carte À prix fixe**

À la carte:
= Individually priced items
Menu à prix fixe:
= Fixed price menu

## Est-ce que vous avez une table libre?

This part's <u>easy</u> — definitely worth learning.

## — Do you have a table free?

*Je voudrais réserver une table pour* quatre *personnes, s'il vous plaît.*

*two:* deux     *three:* trois

= I would like to reserve a table for <u>four</u>, please.

*Nous sommes* quatre .
= There are <u>four</u> of us.

*Nous voudrions nous asseoir* à l'extérieur .

*on the terrace:* sur la terrasse
= We'd like to sit <u>outside</u>.

*Est-ce que je peux avoir la carte, s'il vous plaît?*
= May I have the menu, please?

*Où* sont les toilettes *, s'il vous plaît?*

*is:* est   *the phone:* le téléphone
= Where <u>are</u> <u>the toilets</u>, please?

## I have a dream today, that all tables shall be free...

When a <u>restaurant</u> bit comes up in the exam you'll be kicking yourself if you haven't revised it. And if you're after a <u>top grade</u>, you'll really need to <u>impress</u>. So you have to learn <u>all of it</u>. No missing bits out — if you learn all the stuff on this page (and all the other pages), it'll all be OK.

# At a Restaurant

Now it's time for that all-important part... <u>opinions</u>. You'll need to talk about the <u>foods you prefer</u> and know how to state any <u>problems</u> you have with a meal. Revise this and your <u>French</u> will be complete. Almost.

## Je voudrais... — I would like...

See page 13 for food vocab.

How to give your order, course by course, in perfect French.

**Est-ce que vous avez choisi, monsieur/madame?** = Have you chosen, sir/madam?

*the soup:* la soupe    *the goat's cheese salad:* la salade de chèvre

**Oui, merci. Comme** hors d'œuvre **je prendrai** les crevettes à l'ail **.**

*first course:* entrée (fem.)

= Yes, thank you. For <u>starter</u>, I'll have <u>the garlic prawns</u>.

**Et comme plat principal?** = And for the main course?

**Je voudrais le bifteck.** = I'd like the steak.

*rare:* saignant    *well done:* bien cuit

**Vous le voulez cuit comment?** = How do you want it cooked?

**Je le voudrais** à point **, s'il vous plaît.** = I'd like it <u>medium</u>, please.

## Les boissons et les desserts — Drinks and desserts

**Vous désirez boire quelque chose?** = Would you like something to drink?

**On va prendre deux jus d'orange et une carafe d'eau, s'il vous plaît.** = We'll have two orange juices and a jug of water, please.

**Voulez-vous voir la carte des desserts?** = Would you like to see the dessert menu?

*some cheese:* du fromage

**Non, merci. On va prendre** un café **.** = No, thank you. We're going to have <u>a coffee</u>.

## Est-ce que vous avez fini? — Have you finished?

There's <u>no</u> getting away from having to know <u>this</u>. You can't leave without paying.

**Est-ce que je peux payer?** = May I pay?

**L'addition, s'il vous plaît.** = The bill, please.

**Est-ce que le service est compris?** = Is service included?

## Thanks Mr Federer, the service was ace...

<u>Restaurants</u> — <u>fun</u> to eat at, but a <u>bit of a mouthful</u> when it comes to GCSE French revision. These pages will be <u>really useful</u> in the exam once you've mastered 'em — so go for it...

# Talking About Your Holiday

Everyone wants to bore people by <u>telling</u> them all about their <u>holidays</u>. By the time you've finished this page you'll be able to bore people in <u>French</u>... and get good <u>marks</u>.

## Où es-tu allé(e)? — Where did you go?

This is <u>where</u> you went.

This is <u>when</u> you went.

Other dates and times: pages 2–3.
A bigger list of countries: page 46.

*Je suis allé(e)* aux États-Unis il y a deux semaines .

| | |
|---|---|
| *to Spain:* | en Espagne |
| *to France:* | en France |
| *to Ireland:* | en Irlande |

| | |
|---|---|
| *a week ago:* | il y a une semaine |
| *last month:* | le mois dernier |
| *in July:* | en juillet |
| *in the summer:* | en été |

= I went <u>to the USA</u> <u>two weeks ago</u>.

## Avec qui étais-tu en vacances?

## — Who were you on holiday with?

You'd better <u>answer</u> this question, otherwise there'll be all sorts of gossip.

*J'étais en vacances avec* ma famille *pendant* un mois .

= I was on holiday with <u>my family</u> for <u>a month</u>.

| | |
|---|---|
| *a fortnight:* | quinze jours |
| *two weeks:* | deux semaines |

For past tenses, see pages 104-108.
For more on family, see page 22.

| | |
|---|---|
| *my brother:* | mon frère |
| *my friends:* | mes ami(e)s |
| *my friend's family:* | la famille de mon ami(e) |

## Qu'est-ce que tu as fait? — What did you do?

You need to be able to say what you <u>did</u> on holiday — <u>learn</u> it well.

*Je suis allé(e)* à la plage .

= I went <u>to the beach</u>.

*to the disco:* en discothèque    *to the museum:* au musée

For other sports and activities, see page 29.

This is a reflexive verb — see page 109 for more on these.

*Je me suis détendu(e)* .

= <u>I relaxed</u>.

| | |
|---|---|
| *I enjoyed myself:* | Je me suis amusé(e) |
| *I played tennis:* | J'ai joué au tennis |

## Comment y es-tu allé(e)? — How did you get there?

Remember the little word '<u>y</u>', which means 'there' — it's a useful one (see page 97 for more on this).

*Nous y sommes allé(e)s* en voiture .

= We went there <u>by car</u>.

| | | | |
|---|---|---|---|
| *by plane:* | en avion | *by train:* | par le train / en train |
| *by boat:* | en bateau | *by bike:* | à bicyclette / à vélo |

For more types of transport, see page 49.

## So, celeb Z-list — what's the jungle really like...

One final useful tip before you move on — if you're writing about <u>visiting something</u> while on holiday, e.g. a museum, use '<u>visiter</u>'. If you're writing about <u>visiting a person</u>, it's '<u>rendre visite à</u>'.

# Talking About Your Holiday

Opinions and tales of woe — the examiners love them. So plough on and learn this stuff as well...

## Comment était le voyage? — How was the trip?

Comment étaient tes vacances? = How was your holiday?

Je les ai aimées. = I liked it.

Mes vacances étaient formidables. = My holiday was great.

Je ne les ai pas aimées. = I didn't like it.

Comme ci comme ça. = So-so.

## Quelle catastrophe — What a disaster

Sometimes things don't quite go to plan when you're on holiday.

"Nous avons fait du ski. Ma sœur est tombée, et s'est cassé la jambe." = We went skiing. My sister fell, and broke her leg.

Limb-breakers.

a ski resort: une station de ski

"Nous sommes allés à une station balnéaire, mais mes parents détestent la plage." = We went to a seaside resort, but my parents hate the beach.

Not to everyone's taste.

"J'étais malade pendant le voyage. Nous avons dû nous arrêter pendant une heure dans une aire de repos." = I was ill on the journey. We had to stop for an hour at a motorway services.

a service station: une station-service

For more on the perfect tense, see pages 104-106.

"Ma mère a laissé son passeport à l'hôtel. Elle n'a pas pu prendre l'avion." = My mother left her passport at the hotel. She couldn't take the plane.

"Mon sac à main, mon portable et mon lecteur mp3 ont tous été volés." = My handbag, my mobile phone and my MP3 player were all stolen.

For more on the passive, see page 115.

## Il a plu tous les jours — It rained every day

If they ask you to compare different holidays, the weather's a good place to start...

En Italie, il faisait plus chaud qu' en Écosse. = In Italy it was hotter than in Scotland.

This is the comparative. For more examples, see pages 92-93.

En France, il pleuvait moins qu' en Espagne. = In France, it rained less than in Spain.

For more on weather, see page 60.

## Ça t'a plu? — Non, il a fait très beau...

Watch out with the word 'plu'. It's the past participle of both pleuvoir (to rain) and plaire (to please). 'Ça t'a plu?' means 'Did you like it?', whereas 'A-t-il plu?' means 'Did it rain?'. Tricky.

# Talking About Your Holiday

Accommodation with problems... cockroaches in the bath, rats in the kitchens — that kind of thing.
Like revision, it's not pleasant, but you know the drill — somebody's got to deal with it...

## Il y avait un problème... — There was a problem...

Make sure you can write about at least two problems — safety in numbers.

cold: froid

La télévision était cassée. = The TV was broken.

Il faisait trop chaud.

The chair: La chaise

There's an extra 'e' here because 'télévision' is feminine. If 'cassée' was describing something masculine, there would only be an 'é'. See page 88.

= It was too hot.

The air conditioning: La climatisation     The phone: Le téléphone

La douche ne fonctionnait pas. = The shower didn't work.

Il y avait trop de bruit. Je ne pouvais pas dormir. = There was too much noise. I couldn't sleep.

L'hôtel n'était pas ouvert. Nous sommes arrivé(e)s pendant la fermeture annuelle.

= The hotel wasn't open. We arrived during the annual closure period.

## C'était dégoûtant! — It was disgusting!

Il y avait de l'eau partout. = There was water everywhere.

sand: du sable

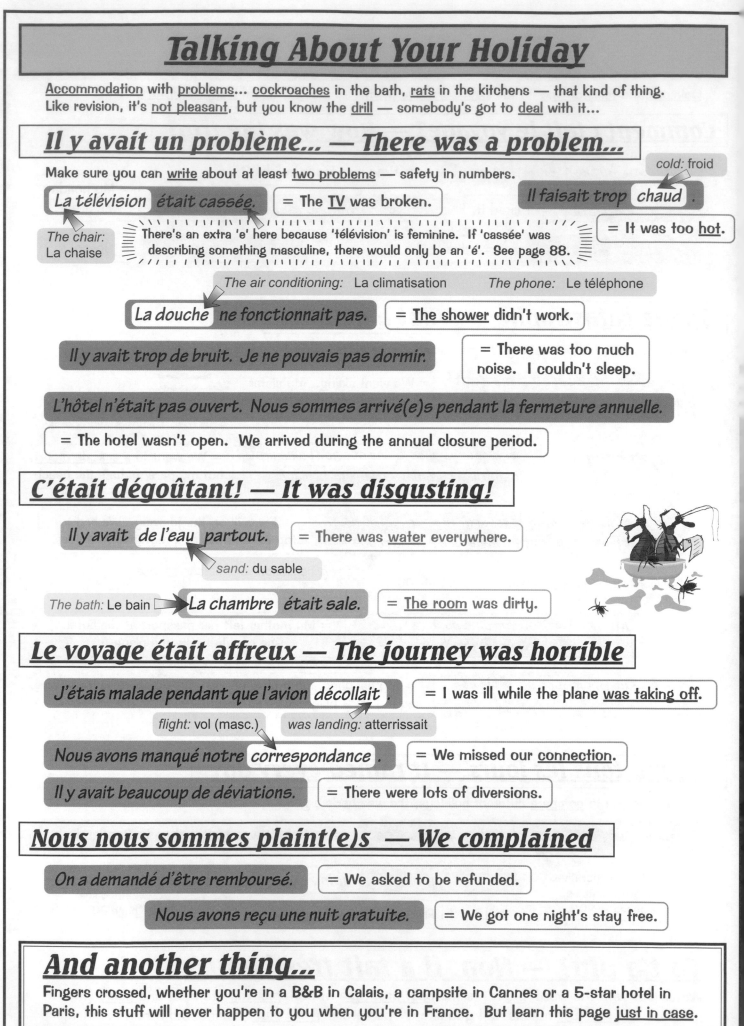

The bath: Le bain    La chambre était sale. = The room was dirty.

## Le voyage était affreux — The journey was horrible

J'étais malade pendant que l'avion décollait. = I was ill while the plane was taking off.

flight: vol (masc.)     was landing: atterrissait

Nous avons manqué notre correspondance. = We missed our connection.

Il y avait beaucoup de déviations. = There were lots of diversions.

## Nous nous sommes plaint(e)s — We complained

On a demandé d'être remboursé. = We asked to be refunded.

Nous avons reçu une nuit gratuite. = We got one night's stay free.

## And another thing...

Fingers crossed, whether you're in a B&B in Calais, a campsite in Cannes or a 5-star hotel in Paris, this stuff will never happen to you when you're in France. But learn this page just in case.

# Talking About Your Holiday

More on holidays — yay. This time though about where you're planning on going, or where you'd like to go.

## Où iras-tu l'année prochaine? — Where will you go next year?

Tricky stuff now — learn to talk about things you will do in the future...

**These are the future tense...**

*For more info about the future tense, see page 103.*

**These are the easy future tense...**

| | |
|---|---|
| Where will you go? <br> *Où est-ce que tu iras?* | I will go to America in two weeks. <br> *J'irai en Amérique dans deux semaines.* |
| How are you going to get there? <br> *Comment vas-tu y aller?* | I'm going to go there by plane. <br> *Je vais y aller en avion.* |

| | |
|---|---|
| What are you going to take? <br> *Qu'est-ce que tu vas prendre?* | I'm going to take some clothes, my sunglasses and some books. <br> *Je vais prendre des vêtements, mes lunettes de soleil et des livres.* |

## Mes vacances de rêve — My dream holiday

This bit's all about what you would do if you could. This uses the conditional (see page 111).

*Comment seraient tes vacances de rêve?* = What would your dream holiday be like?

*Mes vacances de rêve seraient de ...* →

| | |
|---|---|
| stay in a five-star hotel: | rester dans un hôtel cinq étoiles |
| visit a city like... : | visiter une grande ville comme... |
| spend a month in the country: | passer un mois à la campagne |
| go away with my friends: | partir avec mes ami(e)s |
| go away with my family: | partir avec ma famille |

= My dream holiday would be to ...

You might like to start with a fancy "if" — which examiners love, if you get the tenses right.

*Si j'avais beaucoup d'argent ... / Si j'étais riche ...* ...*je ferais du ski tous les ans.*

**Extra marks for style**

= If I had a lot of money ... / If I were rich ... ...I'd go skiing every year.

## Est-ce que les vacances sont importantes pour toi? — Are holidays important to you?

If your speaking assessment's on holidays, you might be asked to give your opinions on holidays in general.

*Bien sûr. Il faut prendre le temps de se détendre.* = Of course. It's essential to take time to relax.

*Est-ce qu'on prend trop de vacances?* = Do we take too many holidays?

*Oui — tous ces* vols *sont mauvais pour l'environnement.* = Yes — all these flights are bad for the environment.

*trips abroad:* voyages à l'étranger

# Holidays — always a tense time...

Like lots of things in GCSE French, talking about holidays comes down to which tense you use. Think of how to say the activity in the infinitive (e.g. 'partir'), and then put it into the correct tense.

# The Weather

You might have to listen to a <u>weather forecast</u> in your <u>listening</u> exam. But don't panic — learn the weather stuff in the present and future tenses given here and you'll be OK. More than OK — stupendous.

## Quel temps fait-il? — What's the weather like?

These <u>short sentences</u> are the ones you definitely <u>can't do without</u> — and they're <u>easy</u>.

**Aujourd'hui il pleut .** = Today <u>it's raining</u>.

It's snowing: il neige

Literally translated, this means 'There is wind.'

Of course, it doesn't <u>always</u> rain, so here are a few others you could use:

**Il fait froid .** = It's <u>cold</u>.

warm: chaud
sunny: du soleil
hot: très chaud

You can use any of these words after 'Il fait...'.

**Il y a du vent .** = It's <u>windy</u>.

icy: de la glace
rainy: de la pluie
cloudy: des nuages (masc.)

thundery: du tonnerre
stormy: une tempête / un orage

## Quel temps fera-t-il demain?

This is quite easy, and it sounds <u>dead impressive</u>:

## — What will the weather be like tomorrow?

It'll snow: Il neigera / Il va neiger

**Il pleuvra / Il va pleuvoir demain .** = <u>It will rain</u> <u>tomorrow</u>.

See page 103 for the future tense.

the day after tomorrow: après-demain
next week: la semaine prochaine

**Il fera froid .** = It will be <u>cold</u>.

nice: beau
bad: mauvais
foggy: du brouillard

**Il y aura des vents forts .**

= There will be <u>strong winds</u>.

showers: des averses (fem.)
sunny intervals: des éclaircies (fem.)
lightning: des éclairs (masc.)

## You need to understand a weather forecast

Here's a <u>real</u> weather forecast — time to show what you can do. You <u>won't know all the words</u>, but don't panic. Work through this one — you should be able to get the gist by looking at the words you <u>do know</u>.

**La météo d'aujourd'hui**
Aujourd'hui il fera chaud en France. Demain il y aura du vent dans le sud et des nuages dans le nord. Il va pleuvoir sur la côte.

**Today's Weather Forecast**
Today it will be warm in France. Tomorrow it will be windy in the south and cloudy in the north. It will rain on the coast.

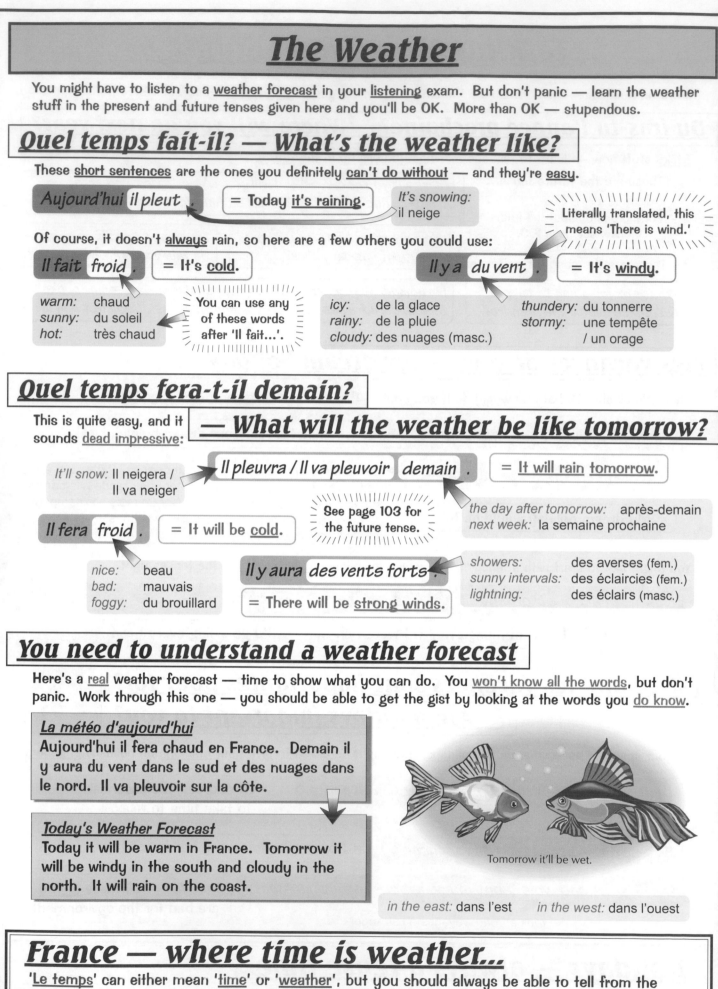

Tomorrow it'll be wet.

in the east: dans l'est      in the west: dans l'ouest

## France — where time is weather...

'<u>Le temps</u>' can either mean '<u>time</u>' or '<u>weather</u>', but you should always be able to tell from the <u>context</u> which one it is. Weather's a favourite with examiners, so you need to <u>learn</u> the <u>examples</u> on this page and the <u>bits of vocab</u> — then you'll be fine. (Just like the weather, with any luck...)

# Revision Summary

It's that time again folks... another dreaded revision summary. Don't dread it. Work in harmony with it, so that by the time you've answered all of these questions (several times), you'll feel like you're a fully-fledged Frenchified person, and ready to take on that exam. OK, cut the 'yoga speak' — just practise these questions till you can answer them in your sleep.

1) Write down four countries in the UK and five other countries, in French. How would you say that you came from each of these places?

2) Write down the nationality to go with each of the places above (but in French).

3) You're at a French train station. How would you do these in French?
   a) Say that you'd like to travel to Marseilles on Sunday.   b) Ask if there are any trains there.

4) How do you say these in French?
   a) the platform   b) the waiting room   c) the timetable   d) the ticket office   e) the departure

5) Ask for three return tickets to Tours, second class. Ask when and what platform the train leaves from and where the left luggage office is.

6) Say that you go to school by car, but your friend walks.

7) You've missed the bus to Pont-Audemer. Ask when the next bus leaves and when it'll arrive.

8) You're at the tourist office and you want more information about the region you're staying in. Ask, in French, for the information, and request a map of the area, too.

9) Imagine that you are a first class impersonator. Impersonate a tourist in France. Ask if the tourist office has any brochures about excursions. Then ask if you can hire a car for two weeks.

10) What are these in French?  a) hotel  b) youth hostel  c) campsite  d) cottage

11) How do you say these in French?   a) key   b) bill   c) stairs   d) tent   e) sleeping bag

12) Your friend announces: 'Je reste chez mon correspondant et je parlerai français tous les jours'. What have they just told you about the school exchange they are set to go on?

13) You arrive at a French hotel. Say you want one double room and two single rooms. You want to stay five nights. Say you'll take the rooms and then ask where the restaurant is, in French.

14) Ask when breakfast is served, out loud and in French.

15) You're telling friends about the grotty hotel you stayed in in France. Your room was dirty, the air conditioning didn't work and the TV was broken. How would you say this in French?

16) You're in a restaurant. You want to order salad for your starter, followed by duck for main course. You want the duck to be well done. How would you say all this in French?

17) How would you ask someone how their holiday was, what they did, how they got there, and how the journey was? Imagine you now have to answer these questions in French.

18) Describe your dream holiday in three French sentences.

19) You've just listened to the forecast. Say that tomorrow it will be hot and sunny.

# Names of Buildings

If you're going to talk about your town, you need to know the names for buildings. Yes, it's a bit dull, but you absolutely <u>have</u> to learn them.

## Learn all these bâtiments — buildings

These are the basic, bog-standard '<u>learn-them-or-else</u>' buildings. (Building = le bâtiment.)

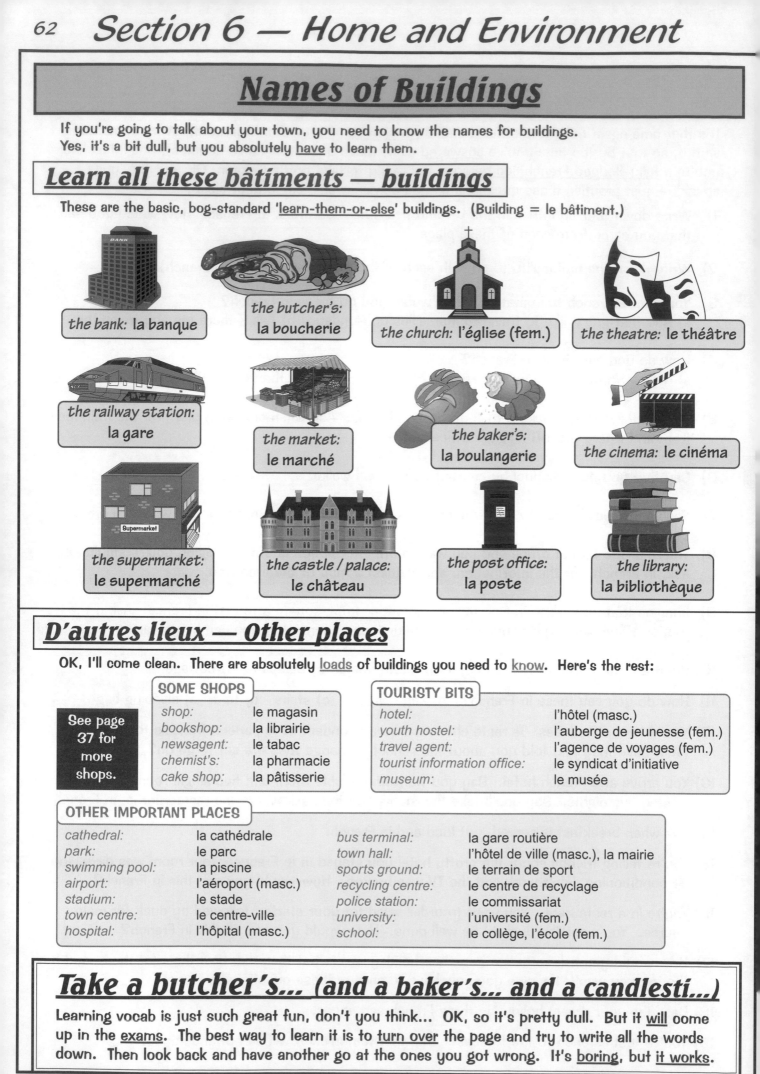

the bank: la banque

the butcher's: la boucherie

the church: l'église (fem.)

the theatre: le théâtre

the railway station: la gare

the market: le marché

the baker's: la boulangerie

the cinema: le cinéma

the supermarket: le supermarché

the castle / palace: le château

the post office: la poste

the library: la bibliothèque

## D'autres lieux — Other places

OK, I'll come clean. There are absolutely <u>loads</u> of buildings you need to <u>know</u>. Here's the rest:

**SOME SHOPS**

See page 37 for more shops.

| | |
|---|---|
| shop: | le magasin |
| bookshop: | la librairie |
| newsagent: | le tabac |
| chemist's: | la pharmacie |
| cake shop: | la pâtisserie |

**TOURISTY BITS**

| | |
|---|---|
| hotel: | l'hôtel (masc.) |
| youth hostel: | l'auberge de jeunesse (fem.) |
| travel agent: | l'agence de voyages (fem.) |
| tourist information office: | le syndicat d'initiative |
| museum: | le musée |

**OTHER IMPORTANT PLACES**

| | | | |
|---|---|---|---|
| cathedral: | la cathédrale | bus terminal: | la gare routière |
| park: | le parc | town hall: | l'hôtel de ville (masc.), la mairie |
| swimming pool: | la piscine | sports ground: | le terrain de sport |
| airport: | l'aéroport (masc.) | recycling centre: | le centre de recyclage |
| stadium: | le stade | police station: | le commissariat |
| town centre: | le centre-ville | university: | l'université (fem.) |
| hospital: | l'hôpital (masc.) | school: | le collège, l'école (fem.) |

## Take a butcher's... (and a baker's... and a candlesti...)

Learning vocab is just such great fun, don't you think... OK, so it's pretty dull. But it <u>will</u> oome up in the <u>exams</u>. The best way to learn it is to <u>turn over</u> the page and try to write all the words down. Then look back and have another go at the ones you got wrong. It's <u>boring</u>, but <u>it works</u>.

# Asking Directions

It's pretty likely you'll get at least <u>one</u> question about <u>asking</u> or <u>understanding directions</u>. If you <u>don't</u> learn this stuff, that's one question you <u>won't</u> be able to answer. That's a good enough reason to learn it.

## Où se trouve... ? — Where is... ?

Asking <u>where something is</u> is dead easy — 'Où est...' or 'Où se trouve' plus the place name:

Où se trouve **la poste** , s'il vous plaît?  = Where is <u>the post office</u>, please?

Est-ce qu'il y a **une bibliothèque** près d'ici?  = Is there <u>a library</u> near here?

## Le cinéma est... — The cinema is...

Le cinéma est **entre la banque et le parc** .  = The cinema is <u>between the bank and the park</u>.

| | | |
|---|---|---|
| *this way:* par ici | *behind the bank:* derrière la banque | *opposite the bank:* en face de la banque |
| *that way:* par là | *in front of the school:* devant l'école | *below the café:* au-dessous du café |
| *here / there:* ici / là-bas | *on the corner:* au coin | *at the end of the road:* au bout de la rue |
| *next to the park:* à côté du parc | *above the bar:* au-dessus du bar | *at the bottom of the garden:* au fond du jardin |

## C'est loin d'ici? — Is it far from here?

It's a good idea to check <u>distance</u>, before letting yourself in for a 3-hour trek:

Est-ce que **le cinéma** est loin d'ici?  = Is <u>the cinema</u> far from here?

*the post office:* la poste
*the park:* le parc

Il est **à deux kilomètres** d'ici.  = It's <u>two kilometres</u> from here.

*a few kilometres:* à quelques kilomètres    *not far:* à deux pas    *far:* loin    *near:* près

## Use 'pour aller à...?' to ask the way

You'll probably hear people asking directions in your <u>listening test</u>.

*(to a woman):* madame    *to the castle:* au château    *to the hospital:* à l'hôpital

Pardon **monsieur** , pour aller **à la banque** , s'il vous plaît?

Use '<u>au</u>' for 'le' words, '<u>à la</u>' for 'la' words, and '<u>à l</u>' for words starting with a vowel and most words which start with an 'h'. See page 87.

= Excuse me <u>sir</u>, how do I get <u>to the bank</u>, please?

Look at page 1 for more stuff on 1st, 2nd, etc.

**LEARN THIS IMPORTANT VOCAB FOR DIRECTIONS**

| | | | |
|---|---|---|---|
| *go straight on:* | allez tout droit | *go / turn right at the traffic lights:* | tournez à droite aux feux rouges |
| *go right:* | tournez à droite | *go straight on, past the church:* | allez tout droit, devant l'église |
| *go left:* | tournez à gauche | *take the first road on the left:* | prenez la première rue à gauche |

## How do you get to Wembley — Practise...

Cover it up, scribble it down, check what you got wrong, and try it again. That's the way to learn this stuff. Keep at it until you know it <u>all</u> — then you'll be really ready for the exam. Just reading the page is <u>nowhere near</u> enough — you wouldn't remember it tomorrow, never mind in the exam.

# Talking About Where You Live

You'll have to understand and answer questions about where you <u>live</u>.
If you've <u>learnt</u> this, you'll be able to understand and answer. Simple as that.

## Où habites-tu? — Where do you live?

You <u>won't</u> get through GCSE
French without needing this <u>vocab</u>
— so make sure you learn it well.

J'habite à  Barrow . = I live in <u>Barrow</u>.

*London:* Londres    *Edinburgh:* Edimbourg

Barrow se trouve dans  le nord-ouest  de l'Angleterre.

See page 46 for more countries.

*the north:* le nord    *the west:* l'ouest (masc.)
*the south:* le sud    *the east:* l'est (masc.)

= Barrow's in <u>the north-west</u> of England.

## You have to write about life 'dans ta ville' — 'in your town'

Practise writing a description of <u>your town</u>, your favourite <u>town</u> or a dream <u>town</u> — <u>know</u> this <u>vocab</u> well...

Qu'est-ce qu'il y a dans ta ville?

= What is there in your town?

Il y a  un marché . = There's <u>a market</u>.

See page 62 for more buildings and places.

Est-ce que tu aimes vivre à Barrow?

= Do you like living in Barrow?

J'aime  vivre à Barrow.

*I don't like:* Je n'aime pas

= <u>I like</u> living in Barrow.

## Comment est Barrow? — What is Barrow like?

Descriptions of <u>towns</u> could come up in any of your <u>assessments</u> — it's need-to-know stuff.

La ville est  très intéressante .

= The town is <u>very interesting</u>.

*boring:* ennuyeuse
*great:* chouette
*dirty:* sale
*clean:* propre
*quiet:* tranquille
*picturesque:* pittoresque

Il y a  beaucoup  à faire.

= There's <u>lots</u> to do.

*enough:* assez    *always something:* toujours quelque chose

Il n'y a rien à faire.

= There's nothing to do.

There's more about where you live on the next page.

Lie if you need to, but make it <u>believable</u>.

<u>Longer descriptions</u> may seem tough at first — they're simply <u>all the bits you already know</u> put together...

J'aime vivre à  Barrow , parce qu'il y a toujours quelque chose à faire.

= I like living in <u>Barrow</u>, because there's always something to do.

Je n'aime pas vivre à  Bogville , parce qu'il n'y a rien à faire.

= I don't like living in <u>Bogville</u>, because there's nothing to do.

## Bogville-sur-mer — celebrity playground...

If you come from a really dreary place which has <u>nothing</u> going for it, you can <u>make things up</u> (within reason) — chances are there'll be <u>something</u> to say about a place near you. Start with <u>where</u> it is and see how much you can note down about it <u>without</u> looking at the page.

# Talking About Where You Live

This page isn't too bad — even the tricky stuff is really just a case of 'learn the sentences and learn what words you can change around in them'. If you spend the time on it, it'll become dead easy.

## Add More Detail about where you live

J'habite au numéro quatre, rue Tub, à Lancaster. = I live at 4 Tub Street, Lancaster.

Lancaster est entouré de collines et de beau paysage. = Lancaster is surrounded by hills and lovely countryside.

*a town:* une ville    *a village:* un village

Lancaster est une grande ville avec quarante-six mille habitants et beaucoup d'industrie. = Lancaster is a city with 46 000 inhabitants and a lot of industry.

## Tu habites avec qui? — Who do you live with?

J'habite avec mes grands-parents. = I live with my grandparents.

*my parents:* mes parents    *my father:* mon père    *my boyfriend:* mon petit ami
*my friends:* mes ami(e)s    *my mother:* ma mère    *my girlfriend:* ma petite amie

J'aime habiter en famille parce que ... = I like living with family because ...

Je n'aime pas habiter en famille parce que ... = I don't like living with family because ...

*My mum does the cooking:* ma mère fais la cuisine.
*we get on well:* nous nous entendons bien.
*I never feel lonely:* je ne me sens jamais seul(e).

*my brother annoys me all the time:* mon frère m'énerve tout le temps.
*I don't have any privacy:* je n'ai pas de vie privée.

## Chez toi — At your home

Being able to write about where you live and understanding others talking about their home is really important too...

*semi-detached house:* maison jumelée    *detached house:* maison individuelle

J'habite une petite maison moderne. = I live in a small, modern house.

*big:* grande    *old:* ancienne
*pretty:* jolie    *green:* verte

In French, you don't need 'dans' when you say where you live. Literally you say, 'I live a house'. It's easiest if you think 'habiter' = 'inhabit'.

Mon appartement se trouve près du parc. 

*the motorway:* de l'autoroute (fem.)
*the shops:* des magasins (masc.)

*My house:* Ma maison    = My flat is near the park.

*on the ground floor:* au rez-de-chaussée

Mon appartement est au premier étage. = My flat is on the first floor.

## Chez — not just for hairdressers...

You need to be able to say where you live — just say "J'habite au numéro..." and then the number of the house or flat, followed by the street name. Easy really. But only if you bother to learn it.

# Inside Your Home

You've got to be able to <u>describe</u> your home. Luckily, you don't need to say <u>everything</u> that's in it — just some things. And you can always pretend you don't have that indoor swimming pool...

## Comment est ta maison? — What's your house like?

It'll look <u>impressive</u> if you can give more <u>details</u> about your home. <u>Details</u> are the <u>answer</u>...

Comment est la cuisine ? = What's the <u>kitchen</u> like?

Est-ce que la cuisine est grande ? = Is the <u>kitchen</u> <u>big</u>?

*the dining room:* la salle à manger

| *comfortable:* confortable | *great:* chouette | *ugly:* laid(e) / |
| *tiny:* tout(e) petit(e) | *beautiful:* beau / belle | moche |

Le salon est joli . = <u>The living room</u> is <u>nice</u>.

*It's not:* Ce n'est pas  C'est ma pièce préférée. = <u>It's</u> my favourite room.

## Est-ce que tu as un jardin? — Have you got a garden?

*My flat:* Mon appartement  Ma maison a un jardin. = <u>My house</u> has a garden.

| *a tree:* un arbre | *a patio:* une terrasse |
| *a lawn:* une pelouse | *a swimming pool:* une piscine |
| | *a hedge:* une haie |

Nous avons des fleurs dans notre jardin.

= We have <u>flowers</u> in our garden.

## Est-ce que tu as une chambre à toi?
## — Have you got your own room?

You'll pick up more juicy <u>marks</u> with these...

J'ai une chambre à moi. = I have my own room.

Je partage une chambre avec mon frère . = I share a room with <u>my brother</u>.

## Décris-moi ta chambre... — Describe your room to me...

<u>Remember</u>, if these aren't in your room, you can be <u>creative</u> (lie) — get the <u>vocab spot on</u>, though.

Il y a quels meubles dans ta chambre? = What furniture is there in your bedroom?

Dans ma chambre, il y a ... = In my bedroom there is / there are ...

| *a wardrobe:* une armoire | *a mirror:* un miroir | *a bed:* un lit | *curtains:* des rideaux (masc.) |
| *a rug:* un tapis | *a (book)shelf:* une étagère | *bunk beds:* des lits superposés | |

Le fauteuil est rouge et les murs sont gris. = <u>The armchair is</u> red and <u>the walls are</u> grey.

'Le fauteuil' is <u>singular</u>, so the verb 'être' is too = <u>est</u>    'Les murs' is <u>plural</u>, so the verb 'être' is too = <u>sont</u>

## For once I wish I lived in a one-room bedsit...

It's all about <u>the little details</u> here. Once you've <u>learnt</u> these <u>phrases</u>, you can go into great detail about your Cliff Richard posters and <u>wow</u> everyone with your <u>descriptive</u> abilities. Super.

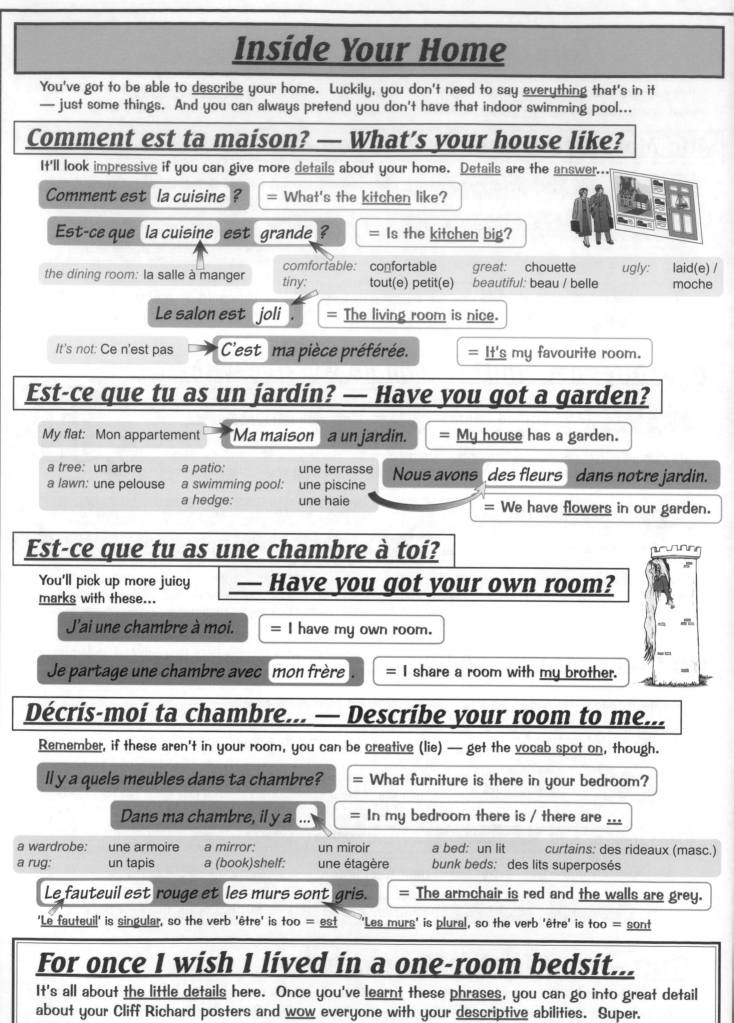

# Daily Routine

Chores and revision — two peas from the same pod. But unlike ironing, once done, <u>revision</u> is <u>done for ever</u>.

## Décris-moi une journée typique...

Daily <u>routine</u>. <u>Learn</u> it. <u>Work</u> it. <u>Know</u> it like it's... um... <u>routine</u>.

## — Describe a typical day to me...

Je me réveille à sept heures . = <u>I wake up</u> at <u>seven o'clock</u>.

| | | | |
|---|---|---|---|
| *I get up:* | Je me lève | *I get dressed:* | Je m'habille |
| *I shower:* | Je me douche | *I relax:* | Je me détends |
| *I get undressed:* | Je me déshabille | *I go to bed:* | Je me couche |

See page 2 for more info about time.

## Est-ce que tu fais le ménage? — Do you do the housework?

Even if you <u>never</u> help at home, <u>learn</u> these words.

Je fais la vaisselle à la maison.

= <u>I wash up</u> at home.

Je dois faire la vaisselle .

= I have to <u>wash up</u>.

| | |
|---|---|
| *I make my bed:* | Je fais mon lit |
| *I do the laundry:* | Je fais la lessive |
| *I do the shopping:* | Je fais les courses |
| *I tidy my room:* | Je range ma chambre |
| *I wash the car:* | Je lave la voiture |
| *I do the gardening:* | Je fais le jardinage |
| *I walk the dog:* | Je promène le chien |

| | |
|---|---|
| *make my bed:* | faire mon lit |
| *do the laundry:* | faire la lessive |
| *do the shopping:* | faire les courses |
| *tidy my room:* | ranger ma chambre |
| *wash the car:* | laver la voiture |
| *do the gardening:* | faire le jardinage |
| *walk the dog:* | promener le chien |

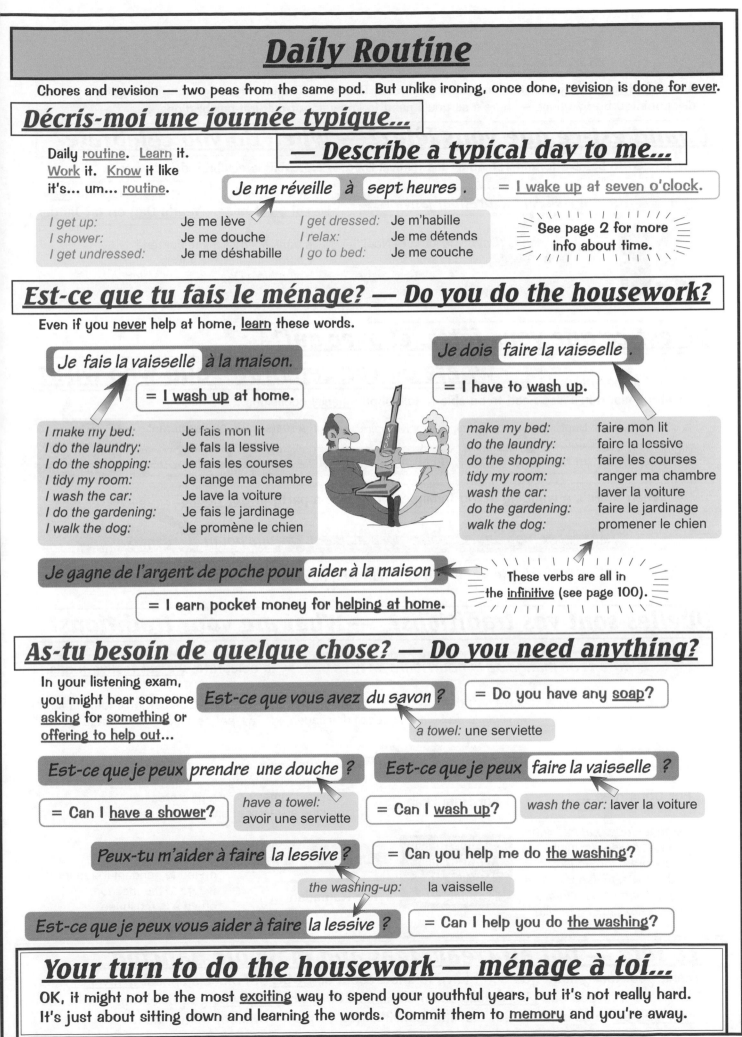

Je gagne de l'argent de poche pour aider à la maison .

= I earn pocket money for <u>helping at home</u>.

These verbs are all in the <u>infinitive</u> (see page 100).

## As-tu besoin de quelque chose? — Do you need anything?

In your listening exam, you might hear someone <u>asking</u> for <u>something</u> or <u>offering to help out</u>...

Est-ce que vous avez du savon ?

= Do you have any <u>soap</u>?

*a towel:* une serviette

Est-ce que je peux prendre une douche ?

= Can I <u>have a shower</u>?

*have a towel:* avoir une serviette

Est-ce que je peux faire la vaisselle ?

= Can I <u>wash up</u>?

*wash the car:* laver la voiture

Peux-tu m'aider à faire la lessive ?

= Can you help me do <u>the washing</u>?

*the washing-up:* la vaisselle

Est-ce que je peux vous aider à faire la lessive ?

= Can I help you do <u>the washing</u>?

## Your turn to do the housework — ménage à toi...

OK, it might not be the most <u>exciting</u> way to spend your youthful years, but it's not really hard. It's just about sitting down and learning the words. Commit them to <u>memory</u> and you're away.

# Festivals and Special Occasions

Ahhhh festivals... If you're thinking music and mud, Glastonbury-style, then you may be slightly disappointed by this page — here's all you'll need to know about cultural celebrations...

## Quand est-ce que vous fêtez? — When do you celebrate?

You'll need to be able to understand all the festival lingo — e.g. what is celebrated and when...

On fête le jour de l'An le premier janvier .

Put a date or time of year here.

= We celebrate New Year's Day on 1st January.

| | | | |
|---|---|---|---|
| Christmas (Day): | (le jour de) Noël | a bank holiday: | un jour férié |
| New Year's Eve: | le réveillon / la Saint-Sylvestre | Easter: | Pâques |
| | | Valentine's Day: | la Saint Valentin |
| All Saints' Day: | la Toussaint | | |

## Où est-ce que vous fêtez, et avec qui?
## — Where do you celebrate, and who with?

As well as cultural celebrations, you'll also need to be able to talk about special occasions...

a christening: un baptême    a birthday: un anniversaire

in a restaurant: au restaurant

See page 42 for more on parties.

Quand il y a un mariage dans ma famille, on organise une fête chez nous .

= When there's a wedding in my family, we organise a party at our house.

a meal: un repas

Pour fêter mon anniversaire, normalement j'ai une boum avec mes amis.

= To celebrate my birthday, I normally have a party with my friends.

## Quelles sont vos traditions? — What are your traditions?

Pour célébrer, on mange de la nourriture de fête .

= To celebrate, we eat festive foods.

we have fun: on s'amuse
we dance: on danse

we give presents: on offre des cadeaux
we receive presents: on reçoit des cadeaux

we sing together: on chante ensemble
we eat as a family: on mange en famille

Pour Noël ...

For Christmas ...

we go to church at midnight: on va à l'église à minuit.
we decorate the house: on décore la maison.
we play games as a family: on joue aux jeux en famille.

Pour la Hanoukka ...

For Hanukkah ...

we light 8 candles — one per day, for 8 days: on allume huit bougies — une par jour, pour huit jours.
we play games and we give presents: on joue aux jeux et on offre des cadeaux.

For how to say 'I am Christian / Muslim etc.' see page 26.

Pour le Ramadan ...

For Ramadan ...

we fast for 30 days: on jeûne pendant trente jours.
we go to the mosque: on va à la mosquée.

## La fête — not all cream teas and maypole dancing...

Thank your lucky stars you don't have to know about all 5000 of France's annual festivals. It's important that you can give details about some sort of celebration, who you celebrate it with and what you do to celebrate. So. Let the festivities (er... I mean revision) commence...

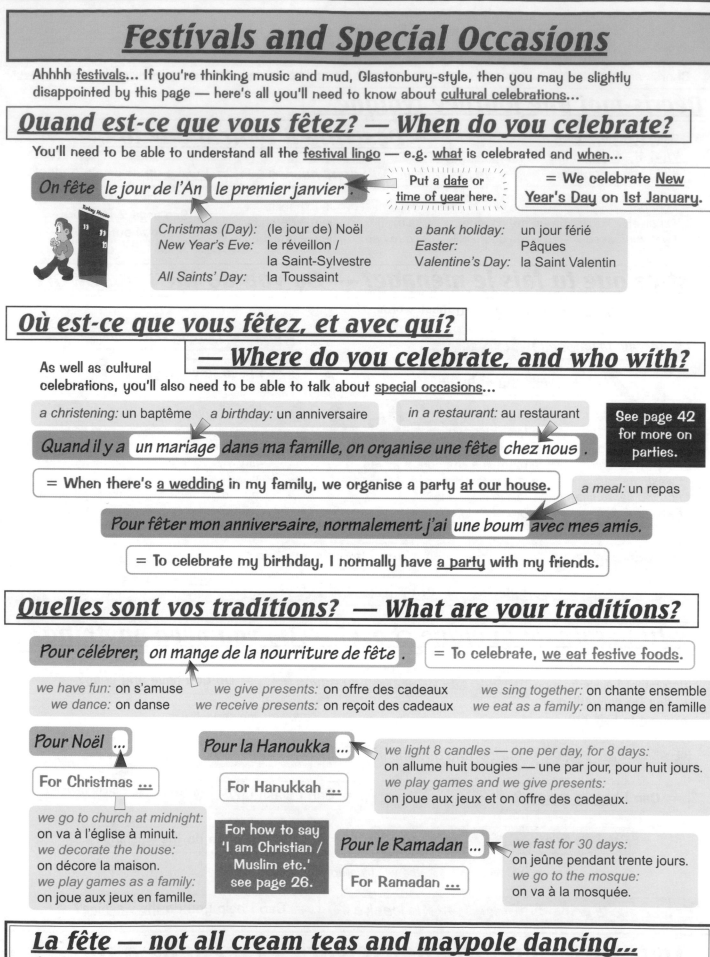

# The Environment

Things get <u>serious</u> when the environment comes up, and you're supposed to have an opinion. It's a chance for you to write or say what you <u>think</u> about something real and <u>important</u>. Go get 'em...

## Il y a de graves problèmes...

Start with the <u>problems</u>...

### — There are some serious problems...

Il y a trop de pollution . = There's too much <u>pollution</u>.

deforestation: déboisement (masc.)
consumption: consommation (fem.)
light: lumière (fem.)
noise: bruit (masc.)

Des gens souffrent d'allergies à cause de la pollution.

= People suffer from allergies because of pollution.

La pollution de l'air par les gaz d'échappement est un danger pour l'environnement.

the hole in the ozone layer : le trou dans la couche d'ozone
global warming: le réchauffement de la terre
the greenhouse effect: l'effet de serre (masc.)
overpopulation: la surpopulation

= <u>Air pollution from exhaust fumes</u> endangers the environment.

forest fires: d'incendies de fôret

On commence à avoir plus d'inondations . = We're starting to have more <u>floods</u>.

## Est-ce que l'environnement est important pour toi?

Then talk about <u>your opinions</u>...

### Is the environment important to you?

**NON!**

Non, ça ne m'intéresse pas du tout .

= No, <u>I'm not at all interested in it</u>.

I'm not worried about the environment:
je ne m'inquiète pas au sujet de l'environnement

Nous n'avons pas le temps de recycler — on travaille tout le temps .

= We don't have time to recycle — <u>we work all the time</u>.

there are other things that are more important:
il y a d'autres choses qui sont plus importantes
governments should find solutions:
les gouvernements devraient trouver des solutions

**OUI!**

Oui, je m'intéresse beaucoup à l'environnement .

= Yes, <u>I'm very interested in the environment</u>.

I think the environment is very important:
je pense que l'environnement est très important

Il y a de la pollution partout parce qu'il y a trop d'embouteillages .

= There is pollution everywhere <u>because there are too many traffic jams</u>.

we don't recycle as much as we should:
on ne recycle pas autant qu'il faut
we use too much packaging:
on utilise trop d'emballage

## My ideal environment has a TV, a bed and pizza...

There are so many <u>different aspects</u> of the environment you could <u>choose</u> to talk about — or not talk about, if you really couldn't give a monkey's. As always, <u>be wise</u> and learn the <u>basics</u>.

# The Environment

Here's some stuff you can do in the home and in the local area to help the environment.

## À la maison... — In the home...

On pourrait ... | = We could ...

recycle packaging instead of throwing it away:
recycler les emballages au lieu de les jeter
grow vegetables in the garden:
cultiver des légumes dans le jardin

turn off the light / television / heating:
éteindre la lumière / la télévision / le chauffage
use less water:
consommer moins d'eau
pick up our rubbish:
ramasser nos déchets

**Here are some things you can recycle:**

box / tin: la boîte
cardboard box: le carton
plastic bag: le sac en plastique
rubbish: les ordures (fem.) / les déchets (masc.)
packaging: les emballages (masc.)
bottles: les bouteilles (fem.)

## Dans les environs... — In the local area...

On devrait ... | = We should ...

buy products with recyclable packaging:
acheter des produits aux emballages recyclables
find the nearest recycling centre:
trouver le centre de recyclage le plus proche

share the journey to work with colleagues:
partager le voyage au travail avec des collègues
use public transport to travel to school:
utiliser les transports en commun pour voyager au lycée
create more pedestrian zones and green spaces:
créer plus de zones piétonnes et d'éspaces verts
build more cycle lanes: construire plus de pistes cyclables

This sentence uses the conditional. See page 111 for more on this.

Si on conduisait moins, il y aurait moins d'émissions, et moins de pluies acides.

= If we drove less, there would be fewer emissions and less acid rain.

Extra marks for style

## À l'avenir... — In the future...

Who knows what the future holds...

À l'avenir, il n'y aura plus de pétrole.

= In the future, there will be no more oil.

we will not have any more natural resources:
on n'aura plus de ressources naturelles
we will use renewable energy sources like solar power:
on utilisera des énergies renouvelables comme l'énergie solaire
the world will be even more overpopulated:
le monde sera encore plus surpeuplé
we will have to reduce carbon dioxide emissions:
il faudra réduire les émissions de gaz carbonique

These sentences are written in the future tense. See page 103 for more on this.

Nous devons sauvegarder l'environnement pour nos enfants.

= We must protect the environment for our children.

Extra marks for style

# Pollution — Load of rubbish...

These pages are hard — there's loads of vocab, and most of it isn't everyday stuff. Still, just think how you'll kick yourself if it comes up in the exam and you haven't learnt it. Shudder.

# _Revision Summary_

Yippee. I don't really know why I said that. Here's another <u>revision</u> summary. You have to do this part to prepare yourself fully for exam time. Do the questions. Get 'em right. Move on with your <u>life</u>. Or do Section Seven — it's all about school and jobs and other extremely uplifting topics.

1) You've arrived in Boulogne and are writing to your penfriend Marie-Claire about the sights. How do you say there's a castle, a swimming pool, a university, a cinema, a cathedral and a theatre?

2) Write down five shops and five other buildings you might find in a town (not the ones above).

3) You need to go to the police station. How do you ask where it is, and if it's far away?

4) What do these directions mean: 'Le commissariat est à un kilomètre d'ici. Tournez à droite, prenez la première rue à gauche et allez tout droit, devant l'église. Le commissariat est à droite, entre la banque et le cinéma.'

5) Tell your French penfriend Jean-Jacques where you live, whereabouts it is (which country and whether it's north-east etc.) and what it's like.

6) Say in French that you like living in your town, there's loads to do and it's quite clean.

7) Say your address and describe the place where you live — is it a town or a village, is the landscape nice, how many people live there, and who do you live with?

8) Your French friend Marie says: 'J'habite avec mes parents et mon frère. J'aime habiter en famille parce que je ne me sens jamais seule.' What does she mean?

9) Marie-Françoise lives in a big, modern house. It's near the town centre, shops and a motorway. How would she say this in French?

10) Write down the names of 3 rooms in the house and 3 describing words. Use these words to create at least 6 sentences to describe the rooms in your house, e.g. La cuisine est jolie.

11) Tom has his own room. He has red walls and a brown wardrobe in his bedroom. He has a bed, a mirror, and some curtains. He doesn't have an armchair. How will he say all this in French?

12) In at least three short sentences, write down in French what you do between your alarm going off in the morning and leaving for school.

13) What festivals do you celebrate? How do you celebrate, where and who with? Answer this interrogation in French.

14) Is the environment important to you? Say why or why not, giving <u>at least two</u> reasons.

15) Sofie's worried about global warming. Give the French for three more examples of environmental problems.

16) There's no stopping Sofie — she's just told you she'd like to live in a remote wooden hut and be at one with nature. Suggest some more realistic options for saving the environment. You'll need to mention at least six — she's very set on the wooden hut idea.

# School Subjects

There's no way to avoid school and jobs, however much they stress you out.  <u>Learn</u> this well — <u>stress</u> less.

## Tu fais quelles matières? — What subjects do you do?

Go over these subjects until
you know them <u>all</u> really well...

**SCIENCES**

| | |
|---|---|
| *science:* | les sciences (fem.) |
| *physics:* | la physique |
| *chemistry:* | la chimie |
| *biology:* | la biologie |

**NUMBERS AND STUFF**

| | |
|---|---|
| *maths:* | les mathématiques (fem.), les maths (fem.) |
| *IT:* | l'informatique (fem.) |

**ARTS AND CRAFTS**

| | |
|---|---|
| *art:* | le dessin |
| *music:* | la musique |
| *D&T:* | les travaux manuels (masc.) |

**PHYSICAL EDUCATION**

*P.E.:* l'éducation physique (fem.) / l'EPS (l'éducation physique et sportive) (fem.)

**LANGUAGES**

| | |
|---|---|
| *French:* | le français |
| *German:* | l'allemand (masc.) |
| *Spanish:* | l'espagnol (masc.) |
| *Italian:* | l'italien (masc.) |
| *English:* | l'anglais (masc.) |

**HUMANITIES**

| | |
|---|---|
| *history:* | l'histoire (fem.) |
| *geography:* | la géographie |
| *religious studies:* | l'instruction religieuse (fem.) |
| *PSHE:* | l'instruction civique (fem.) |

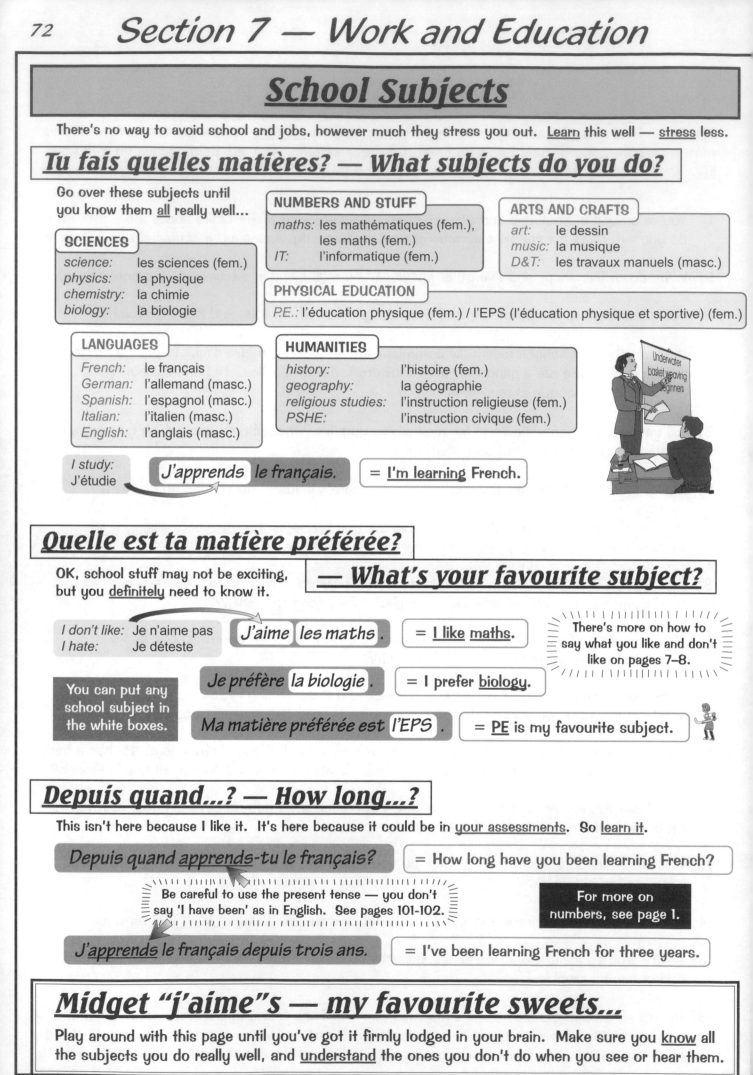

*I study:*
J'étudie

**J'apprends** le français.    = <u>I'm learning</u> French.

## Quelle est ta matière préférée? — What's your favourite subject?

OK, school stuff may not be exciting,
but you <u>definitely</u> need to know it.

*I don't like:* Je n'aime pas
*I hate:*       Je déteste

**J'aime** les maths .    = <u>I like</u> <u>maths</u>.

There's more on how to
say what you like and don't
like on pages 7–8.

You can put any
school subject in
the white boxes.

**Je préfère** la biologie .    = I prefer <u>biology</u>.

**Ma matière préférée est** l'EPS .    = <u>PE</u> is my favourite subject.

## Depuis quand...? — How long...?

This isn't here because I like it.  It's here because it could be in <u>your assessments</u>.  So <u>learn it</u>.

**Depuis quand** <u>apprends</u>-tu le français?    = How long have you been learning French?

Be careful to use the present tense — you don't
say 'I have been' as in English.  See pages 101-102.

For more on
numbers, see page 1.

**J'**<u>apprends</u> le français depuis trois ans.    = I've been learning French for three years.

# Midget "j'aime"s — my favourite sweets...

Play around with this page until you've got it firmly lodged in your brain.  Make sure you <u>know</u> all
the subjects you do really well, and <u>understand</u> the ones you don't do when you see or hear them.

# The School Routine

Not the most exciting of pages ever, but it's <u>worth</u> all the effort when you get <u>tricky questions</u> on <u>school routine</u>. Make sure you really <u>master the basics</u> before moving on to the longer sentences.

## Comment vas-tu au collège? — How do you get to school?

This bit's <u>basic</u> — know the basics...

*by bus:* en bus    *by train:* en train

*Je vais au collège* en voiture. = I go to school <u>by car</u>.

For more on forms of transport, see page 49.

*Je vais au collège à pied.* = I go to school on foot.

## L'horaire — The timetable

It's important you know how to describe a <u>school day</u> — une <u>journée scolaire</u>.

You're right, this timetable is a bit much.

*finish:* finissent

*Les cours* commencent *à neuf heures.* = Lessons <u>begin</u> at 9.00.

For more on times, see page 2.

*Nous avons huit cours par jour.* = We have 8 lessons per day.

*Chaque cours dure trente minutes.* = Each lesson lasts 30 minutes.

*Nous faisons une heure de devoirs par jour.* = We do one hour of homework every day.

*Lunch break:* La pause déjeuner

*La récréation* est à onze heures. = <u>Break</u> is at 11.00.

*I talk to my friends:* Je parle avec mes ami(e)s
*I do my homework:* Je fais mes devoirs
*I play football:* Je joue au football
*I go in the computer room:* Je vais dans la salle d'informatique

*Je mange un fruit* dans la cour pendant la récré. = <u>I eat a piece of fruit</u> in the playground at break time.

## L'année scolaire — The school year

This is all a bit more <u>tricky</u> but, if you want a top mark, you need to <u>learn it</u>.

*Il y a trois trimestres.* = There are three terms.

Slow motion made the school year pass even more slowly...

*Nous avons* six semaines *de vacances* en été. = We have <u>six weeks</u>' holiday <u>in the summer</u>.

*eight weeks:* huit semaines    *five days:* cinq jours    *at Christmas:* à Noël    *at Easter:* à Pâques

J'adore *la rentrée parce que* ... = <u>I love</u> the start of the new school year because...

*I hate:* Je déteste

*I want to see my friends again:* j'ai envie de revoir mes ami(e)s.
*I feel ready to go back to school:* je me sens prêt(e) à retourner au lycée.
*I have no desire to study again:* je n'ai aucun désir de recommencer mes études.

## I've got a real horaire of a timetable this year...

Don't forget the phrases for your exciting <u>school routine</u>, and the sentences for saying how you <u>go</u> to school. Remember the handy phrase '<u>par jour</u>' — you can stick it in loads of sentences.

# More School Stuff

OK, I know this school stuff is a bit close to home and it's a bit boring. (Well, properly boring actually.) But it's revision — it's unlikely to ever get really good. Power through and you'll reap exam rewards galore.

## Portez-vous un uniforme? — Do you wear a uniform?

You may have to understand others talking about the differences between schools in the UK and in France...

Les élèves anglais portent d'habitude un uniforme à l'école.

= English pupils usually wear a uniform to school.

See page 39 for more on clothes and colours.

Notre uniforme est un pull rouge, un pantalon gris, une chemise blanche et une cravate verte.

= Our uniform is a red jumper, grey trousers, a white shirt and a green tie.

| | |
|---|---|
| we go to nursery school from the age of 3 to 6: | on va à la maternelle de l'âge de trois à six ans |
| we go to secondary school from the age of 11 to 15: | on va au collège de l'âge de onze à quinze ans |
| we study for the 'baccalauréat' at a 'lycée': | on étudie pour le bac au lycée |
| we have to go there on Saturday mornings: | on doit y aller le samedi matin |
| the school day is longer: | la journée scolaire est plus longue |

En France, on ne va pas au collège le mercredi après-midi .

= In France, we don't go to school on Wednesday afternoons.

For more information on times, see page 2.

## Les règles sont strictes — The rules are strict

On n'a pas le droit de parler dans les couloirs .

= We're not allowed to talk in the corridors.

| | |
|---|---|
| to go in the staff room: | d'entrer dans la salle des professeurs |
| to write on the (interactive white)board: | d'écrire sur le tableau (blanc intéractif) |
| to eat in the lab: | de manger au laboratoire |
| to wear jewellery: | de porter des bijoux |

En France , on doit passer un examen à l'âge de quinze ans .   16 : seize ans

In Great Britain: En Grande-Bretagne

= In France, we have to take an exam at the age of 15.

## Mes affaires — My stuff

Learn this list of stuff you find in your school bag — and I'm not talking about half-eaten sandwiches, an unwashed P.E. kit, or the crumpled-up newsletter you should have given your mum last week.

| | | | |
|---|---|---|---|
| ruler: | une règle | pen: | un stylo |
| pencil: | un crayon | calculator: | une calculatrice |
| (text)book: | un livre | exercise book: | un cahier |

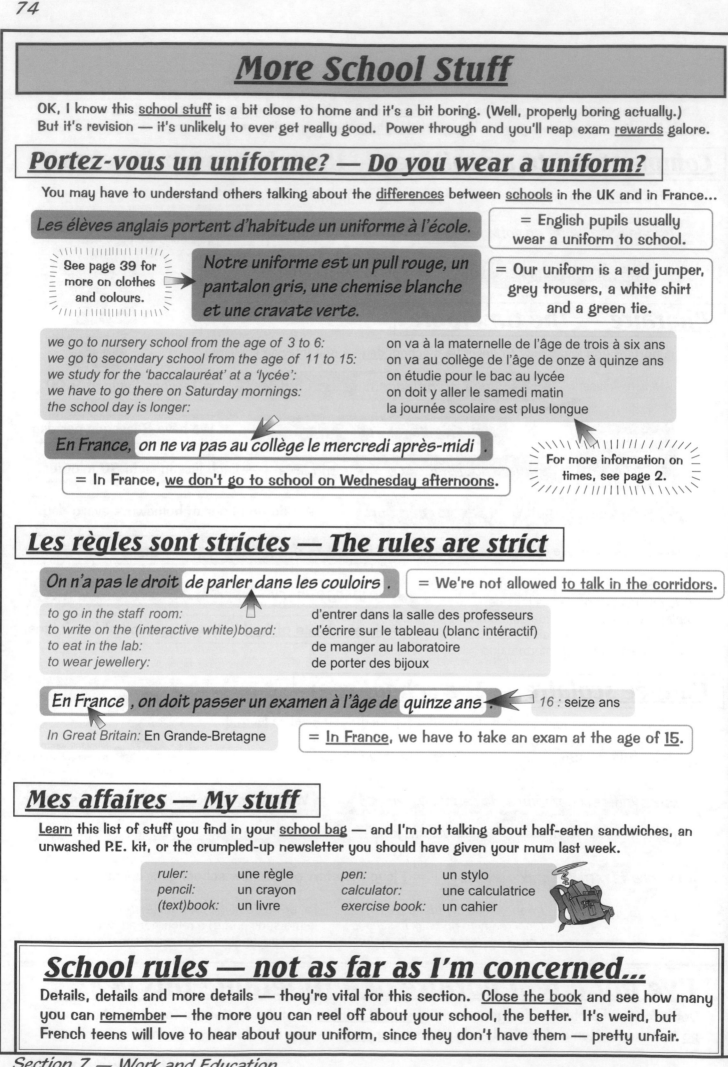

## School rules — not as far as I'm concerned...

Details, details and more details — they're vital for this section. Close the book and see how many you can remember — the more you can reel off about your school, the better. It's weird, but French teens will love to hear about your uniform, since they don't have them — pretty unfair.

# Classroom Language

We all have our 'off' days, so it's really <u>useful</u> to be able to ask someone to <u>repeat</u> something, or <u>spell out</u> a word you're not sure about. This stuff could get you out of a sticky mess in your <u>speaking assessment</u>.

## Asseyez-vous! — Sit down!

<u>Learn</u> these 6 phrases to avoid teacherly wrath. The '<u>vous</u>' ones are <u>formal</u> and the '<u>tu</u>' ones are <u>informal</u>.

| | | | |
|---|---|---|---|
| *Levez-vous!* | = Stand up! | *Asseyez-vous!* | = Sit down! | *Taisez-vous!* | = Be quiet! |
| *Lève-toi!* | = Stand up! | *Assieds-toi!* | = Sit down! | *Tais-toi!* | = Be quiet! |

## Parlez-vous français? — Do you speak French?

We all make <u>mistakes</u> and <u>misunderstand</u> things sometimes, but if you can ask for help you just might never make the same mistake twice. So this stuff can <u>help</u> you <u>understand</u> better — it's really worth <u>learning</u>.

*Comment est-ce qu'on prononce ça?*  = How do you pronounce that?

*Comment ça s'écrit?*  = How do you spell that?

*Comment est-ce qu'on dit ça en français?*  = How do you say that in French?

*Pouvez-vous répéter, s'il vous plaît?*  = Can you repeat that, please?

## If you don't understand, say 'Je ne comprends pas'

These phrases can be <u>vital</u> in your <u>speaking assessments</u>. Even if the worst happens, it's far better to say 'I don't understand' <u>in French</u> than to shrug, give a cheesy smile and mumble something in English.

*Je (ne) comprends (pas).*  = I (don't) understand.

*Que veut dire...?*  = What does ... mean?

Can you (informal): Peux-tu →  *Pouvez-vous expliquer ce mot?*  = <u>Can you</u> explain this word? (formal)

## Est-ce que j'ai fait une erreur? — Did I make a mistake?

| | | | |
|---|---|---|---|
| *Je ne sais pas.* | = I don't know. | *Je me suis trompé(e).* | = I was wrong. |
| *C'est vrai.* | = That's right. | *C'est faux.* | = That's wrong. |
| *Tu as raison.* | = You're right. | *Tu as tort.* | = You're wrong. |

## "Comment ça s'écrit?" — "Ç-A"

You can <u>save</u> yourself from an embarrassing silence by asking the person you're talking to if they can repeat or clarify something — there's no shame in it. All you have to do is learn these <u>dead useful</u> phrases. Remember, bouts of forgetfulness happen to everyone — <u>DON'T PANIC</u>.

# Problems at School

If you're anything like me, you'll love to <u>complain</u> about stuff — this is your chance. This page gives you all manner of ways to vent school-related <u>stresses</u> and <u>gripes</u>. Go on, folks — indulge...

## J'en ai marre... — I'm fed up...

Est-ce que tout va bien au collège? = Is everything going well at school?

Oui, tout va bien. = Yes, everything's going well.

Non, j'ai beaucoup de problèmes à l'école... = No, I've got lots of problems at school...

Je suis vraiment malheureux / malheureuse . = I'm really <u>unhappy</u>.

*depressed:* déprimé(e)

J'ai commencé à manquer les cours. = I've started to play truant.

Il n'y a personne à qui je peux parler. = There's nobody I can talk to.

## Mes parents m'en demandent trop
## — My parents expect too much of me

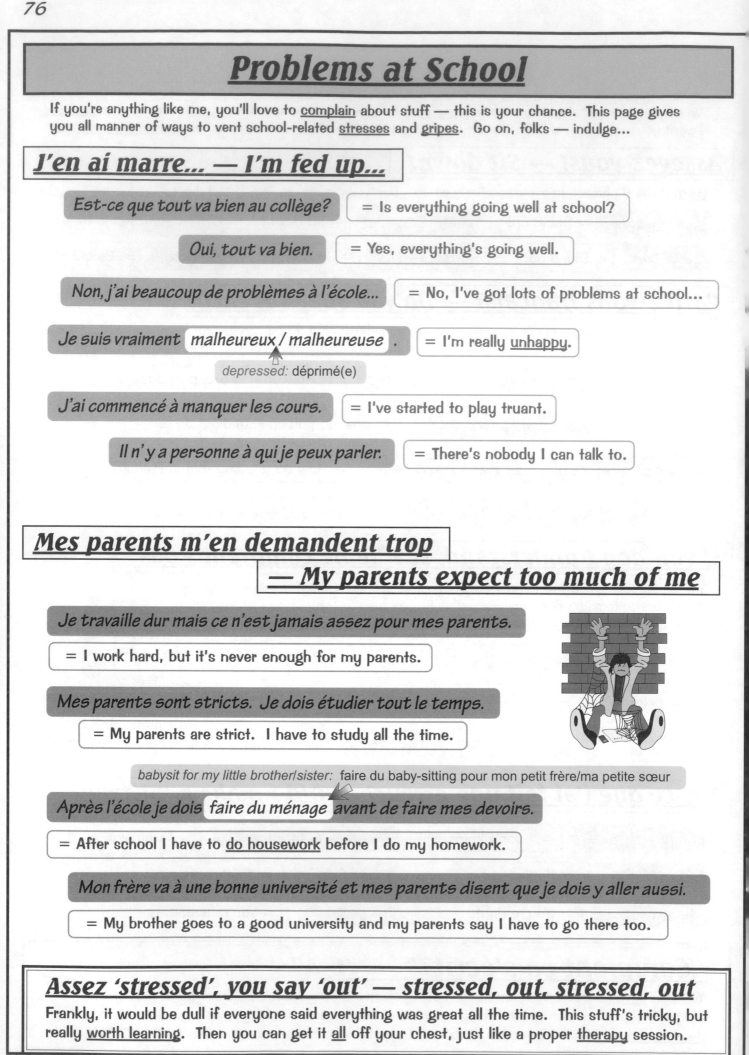

Je travaille dur mais ce n'est jamais assez pour mes parents.

= I work hard, but it's never enough for my parents.

Mes parents sont stricts. Je dois étudier tout le temps.

= My parents are strict. I have to study all the time.

*babysit for my little brother/sister:* faire du baby-sitting pour mon petit frère/ma petite sœur

Après l'école je dois faire du ménage avant de faire mes devoirs.

= After school I have to <u>do housework</u> before I do my homework.

Mon frère va à une bonne université et mes parents disent que je dois y aller aussi.

= My brother goes to a good university and my parents say I have to go there too.

## Assez 'stressed', you say 'out' — stressed, out, stressed, out

Frankly, it would be dull if everyone said everything was great all the time. This stuff's tricky, but really <u>worth learning</u>. Then you can get it <u>all</u> off your chest, just like a proper <u>therapy</u> session.

# Problems at School

Yup, there's <u>more</u>...

## Je ne me fais pas facilement des amis
## — I don't make friends easily

Je connais beaucoup de gens mais je n'ai pas de vrai(e)s ami(e)s.

= I know lots of people but I don't have any real friends.

On me brutalise. = I get bullied.

J'ai de bonnes notes mais je ne peux pas sortir avec mes ami(e)s parce que je n'ai jamais le temps.

= I get good marks, but I can't go out with my friends because I never have time.

a boyfriend: un copain

Tout le monde a une copine sauf moi. = Everyone has <u>a girlfriend</u> except me.

## J'ai du mal à suivre — I have difficulty following

Au collège, les explications sont toujours trop rapides pour moi.

= At school, <u>the explanations are always too quick for me.</u>

failing: d'échouer

I have difficulties understanding: j'ai des difficultés à comprendre
I'm snowed under with work: je suis surchargé(e) de travail

J'ai peur de devoir redoubler. = I fear <u>having to repeat a year</u>.

Les profs ne m'aiment pas et me mettent toujours en retenue.

= The teachers don't like me and always put me in detention.

Je ne suis pas doué(e) pour les études. = I'm not academic.

## Je ne peux pas être moi-même — I can't be myself

On doit porter un uniforme démodé et on n'a pas le droit de porter du maquillage.

= We have to wear an old-fashioned uniform and we aren't allowed to wear make-up.

Je veux un tatouage mais ils sont interdits. = I want <u>a tattoo</u> but they're banned.

a piercing: un piercing

Il faut toujours porter les vêtements à la mode et ça coûte vraiment cher.

= You always have to wear fashionable clothes and it's really expensive.

## And you thought you had problems...

Even if you don't always find school a <u>piece of cake</u>, I'll bet you anything you like that you don't have as many issues as are covered on these two pages. Now you're feeling better, learn them all.

# Work Experience

These pages make you think even more about your <u>future</u> — it's nearly a public service. If you can't see your future without the aid of a crystal ball, then start exercising your <u>imagination</u>.

## As-tu fait un stage? — Have you done work experience?

Work experience is <u>great</u> — I remember my week spent bored to death in a certain high street bank...

J'ai fait mon stage en entreprise chez Peugeot .

= I did my work experience at <u>Peugeot</u>.

*Put any company name here.*

J'y ai travaillé pendant une semaine, du deux au six mars.

= I worked there for a week, from 2nd to 6th March.

Je n'ai jamais fait un stage.

*haven't yet: n'ai pas encore*

= I <u>have never</u> done work experience.

## Est-ce que tu as aimé le travail? — Did you like the work?

More <u>opinions</u> wanted here...

*comfortable: confortable*

Le travail était amusant .

= The work was <u>fun</u>.

Je me suis senti(e) seul(e) .

*stressful: stressant*
*interesting: intéressant*

*were boring: étaient barbants*
*were interesting: étaient intéressants*

= I felt <u>lonely</u>.

Mes collègues de travail n'étaient pas sympa .

= My colleagues <u>were unfriendly</u>.

## C'est une journée très longue... — It's a very long day...

Imagine that your work experience job is your <u>career</u> for life. Does that change your <u>opinions</u>?

Les conditions sont terribles .

= The <u>conditions</u> are <u>terrible</u>.

*hours: horaires (masc.)*

*comfortable: confortables*   *fantastic: fantastiques*

*It is: C'est*   Ce n'est pas très bien payé.

= <u>It's not</u> very well paid.

## J'ai un emploi à mi-temps — I have a part-time job

Make these easier by choosing <u>easy-to-say</u> jobs and <u>simple</u> values — if only the rest of life was like that.

J'ai un travail à mi-temps .

= I've got <u>a part-time job</u>.

*holiday / temporary job: un emploi temporaire*   *£15 per week: quinze livres par semaine*

Je gagne cinq livres par heure .

= I earn <u>£5 per hour</u>.

Je suis boucher/bouchère .

= I am <u>a butcher</u>.

You can find plenty more jobs on page 80.

## Are you experienced?...

You <u>might</u> have to comment on your <u>work experience</u> or part-time <u>jobs</u> in the speaking assessment. Talk about anything work-related that you've done in your life, and give your <u>opinions</u> about it too.

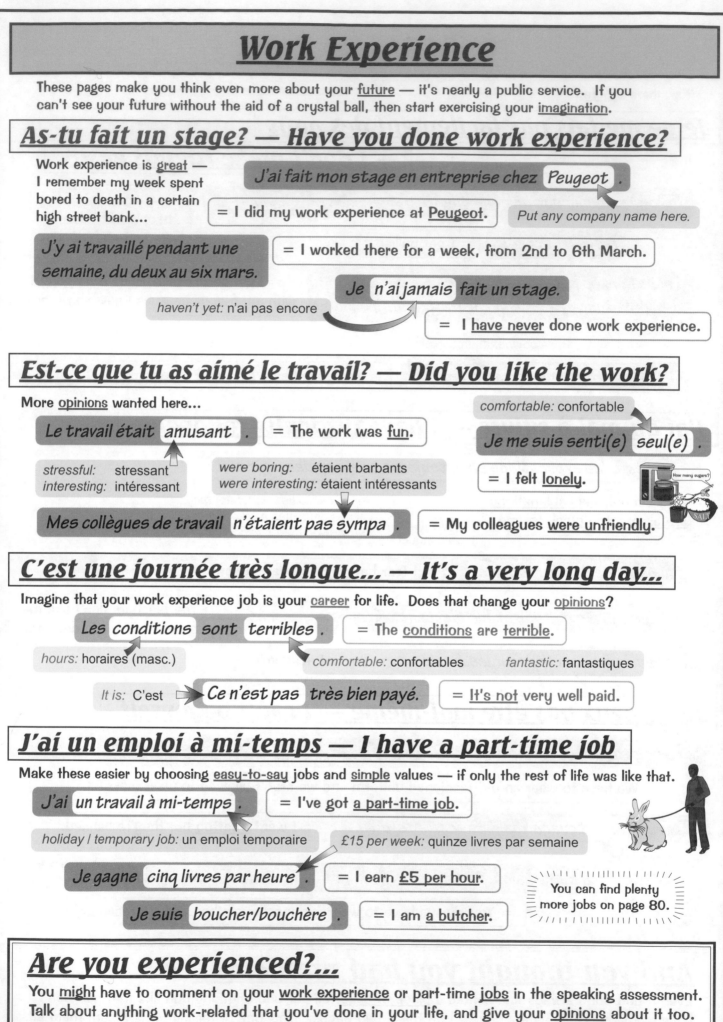

# Plans for the Future

If your idea of future plans is what you're doing next weekend, then try thinking a bit further ahead...

## La vie après les examens... — Life after the exams...

There are loads of things to do after GCSEs. Here's the basic vocab.

Je voudrais **préparer le bac**.

= I would like to do A-levels.

'Bac' is short for 'baccalauréat', the French equivalent of A-levels — except that they do more subjects than we do.

to study geography:  étudier la géographie.
to continue my studies:  continuer mes études.

I have some good friends there:
j'ai de bon(ne)s ami(e)s là.
I'll be able to do my favourite subjects:
je pourrai faire mes matières préférées.

J'ai choisi d'entrer en première parce que ...

= I've chosen to go into the Sixth Form because...

J'ai pris la décision de quitter l'école.

= I've made the decision to leave school.

Je voudrais **faire un stage en entreprise**.

= I'd like to do a placement at a company.

to get married and have children:  me marier et avoir des enfants

Je vais chercher un emploi.

= I'm going to look for a job.

If you'd like to do a particular job after leaving school, use some of the vocabulary from page 80.

Je voyagerai.

= I will travel.

## Always say Why you want to do something

When you're commenting on your future plans, give a reason for them each time.
For example, 'I want to take a year out so that I can travel'.

Je voudrais étudier **la musique**, parce que je veux devenir **musicien(ne)** plus tard.

Remember to get the gender (le or la) right for the school subjects. Refresh your memory on page 72.

accountant: comptable          teacher: prof(esseur)

= I would like to study music, because I want to be a musician afterwards.

Je voudrais préparer le bac car après je veux étudier la biologie à l'université.

= I would like to do A-levels because afterwards I want to study biology at university.

## Life after GCSE — hard to imagine....

I know GCSE French seems like a scary mystery, but this sort of stuff comes up year after year...
Learn all this and you'll be laughing. Use words like 'je voudrais' and 'parce que' for extra marks.

# Types of Job

There are more jobs here than you can shake a stick at — and you <u>do</u> need to <u>recognise all</u> of them because any of the little blighters could pop up in your <u>listening</u> and <u>reading</u> exams.

## Female versions of jobs can be tricky

Often, job titles in French are <u>different for men and women</u>. You need to recognise <u>both</u> versions...

### Masculine/Feminine
Watch out for the feminine versions of jobs. Although there are lots which just add an 'e' in the feminine, some follow different rules. For example, '<u>-er</u>' often becomes '<u>ère</u>', '<u>-teur</u>' often becomes '<u>-trice</u>' and '<u>-eur</u>' often becomes '<u>-euse</u>'. If you're not sure, check in a dictionary.

| | | |
|---|---|---|
| Le musicien (masc.) | La musicienne (fem.) | = Musician |
| Le boucher (masc.) | La bouchère (fem.) | = Butcher |
| L'acteur (masc.) | L'actrice (fem.) | = Actor / actress |
| Le coiffeur (masc.) | La coiffeuse (fem.) | = Hairdresser |

## The gender of a job depends on who is doing it

Even if you've no interest in doing any of these jobs, make sure you learn them for the <u>reading</u> and <u>listening</u> exams...

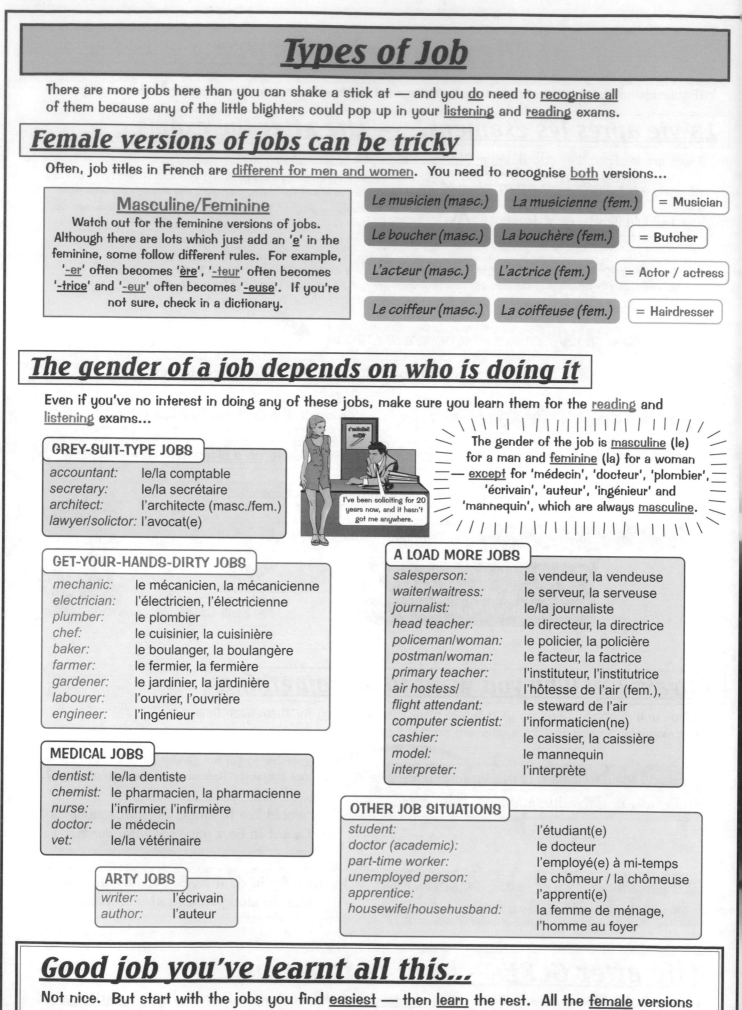

I've been soliciting for 20 years now, and it hasn't got me anywhere.

The gender of the job is <u>masculine</u> (le) for a man and <u>feminine</u> (la) for a woman — <u>except</u> for 'médecin', 'docteur', 'plombier', 'écrivain', 'auteur', 'ingénieur' and 'mannequin', which are always <u>masculine</u>.

### GREY-SUIT-TYPE JOBS
| | |
|---|---|
| accountant: | le/la comptable |
| secretary: | le/la secrétaire |
| architect: | l'architecte (masc./fem.) |
| lawyer/solicitor: | l'avocat(e) |

### GET-YOUR-HANDS-DIRTY JOBS
| | |
|---|---|
| mechanic: | le mécanicien, la mécanicienne |
| electrician: | l'électricien, l'électricienne |
| plumber: | le plombier |
| chef: | le cuisinier, la cuisinière |
| baker: | le boulanger, la boulangère |
| farmer: | le fermier, la fermière |
| gardener: | le jardinier, la jardinière |
| labourer: | l'ouvrier, l'ouvrière |
| engineer: | l'ingénieur |

### MEDICAL JOBS
| | |
|---|---|
| dentist: | le/la dentiste |
| chemist: | le pharmacien, la pharmacienne |
| nurse: | l'infirmier, l'infirmière |
| doctor: | le médecin |
| vet: | le/la vétérinaire |

### ARTY JOBS
| | |
|---|---|
| writer: | l'écrivain |
| author: | l'auteur |

### A LOAD MORE JOBS
| | |
|---|---|
| salesperson: | le vendeur, la vendeuse |
| waiter/waitress: | le serveur, la serveuse |
| journalist: | le/la journaliste |
| head teacher: | le directeur, la directrice |
| policeman/woman: | le policier, la policière |
| postman/woman: | le facteur, la factrice |
| primary teacher: | l'instituteur, l'institutrice |
| air hostess/ | l'hôtesse de l'air (fem.), |
| flight attendant: | le steward de l'air |
| computer scientist: | l'informaticien(ne) |
| cashier: | le caissier, la caissière |
| model: | le mannequin |
| interpreter: | l'interprète |

### OTHER JOB SITUATIONS
| | |
|---|---|
| student: | l'étudiant(e) |
| doctor (academic): | le docteur |
| part-time worker: | l'employé(e) à mi-temps |
| unemployed person: | le chômeur / la chômeuse |
| apprentice: | l'apprenti(e) |
| housewife/househusband: | la femme de ménage, l'homme au foyer |

## Good job you've learnt all this...

Not nice. But start with the jobs you find <u>easiest</u> — then <u>learn</u> the rest. All the <u>female</u> versions too — ooh, I don't envy you. But think how knowledgeable you'll be at the end of it all.

# Jobs: Advantages and Disadvantages

What a page title... It pretty much sums up what's <u>important</u> here, I think.

## Say what job you'd like to do and why

Use 'devenir' (to become) to say what job you'd like to do.

State the job you'd like to do with a <u>short</u> and <u>simple</u> reason why — easy.

*I hope:* J'espère ➡ **Je voudrais devenir médecin, ...** = <u>I would like</u> to become a doctor, ...

**IMPORTANT:** In French you DON'T use 'un'/'une' when you're talking about a job you have or want to have.

**... parce que le travail serait *intéressant* .**

*varied:* varié    *fun:* amusant    *easy:* facile

See page 80 for more jobs.

= ... because the work would be <u>interesting</u>.

**Dans mon travail, je voudrais *aider les personnes défavorisées* .** = In my job, I'd like <u>to help disadvantaged people</u>.

*work with people/numbers:* travailler avec les gens/les chiffres

## Je n'aimerais pas être... — I wouldn't like to be...

**Je n'aimerais pas être *avocat(e)* .** = I wouldn't like to be a <u>lawyer</u>.

**Je serais toujours *fatigué(e)* .** You can put any job from page 80 here.

= I'd always be <u>tired</u>.    *unhappy:* malheureux(euse)    *snowed under with work:* surchargé(e) de travail

**Le travail serait trop difficile.** = The work would be too difficult.

**Les heures *au bureau* seraient trop longues.** = The hours <u>in the office</u> would be too long.

*at work:* au travail    *in the classroom:* dans la salle de classe    *in the factory:* à l'usine

## Je préférerais travailler comme... — I'd prefer to work as...

**Je préférerais travailler comme *écrivain* .** = I would prefer to work as a <u>writer</u>.

For comparisons with 'more' or 'less', see page 92. You can put any job from page 80 here.

**Ce serait plus intéressant et moins stressant.** = It'd be more interesting and less stressful.

See pages 88-90 for more adjectives.

**Je pourrais *voyager* .** = I'd have the chance <u>to travel</u>.

*to be creative:* être créatif / créative    *to work with animals:* travailler avec des animaux
*to be myself:* être moi-même    *to work in a hospital:* travailler dans un hôpital

## I'll take the pros and leave the cons...

Valuable stuff. Saying <u>what job</u> you want to do and <u>why</u> is pretty <u>essential</u>. If the truth's too hard to say, e.g. you want a job in inverse-polarity-dynamo maintenance, then say something <u>simpler</u>. Don't forget these little bits and pieces for the assessments — they could be useful...

# Getting a Job

Hate to break it to you, but stuff on getting a job could come up <u>anywhere</u> in the exam/assessments.

## Je cherche un emploi... — I'm looking for a job...

Je cherche un emploi dans un hôtel .

= I'm looking for a job in <u>a hotel</u>.

See page 1 for more numbers.

| | | | |
|---|---|---|---|
| *a restaurant:* | un restaurant | *an office:* | un bureau |
| *a sports centre:* | un centre sportif | *a shop:* | un magasin |

J'ai déjà deux ans d'expérience.

= I already have <u>two</u> years' experience.

Je serais idéal(e) pour ce poste parce que je suis bilingue .

= I'd be ideal for this job because <u>I'm bilingual</u>.

*I speak English / French / Italian / Spanish:*
je parle anglais / français / italien / espagnol.
*I like working with children / animals / people:*
j'aime travailler avec les enfants / les animaux / les gens.
*I have lots of experience:* j'ai beaucoup d'expérience.

| | |
|---|---|
| *I am practical:* | je suis pratique |
| *I am hard-working:* | je suis travailleur / travailleuse |
| *I am always nice:* | je suis toujours agréable |
| *I am always polite:* | je suis toujours poli(e) |

## On cherche... — We are looking for...

See page 23 for more character traits.

Offre d'emploi: On cherche
un serveur / une serveuse
Lundi et vendredi soir
19 - 21:00

Vous aimez travailler avec les animaux?
On cherche un(e) assistant(e).
20 heures par semaine.
Appelez Jean au
03-12-24-38-42

On cherche quelqu'un pratique,
travailleur(euse), honnête et aimable
pour vendre et organiser.
Entrez pour plus d'infos.

= Wanted:
We're looking for a waiter/waitress.
Monday and Friday evening.
7 - 9pm.

= Do you like working with animals?
We're looking for an assistant.
20 hours per week.
Call Jean on 03-12-24-38-42

= We're looking for someone
practical, hard-working, honest and
nice to sell products and organise.
Come in for more info.

## Je m'intéresse au poste — I'm interested in the position

So, you've <u>applied</u>. Hopefully they'll <u>call back</u> and say something like this:

Est-ce que vous pouvez venir pour un entretien ...

= Can you come <u>for an interview</u>...

*the boss:* le / la patron(ne)

*and meet us:* nous rencontrer

... avec Monsieur LeBrun ...

= ...with <u>Mr LeBrun</u> ...

... lundi le 7 mars à 9h?

= ...on Monday,
7th March
at 9am?

Apportez une copie de votre CV , s'il vous plaît.

= Please bring <u>a copy of your CV</u>.

| | |
|---|---|
| *a photo:* | une photo |
| *your passport:* | votre passeport (masc.) |
| *your driving licence:* | votre permis de conduire (masc.) |

## I'm perfect because I'm blingin' — oops, bilingue

It's useful stuff this — <u>rip</u> this <u>page</u> out, tuck it in your rucksack and you could go and get a
<u>summer job</u> in Paris. No ripping 'til you've <u>learnt</u> it, though — you've got exams to pass first...

# Getting a Job

Good <u>covering letter</u>, dazzling <u>CV</u>, nice <u>tie</u>, job's <u>yours</u>.

## J'ai lu votre annonce — I read your advertisement

Every job application needs a good letter...

Rachael Johnson
46 Loxley Road,
Ambridge,
Borsetshire.  BO12 2AM

Madame de Villiers
Commerce Tapisserie,
19 rue du Conquérant,
14066 Bayeux

*See p.11 for more on writing formal letters.*

Madame,                    Bayeux, le 8 février 2009

J'ai lu votre annonce dans *Le Monde* hier, et je m'intéresse au poste de Chef de Projet.

Vous verrez dans mon CV que ma carrière a été variée, puisque j'ai travaillé dans les secteurs privé et publique.  Je pense que j'ai l'expérience nécessaire pour ce rôle.

Je suis disponible pour un entretien dès que vous le souhaiterez.  N'hésitez pas de me contacter si vous avez besoin de plus d'informations.

Je vous prie d'agréer, Madame, l'expression de mes sentiments distingués.

Rachael Johnson

I read your advertisement in *Le Monde* yesterday, and I'm interested in the position of Project Manager.

You will see in my CV that my career has been varied, as I have worked in the private and public sectors.  I think that I have the necessary experience for this role.

I am available for an interview as soon as you wish.  Don't hesitate to contact me if you need more information.

## Vous verrez dans mon CV...

And every applicant needs a good CV...

## — You will see in my CV...

### CURRICULUM VITAE

Rachael Johnson
46 Loxley Road, Ambridge, Borsetshire.  BO12 2AM
Téléphone 02 40 54 10 66
Nationalité anglaise

ÉDUCATION
1998:   Licence d'Histoire (première classe)
1995:   A-levels (équivalence Baccalauréat):
        Histoire (B), Anglais (B), Mathématiques (C)

EXPÉRIENCE PROFESSIONNELLE
Depuis 2005:  Directeur des ventes chez 'Sales Albion', Loxley.
1998-2005:    Vendeuse chez 'Grant Russell Ltd,' Foxford

AUTRES RENSEIGNEMENTS
Programme de formation d'informatique (mars 2007)
Permis de conduire
Je parle couramment anglais, français et gallois.

EDUCATION
1998: History degree (first class)
1995: A-levels (equivalent to Bac)
        History (B), English (B), Maths (C)

PROFESSIONAL EXPERIENCE
Since 2005: Sales manager at 'Sales Albion', Loxley.
1998-2005: Salesperson at 'Grant Russell Ltd', Foxford

OTHER INFORMATION
Training course in IT (March 2007)
Driving licence
I speak fluent English, French and Welsh.

## Et une belle cravate...

Work — a necessary part of life, alas, and a necessary part of GCSE French.  Work/job-related tasks could crop up <u>anywhere</u>, so it's a good idea to get all this stuff well and truly <u>off pat</u>.

# Telephones

You have to know <u>French phone vocab</u> and understand <u>messages</u> and stuff — it's <u>simple</u>. No. Really it is.

## Je dois faire un appel — I have to make a call

This is easy marks — <u>learn it</u>.

Use 'ton' for someone you know well.
If you need to be more formal, use 'votre'.

*Quel est* ton *numéro de téléphone?* | = What is <u>your</u> telephone number?

*See page 1 for all the numbers.*

*Mon numéro de téléphone est le* vingt-huit, dix-neuf, cinquante-six .

= My telephone number is <u>28 19 56</u>.

Phone numbers are always given in 2-digit numbers, e.g. <u>twenty-eight</u> rather than <u>two-eight</u>. And don't ask me why they stick a 'le' in front of it — they <u>just do</u>.

*Vous n'avez pas le bon numéro.* | = You don't have the right number.

## When you make a call, say 'ici Bob' — 'It's Bob here'

You <u>need</u> to be able to <u>understand</u> the general phone vocab used in France.

You might hear this when someone <u>answers</u> the phone:

*Allô! C'est* Philippe *à l'appareil.* | = Hello! <u>Philippe</u> speaking.

These questions are common <u>phone enquiries</u>:

*Est-ce que* Bob *est là?* | = Is <u>Bob</u> there?

*Est-ce que je peux parler à* Joanie ? | = Can I speak to <u>Joanie</u>?

These are common <u>phone responses</u>:

to her: la | *Je vous* le *passe.* | = I'll put you through <u>to him</u>.

*Je vous écoute.* | = I'm listening.

*Allô?*

*Allô?*

These are common conversation <u>closers</u>:

*À bientôt.* | = See you soon. | *À plus tard.* | = See you later. | *Appelle-moi.* | = Call me.

## Je voudrais laisser un message — I'd like to leave a message

You have to be able to understand phone <u>messages</u>. This is a typical <u>run-of-the-mill</u> one:

Hello, this is Nicole Smith.

The caller's name should go here.

I have a message for Jean-Claude.

This is who needs to call back.

*Allô, ici* Nicole Smith . *J'ai un message pour* Jean-Claude .
*Est-ce qu'il peut me rappeler vers* dix-neuf heures *ce soir?*
*Mon numéro de téléphone est le* cinquante-neuf,
dix-huit, quarante-sept . *Merci beaucoup. Au revoir.*

My phone number is 591847.

Can he call me back at around 7pm tonight?

This is what time he should call back.

This is the phone number he should return the call to.

Thank you. Goodbye.

## Le téléphone — sounds phoney to me...

I wouldn't rate your chances with French GCSE if you don't <u>learn</u> this stuff — <u>phones</u> come up pretty frequently. But, with this lot under your belt, you'll have more than a <u>fighting chance</u>.

# *Revision Summary*

This is an <u>extremely important</u> page. You should <u>stop</u> and spend some minutes here and only trek on when you can recall all of this stuff effortlessly. OK, rant over. Now just learn this stuff, then go and have a nice cold drink and play on one of those new-fangled games consoles...

1) Say what your GCSE subjects are in French. I guess one of them will be 'le français'...

2) What's your favourite subject? What subject(s) don't you like? Answer in French.

3) Depuis quand apprends-tu le français? Translate the question. And then answer it in French.

4) How would you say that your lunch break begins at 12.30pm and that you eat a sandwich and then play volleyball?

5) How would you say that you have six lessons every day and each lesson lasts 50 minutes?

6) Pete is describing his school to his French penfriend Christophe. How would he say that there are three terms, that he wears a school uniform and that the rules are very strict?

7) Au collège, on n'a pas le droit de porter un pull à capuche et on ne peut pas parler dans les couloirs. Your French friend has just told you this in her latest email. What does she say?

8) Décris-moi ton uniforme.

9) Your teacher has just said a very long sentence in French and you don't understand. What three questions could you ask to help clarify the situation?

10) Imagine your parents are the bane of your life (shouldn't be too difficult). How would you say that they're strict, you have to study all the time, and they think you should go to university like your sister?

11) Stéphanie says, 'J'ai des difficultés à comprendre au collège — les explications sont toujours trop rapides pour moi et j'ai peur de devoir redoubler.' What does she mean?

12) Write a full French sentence explaining where you did your work experience. If you didn't do work experience anywhere then write that down. Also answer: 'As-tu un emploi à mi-temps?'

13) Qu'est-ce que tu voudrais faire après les examens?

14) Tell a French passer-by what you look for in a job, what job you'd most like to do and why.

15) Complete this tiebreaker question (in no more than 30 French words): Je serais idéal(e) pour ce poste parce que...

16) Translate into French: "He's looking for a job in a restaurant. He has two years' experience."

17) Quel est ton numéro de téléphone? *(No cheating and writing it in numerals — do it in French. And say it out loud.)*

18) What would you say in French when:
    a) you answer the phone in French?    b) you want to put someone through?
    c) you tell someone you'll see them later?    d) you have a message for Daniel Craig?

**NOUNS**      <u>**Words for People and Objects**</u>

Stop — before you panic, this stuff is a lot less scary than it looks.  It's all <u>pretty</u>
<u>simple</u> stuff about words for <u>people</u> and <u>objects</u> — nouns.  This is <u>really important</u>.

## Every French noun is masculine or feminine

Whether a word is <u>masculine</u>, <u>feminine</u>, <u>singular</u> or <u>plural</u> affects a heck of a lot of things.  All '<u>the</u>' and
'<u>a</u>' words change and, if that wasn't enough, the adjectives (like 'new', 'shiny') change to fit the word.

EXAMPLES:  an interesting book: <u>un</u> livre intéressant  (masculine)
                an interesting programme: <u>une</u> émission intéressante  (feminine)

*For details on changing
stuff like this, see
pages 87 and 88.*

It's no good just knowing the French words for things — you
have to know whether each one's <u>masculine</u> or <u>feminine</u> too...

> **THE GOLDEN RULE**
>
> Each time you <u>learn</u> a <u>word</u>, remember a <u>le</u> or <u>la</u> to go
> with it — don't think 'dog = chien', think 'dog = <u>le</u> chien'.

> **LE AND LA**
>
> <u>LE</u> in front of a noun means it's
> <u>masculine</u>.  <u>LA</u> in front = <u>feminine</u>.

## These rules help you guess what gender a word is

If you have to
guess whether a
word is <u>masculine</u>
or <u>feminine</u>, these
are good rules of
thumb.

> **RULES OF THUMB FOR MASCULINE AND FEMININE NOUNS**
>
> **MASCULINE NOUNS:**
> most nouns that end:
> -age  -er  -eau  -ing    -ment  -ou
> -ail  -ier  -et  -isme  -oir    -eil
> also: male people, languages, days,
> months, seasons
>
> **FEMININE NOUNS:**
> most nouns that end:
> -aine  -ée  -ense  -ie  -ise  -tion
> -ance  -elle  -esse  -ière  -sion  -tude
> -anse  -ence  -ette  -ine  -té  -ure
> also: female people

## Making Nouns Plural

1) Nouns in French are usually made plural by
adding an '<u>s</u>' — just like English, really.

 e.g. une orange → des oranges
           an orange → oranges

2) But there are always <u>exceptions</u> to the rule in French.  Nouns with the endings in
the table below have a <u>different</u> plural form — and this lot are just the beginning.

| <u>Noun ending</u> | <u>Irregular plural ending</u> | <u>Example</u> |
|---|---|---|
| -ail | -aux | travail → travaux |
| -al | -aux | journal → journaux |
| -eau | -eaux | bureau → bureaux |
| -eu | -eux | jeu → jeux |
| -ou | -oux | chou → choux |

> **TOP TIP FOR PLURALS**
>
> Each time you <u>learn</u> a new word,
> make sure you know <u>how</u> to
> make it into a plural too.

3) Some nouns <u>don't change</u> in the plural.
These are usually nouns that end in <u>-s</u>, <u>-x</u> or <u>-z</u>.

*un nez → des nez
a nose → noses
un mois → des mois
a month → months*

4) When you make a noun plural, instead of 'le' or 'la' to
say '<u>the</u>', you have to use '<u>les</u>' — see page 87.

### Gender reassignment — don't try it in the exam...
The bottom line is — <u>every time</u> you learn a word in French, you <u>have</u> to learn whether it's <u>le</u> or <u>la</u>,
and how to make it <u>plural</u>.  If you get it wrong, you'll <u>lose marks</u> for accuracy — and then I'll cry.

# 'The' and 'A'

'<u>The</u>' and '<u>a</u>' — you use these words more than a mobile phone. They're tricky. <u>Revise</u> 'em well.

## 'A' — un, une

*Grammar Fans: these are called '<u>Indefinite Articles</u>'.*

1) In English we don't have <u>genders</u> for nouns — simple.
2) In French, you need to know whether a word is <u>masculine</u> or <u>feminine</u>.

| masculine | feminine |
|-----------|----------|
| un | une |

**EXAMPLES:**

Masculine — *J'ai un frère.* = I have a brother.

Feminine — *J'ai une sœur.* = I have a sister.

## 'The' — le, la, l', les

*Grammar Fans: these are called '<u>Definite Articles</u>'.*

1) Like the French for 'a', the word for 'the' is different for <u>masculine</u> and <u>feminine</u>. This one has a <u>plural</u> form as well, though.
2) For words starting with a <u>vowel</u> (a, e, i, o, u) the '<u>le</u>' or '<u>la</u>' are shortened to <u>l'</u>, e.g. l'orange.
3) Some words starting with an '<u>h</u>', also take '<u>l''</u>' instead of 'le' or 'la'. Sadly there's no rule for this — you just have to learn which ones take 'l'' and which ones take 'le' or 'la'.

| masculine singular | feminine singular | in front of a vowel /some words beginning with 'h' | masculine or feminine plural |
|-----|-----|-----|-----|
| le | la | l' | les |

*That's an affirmative*
*Absolutely! No doubt at all.*
*100% positive. Couldn't be surer.*

**EXAMPLES:**

*Le garçon.* = <u>The</u> boy.

*La fille.* = <u>The</u> girl.

*L'homme.* = <u>The</u> man.

*Les hommes.* = <u>The</u> men.

*Le hamster.* = <u>The</u> hamster.

*Les hamsters.* = <u>The</u> hamsters

## 'De' and 'à' change before 'le' and 'les'

1) Weird stuff happens with '<u>à</u>' (to) and '<u>de</u>' (of).
2) You <u>can't</u> say 'à le', 'à les', 'de le' or 'de les'.
3) '<u>À</u>' and '<u>de</u>' combine with '<u>le</u>' and '<u>les</u>' to make new words — '<u>au</u>', '<u>aux</u>' (usually meaning 'to the'), and '<u>du</u>' and '<u>des</u>' (usually meaning 'of the').

|  | le | la | l' | les |
|------|------|------|------|------|
| à + | au | à la | à l' | aux |
| de + | du | de la | de l' | des |

**EXAMPLES :**

*Je vais à* + *le café* = *Je vais au café.* = I go to the café.

*Je viens de* + *le Canada* = *Je viens du Canada.* = I come from Canada.

## 'Some' or 'any' — du, de la, de l', des

*Grammar Fans: these are called '<u>Partitive Articles</u>'.*

These don't just mean '<u>of the</u>' — they can also mean '<u>some</u>' or '<u>any</u>'.

**EXAMPLES:**

*J'ai <u>des</u> pommes.* = I have <u>some</u> apples.

*Avez-vous <u>du</u> pain?* = Have you got <u>any</u> bread?

| masculine singular | feminine singular | in front of a vowel / 'h' which takes 'l'' | masculine or feminine plural |
|-----|-----|-----|-----|
| du | de la | de l' | des |

**N.B.** In <u>negative</u> sentences, like 'I don't have any apples', you just use '<u>de</u>' — 'Je n'ai pas <u>de</u> pommes'.

## A page on 'the' — not the most fun...

Phew, am I glad I speak English — just one word for '<u>the</u>' and no genders (in grammar anyway). But there's no getting around it — you <u>need</u> this stuff to get your <u>French right</u> in the <u>assessments</u>. <u>Cover up</u> the page and write out <u>all four tables</u> — keep on scribbling till you can do it in your sleep.

| ADJECTIVES | ## Words to Describe Things |
|---|---|

Gain <u>more marks</u> and show what an interesting person you are by using some <u>juicy describing</u> words.

## Adjectives must 'agree' with the thing they're describing

1) In <u>English</u>, the describing word (adjective) stays the <u>same</u> — like <u>big</u> bus, <u>big</u> bananas...

2) In <u>French</u>, the describing word has to <u>change</u> to <u>match</u> whether what it's describing is <u>masculine</u> or <u>feminine</u> and <u>singular</u> or <u>plural</u>. Look at these examples where 'intéressant' has to change:

| *Masculine Singular* | *Masculine Plural* | *Feminine Singular* | *Feminine Plural* |
|---|---|---|---|
| le garçon intéressant | les garçons intéressants | la fille intéressante | les filles intéressantes |
| (the <u>interesting</u> boy) | (the <u>interesting</u> boys) | (the <u>interesting</u> girl) | (the <u>interesting</u> girls) |

The Rules Are:

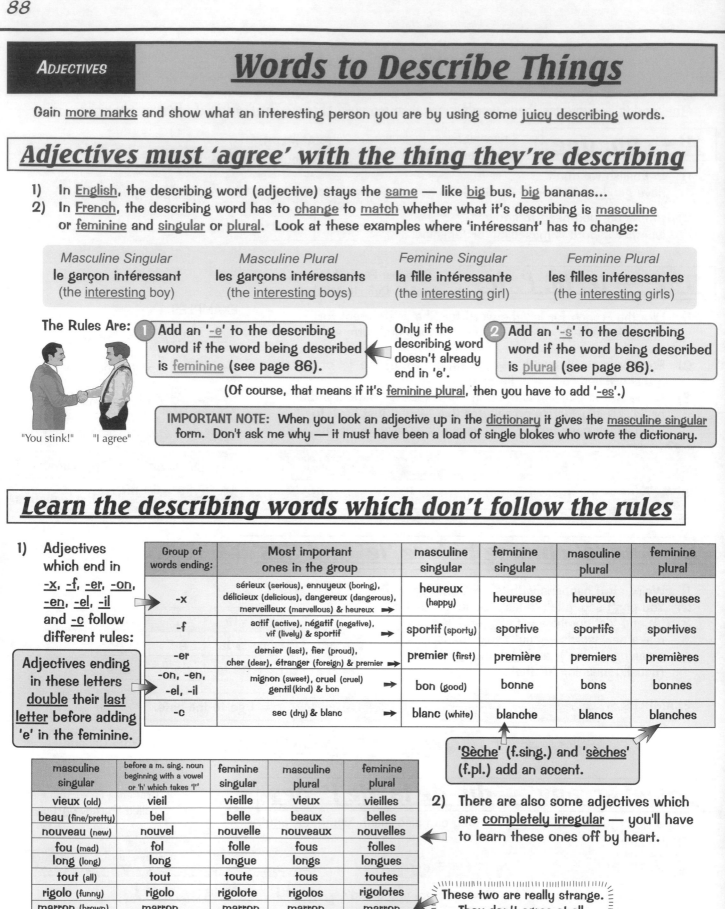

"You stink!"  "I agree"

**1** Add an '<u>-e</u>' to the describing word if the word being described is <u>feminine</u> (see page 86).

Only if the describing word doesn't already end in 'e'.

**2** Add an '<u>-s</u>' to the describing word if the word being described is <u>plural</u> (see page 86).

(Of course, that means if it's <u>feminine plural</u>, then you have to add '<u>-es</u>'.)

IMPORTANT NOTE: When you look an adjective up in the <u>dictionary</u> it gives the <u>masculine singular</u> form. Don't ask me why — it must have been a load of single blokes who wrote the dictionary.

## Learn the describing words which don't follow the rules

1) Adjectives which end in <u>-x</u>, <u>-f</u>, <u>-er</u>, <u>-on</u>, <u>-en</u>, <u>-el</u>, <u>-il</u> and <u>-c</u> follow different rules:

Adjectives ending in these letters <u>double</u> their <u>last letter</u> before adding 'e' in the feminine.

| Group of words ending: | Most important ones in the group | masculine singular | feminine singular | masculine plural | feminine plural |
|---|---|---|---|---|---|
| -x | sérieux (serious), ennuyeux (boring), délicieux (delicious), dangereux (dangerous), merveilleux (marvellous) & heureux ➡ | heureux (happy) | heureuse | heureux | heureuses |
| -f | actif (active), négatif (negative), vif (lively) & sportif ➡ | sportif (sporty) | sportive | sportifs | sportives |
| -er | dernier (last), fier (proud), cher (dear), étranger (foreign) & premier ➡ | premier (first) | première | premiers | premières |
| -on, -en, -el, -il | mignon (sweet), cruel (cruel) gentil (kind) & bon ➡ | bon (good) | bonne | bons | bonnes |
| -c | sec (dry) & blanc ➡ | blanc (white) | blanche | blancs | blanches |

'Sèche' (f.sing.) and 'sèches' (f.pl.) add an accent.

| masculine singular | before a m. sing. noun beginning with a vowel or 'h' which takes 'l' | feminine singular | masculine plural | feminine plural |
|---|---|---|---|---|
| vieux (old) | vieil | vieille | vieux | vieilles |
| beau (fine/pretty) | bel | belle | beaux | belles |
| nouveau (new) | nouvel | nouvelle | nouveaux | nouvelles |
| fou (mad) | fol | folle | fous | folles |
| long (long) | long | longue | longs | longues |
| tout (all) | tout | toute | tous | toutes |
| rigolo (funny) | rigolo | rigolote | rigolos | rigolotes |
| marron (brown) | marron | marron | marron | marron |
| orange (orange) | orange | orange | orange | orange |

2) There are also some adjectives which are <u>completely irregular</u> — you'll have to learn these ones off by heart.

These two are really strange. They don't agree at all.

## Even 'désagréable(s)' agrees...

Aaaargh — more tables to learn, but then that's the nature of French grammar. For these endings to be of any <u>use</u> to you, you need to learn the <u>genders</u> of the nouns in the first place — you have to know <u>what</u> your adjective needs to <u>agree</u> with. To get it right, <u>get learning</u>.

# Words to Describe Things

**ADJECTIVES**

Details and descriptions are key to doing well in the exam — so, words to <u>describe</u> things are quite <u>important</u>.

## Top 21 Describing Words

Here are 21 <u>describing words</u> — they're the ones you really <u>have</u> to know.

Grammar Fans:
These are '<u>Adjectives</u>'.

| | | | | | |
|---|---|---|---|---|---|
| *good:* | bon(ne) | *normal:* | normal(e) | *old:* | vieux / vieille |
| *bad:* | mauvais(e) | *interesting:* | intéressant(e) | *young:* | jeune |
| *beautiful:* | beau / belle | *boring:* | ennuyeux / ennuyeuse | *new:* | nouveau / nouvelle |
| *happy:* | heureux / heureuse | *terrible:* | affreux / affreuse | *fast:* | rapide |
| *sad:* | triste | *long:* | long(ue) | *slow:* | lent(e) |
| *easy:* | facile | *big/tall:* | grand(e) | *practical:* | pratique |
| *difficult:* | difficile | *small/short:* | petit(e) | *funny:* | amusant(e) |

## Most describing words go after the word they describe

It's the opposite of English — in French <u>most</u> describing words
(adjectives) <u>go after</u> the word they're describing (the noun).

**EXAMPLES:**

*J'ai une voiture <u>rapide</u>.* = I have a <u>fast</u> car.

*J'ai lu un livre <u>intéressant</u>.* = I read an <u>interesting</u> book.

noun (dress)

la robe rouge

adjective (red)

You can also use describing words in sentences with verbs like '<u>être</u>' (to be) and
'<u>devenir</u>' (to become). The adjective still needs to <u>agree</u> with the noun though.

**EXAMPLES:**

*Ils sont <u>prêts</u>.* = They are <u>ready</u>.

*Elle est devenue <u>belle</u>.* = She has become <u>beautiful</u>.

Adjectives are always
<u>masculine singular</u> after
'<u>ce</u>'. E.g. 'C'est nouveau'
(It's new), 'Ce sera cher'
(It will be expensive), etc.

## There are some odd ones out that go in front

These describing words almost always go <u>before</u> the noun — a real pain:

| | | | | | |
|---|---|---|---|---|---|
| *good:* | bon(ne) | *new:* | nouveau / nouvel(le) | *small:* | petit(e) |
| *bad:* | mauvais(e) | *fine / pretty:* | beau / belle | *high:* | haut(e) |
| *young:* | jeune | *better / best:* | meilleur(e) | *first:* | premier / première |
| *old:* | vieux / vieil(le) | *nice / pretty:* | joli(e) | | |

**EXAMPLES:** *J'ai un <u>nouveau</u> chat.* = I have a <u>new</u> cat.

*J'ai une <u>petite</u> maison, avec un <u>joli</u> jardin et une <u>belle</u> vue.*

= I have a <u>small</u> house, with a <u>pretty</u> garden and a <u>beautiful</u> view.

Adjectives still have to
agree, regardless of
whether they come
before or after the noun.

'<u>Cher</u>' is a strange adjective. It can go <u>in front</u> of or <u>after</u> the noun, but its <u>meaning changes</u> according to
its position. <u>Before</u> the noun it means '<u>dear</u>', e.g. 'my dear friend' and <u>after</u> the noun it means '<u>expensive</u>'.

## Good, bad... indifferent?

By now you're probably thinking you could get through life without adjectives and you could well
be right — as long as you never want to tell anyone how <u>interesting</u>, <u>beautiful</u> and <u>happy</u> you are.
Start by learning those <u>21 key words</u> at the top of the page — they'll <u>spice</u> your writing up no end.

## ADJECTIVES
# Words to Describe Things

More really important stuff on describing words, including words that show who something belongs to...

## My, your, our — words for who it belongs to

You have to be able to use and understand these words
to say that something belongs to someone:

Like in English, these go before the noun.
E.g. 'mon ami', 'notre cousin', etc.

| | masculine singular | feminine singular | plural |
|---|---|---|---|
| my | mon | ma | mes |
| your (informal, sing.) | ton | ta | tes |
| his/her/its | son | sa | ses |
| our | notre | notre | nos |
| your (formal/pl.) | votre | votre | vos |
| their | leur | leur | leurs |

Grammar Fans: These are 'Possessive Adjectives'.

The word you use from the table above has to match the thing it's describing, and NOT the person that thing belongs to. So in the example below, it's always 'mon père' even if it's a girl talking.

| Mon père est petit, ma mère est grande. | = My father is short, my mother is tall. |

This means that son/sa/ses could mean either 'his' or 'her'. You can usually tell which one it is by the context.

| J'ai vu Pierre avec sa sœur. | = I saw Pierre with his sister. |

| Marie et sa sœur sont inséparables. | = Marie and her sister are inseparable. |

## 'Ma amie' becomes 'mon amie'

Before a noun beginning with a vowel or words beginning with 'h' that take 'l'', always use the masculine form. You do this because it's easier to say.

| Mon amie s'appelle Helen. | = My friend's called Helen. |

| Écoutez son histoire. | Listen to his/her story. |

## Quelque and chaque — rule-breakers...

Grammar Fans: 'Indefinite Adjectives'.

1) 'Quelque' (some) and 'chaque' (each) don't have a whole set of different forms for when they're feminine or plural.
2) 'Quelque' doesn't have a feminine form, but it does add an '-s' when it changes from singular to plural.
3) 'Chaque' never changes — it's always the same whether its describing something masculine or feminine.

EXAMPLES:

| J'ai acheté quelques bonbons. | = I bought some sweets. |

| Chaque personne ici aime le chocolat. | = Each person here likes chocolate. |

## My, oh my...

...what fun we're having. It's so important, all this — especially that the possessive adjectives change according to the thing being described, NOT the owner. And when you're using 'quelque' or 'chaque' to describe something feminine don't ever add an '-e' — that would just be silly.

# Words to Describe Actions

**ADVERBS**

The three previous pages describe <u>objects</u>, e.g. the bus is <u>red</u>. This page is about describing things you <u>do</u>, e.g. 'I speak French <u>perfectly</u>', and about adding <u>more info</u> — 'I speak French <u>almost</u> perfectly'.

## Make your sentences better by saying how you do things

1) In <u>English</u>, you don't say 'I talk slow' — you have to <u>add</u> a '<u>ly</u>' on the end to say 'I talk slow<u>ly</u>'.
2) In <u>French</u>, you have to <u>add</u> a '<u>ment</u>' on the end, but first you have to make sure the describing word is in the <u>feminine</u> form (see page 88).

*Grammar Fans: These are '<u>Adverbs</u>'.*

**EXAMPLES:** *Il parle* lentement . = He speaks <u>slowly</u>.

*normally:* normalement
*strangely:* bizarrement

The French word for 'slow' is '<u>lent</u>', but the feminine form is '<u>lente</u>'. Add '<u>ment</u>' and you get '<u>lentement</u>' = slowly.

3) <u>Unlike adjectives</u> (pages 88-90) you <u>don't</u> ever have to <u>change</u> these words — they're describing the <u>action</u>, not the person doing it.

Always the same.

Feminine *Elle parle* lentement . Plural *Nous parlons* lentement .

## Learn these odd ones out off by heart

Just like in English there are <u>odd ones out</u> — for example, you <u>don't</u> say 'I sing <u>goodly</u>'. The adjective 'good' changes to 'well' when it becomes an adverb. Have a look at the other odd ones out in the table:

| ENGLISH | FRENCH |
|---|---|
| good → well | bon(ne) → bien |
| bad → badly | mauvais(e) → mal |
| fast → fast | rapide → vite |

*Je chante.*
*I sing.*

*Je chante bien.* *Je chante mal.*
*I sing <u>well</u>.* *I sing <u>badly</u>.*

## Use one of these fine words to give even more detail

Add any one of these simple <u>words</u> or <u>phrases</u> to make that impressive sentence even more so... You can use them for sentences saying <u>how something is done</u>:

*Je cours* trop *lentement.* = I run <u>too</u> slowly.

*very:* très   *quite:* assez   *too:* trop   *really:* vraiment

...and for saying <u>what you think about something</u>...

*too much:* trop

*J'aime* beaucoup *la glace.* = I like ice cream <u>a lot</u>.

...and for sentences about <u>what something is like</u>...

*Bob est* très *heureux.* = Bob is <u>very</u> happy.

*almost:* presque   *Il est* peu *intéressant.* = He is <u>not very</u> interesting.

*sometimes:* quelquefois   *often:* souvent

...and for saying <u>how often something is done</u>...

*Je joue* de temps en temps *au football.* = I play football <u>from time to time</u>.

## I eat too quickly and run too slowly...

Alrighty — this is <u>a bit like</u> English — you have a set ending (-ment) to learn and stick on, and it's not too tricky either. Make sure you <u>really know</u> the standard <u>rule</u> and all the <u>exceptions</u>. <u>Practise</u> taking a few French sentences and <u>adding</u> detail... then use them when you're doing your <u>assessments</u>.

**COMPARATIVES & SUPERLATIVES**

# Comparing Things

Often you don't just want to say that something is <u>tasty</u>, <u>juicy</u> or whatever — you want to say that it's the <u>tastiest</u>, or (to create a nice amount of jealousy) that it's <u>juicier than</u> someone else's...

## How to say more weird, most weird

In French you can't say '<u>weirder</u>' or '<u>weirdest</u>' — you have to say '<u>more weird</u>' or '<u>the most weird</u>':

Dave est **bizarre** .

= Dave is <u>weird</u>.

Dave est **plus bizarre** .

= Dave is <u>more weird/weirder</u>.

Dave est **le plus bizarre** .

= Dave is the <u>most weird/weirdest</u>.

You can do this with any <u>describing word</u>. Check out pages 88 to 90.

| | | | | | |
|---|---|---|---|---|---|
| *old:* | vieux | *older:* | plus vieux | *oldest:* | le plus vieux |
| *big (or tall):* | grand | *bigger:* | plus grand | *biggest:* | le plus grand |

Add 'plus'.

Add 'le plus'.

## Don't forget agreement

The adjectives still need to <u>agree</u> as normal:

*See page 88 for more on how adjectives <u>agree</u>.*

*less pretty:* moins jolie

Cette robe est **plus jolie** . = This dress is <u>prettier</u>.

*less strong:* moins forts

Ils sont **plus forts** . = They're <u>stronger</u>.

When you're saying 'the most ...', you need to say '<u>le</u> plus', '<u>la</u> plus' or '<u>les</u> plus' to match the word you're describing (see page 87).

*the least funny:* la moins amusante

Liz est <u>**la plus amusante**</u> . = Liz is <u>the funniest</u>.

*the least strong:* les moins forts

Ed et Jo sont <u>**les plus amusants**</u> . = Ed and Jo are <u>the funniest</u>.

## The three ways of comparing things — More, Less and As

If you want to say '<u>less ...</u>' or '<u>as ... as</u>', you just use the words '<u>moins</u>' and '<u>aussi</u>' instead of '<u>plus</u>'. And the word for '<u>than</u>' is '<u>que</u>'.

Ed est <u>plus grand que</u> Tom. = Ed is tall<u>er</u> <u>than</u> Tom.

Ed est <u>moins grand que</u> Tom. = Ed is <u>less</u> tall <u>than</u> Tom.

Ed est <u>le moins</u> grand. = Ed is <u>the least</u> tall.

To say '<u>the least ...</u>', you just say '<u>le/la/les moins ...</u>':

## Mirror, mirror on the wall...

Yup, the stuff on this page is a favourite of wicked stepmothers and it's a favourite with French teachers too — they simply adore it when you get it <u>right</u>. To learn this kind of thing you just need to <u>repeat some examples</u> to yourself about 30 times in a kind of <u>weird chant</u> until it <u>sticks</u>.

# Comparing Things

Right, just a bit more on comparisons. A few common exceptions, and also how to compare the way people do things. Chomping at the bit? Trois, deux, un... go.

## Pour le meilleur et pour le pire... — For better or worse...

Just like in English, there are some odd ones out when it comes to comparing things, and these tend to be the ones that crop up a lot. With these ones, you don't say 'plus ...' or 'moins ...'.

| | | | | | | |
|---|---|---|---|---|---|---|
| good: | bon(ne)(s) | ➡ | better: | meilleur(e)(s) | ➡ best: | le meilleur |
| bad: | mauvais(e)(s) | ➡ | worse: | pire(s) | ➡ worst: | le pire |
| lots: | beaucoup | ➡ | more: | plus | ➡ most: | le plus |
| little: | peu | ➡ | less: | moins | ➡ least: | le moins |

With these four, the 'le' can be replaced with 'la' or 'les' if the thing that's being described is feminine or plural. 'Meilleur' still takes an 'e' in the feminine and an 's' in the plural, and 'pire' still takes an 's' in the plural.

**EXAMPLES:**  *Ce livre est meilleur que le dernier.*  = This book is better than the last (one).

*Le chien bleu est le pire.*  = The blue dog is the worst.

## More or most weirdly is pretty much the same...

When you're comparing how people do things, it works pretty much how you'd expect.

*Dave parle bizarrement.*  = Dave talks weirdly.

*Dave parle plus bizarrement.*  = Dave talks more weirdly.

*Dave parle le plus bizarrement.*  = Dave talks the most weirdly.

'Bizarrement' is an adverb. See page 91 for more on this.

Words like 'bizarrement' (adverbs) don't agree, and you always use 'le'.

*Jessica court le plus vite.*  = Jessica runs the fastest.

DON'T fall into the trap of saying 'vitement' for fast. The adverb is always 'vite' and the adjective is 'rapide'.

## Je chante mieux que toi — I sing better than you

There are some odd ones out you need to know with comparative adverbs:

| | | | | | |
|---|---|---|---|---|---|
| well: | bien | ➡ | better: | mieux | ➡ best: le mieux |
| badly: | mal | ➡ | worse: | pire | ➡ worst: le pire |

In English we might say "I'm a better singer than you" and "You're a good player, but Henri's the best."

*Tu joues bien, mais c'est Henri qui joue le mieux.*  = You play well, but Henri plays the best.

## And that's more or less it...

This'll help you sound much more sophisticated when you talk French. Instead of saying "It's a good film", you can say "It's a better film than...", or "It's the best film of this year". 'Mieux' comes up all the time, like when people say, 'Ça va mieux' meaning 'I'm feeling better'.

## PREPOSITIONS — Sneaky Wee Words

It all looks terrifying.  But you've got to learn it if you want tip-top marks.  It's really only a few words.

### TO — à or en

Where we use 'to', the French usually use 'à':  **Il va à Paris.**  = He's going to Paris.

But for feminine countries and ones beginning with a vowel, it's usually 'en':

**Il va en France.**  = He's going to France.

*For 'the train to Calais' see 'the train for Calais' on page 95.  For times, like '10 to 4', see page 2.*

For things like to go, to do, just use the infinitive (see page 100) — you don't need an extra word for 'to'.  E.g. aller = to go, faire = to make.

### ON — sur or à

For 'on top' of something, it's 'sur':

**Sur la table.**  = On the table.

For days of the week, it's left out:

**Je pars lundi.**  = I'm leaving on Monday.

When it's not 'on top', it's usually 'à':

**Je l'ai vu à la télé.**  = I saw it on TV.

**J'irai à pied.**  = I'll go on foot.

### IN — dans, à or en

If it's actually inside something, then it's usually 'dans':  **C'est dans la boîte.**  = It's in the box.

If it's in a town, it's 'à':  **J'habite à Marseille.**  = I live in Marseilles.

If you want to say in a feminine country, or one beginning with a vowel, then it's usually 'en':  **J'habite en France.**  = I live in France.

### FROM — de or à partir de

Where we use 'from', they usually use 'de':

**De Londres à Paris.**  = From London to Paris.

**Je viens de Cardiff.**  = I come from Cardiff.

For dates, it's 'à partir de':

**À partir du 4 juin.**

= From the 4th of June.

### OF — de or en

Where we use 'of', they usually use 'de':  **Une bouteille de lait.**  = A bottle of milk.

*Watch out: sometimes it's hard to spot the 'de' in a sentence, because 'de' + 'le' = du, and 'de' + 'les' = 'des' — see page 87.*

*You don't say 'of' with dates (see page 3):*

'Made of' is 'en':  **C'est en cuir.**  = It's made of leather.

**Le 2 juin.**  = The 2nd of June.

### Tiny but deadly...

There's so much on this page that catches people out.  Before carrying on, go back over this page and cover up all the boxes with French in them, and translate back all the English sentences.

# Sneaky Wee Words

A couple more sneaky words, and then the dreaded <u>qui</u> and <u>que</u>...

## FOR — pour or depuis

Where we use '<u>for</u>', they usually use '<u>pour</u>':

| Un cadeau <u>pour</u> moi. | = A present <u>for</u> me. |

For 'the train for...', it's '<u>pour</u>':

| Le train <u>pour</u> Calais. | = The train <u>for</u> Calais. |

To say how long you're going to do something for in the future, use '<u>pour</u>':

| Je vais aller en France <u>pour</u> le week-end. | = I'm going to go to France <u>for</u> the weekend. |

To say things like 'I've studied French for 5 years', use the <u>present tense</u> and '<u>depuis</u>':

| J'apprends le français <u>depuis</u> cinq ans. | = I've studied French <u>for</u> 5 years. |

To say how long you were doing something for in the past, use the <u>imperfect tense</u> and '<u>pendant</u>':

| J''apprenais l'allemand <u>pendant</u> un an. | = I learnt German <u>for</u> a year. |

## AT — à

| <u>À</u> six heures. | = <u>At</u> six o'clock. |

| Elle est <u>à</u> l'école. | = She is <u>at</u> school. |

<u>Watch out</u>: It can be hard to spot the 'à' in a sentence, because 'à' + 'le' = 'au' and 'à' + 'les' = 'aux' — see page 87.

## Qui and que — Which / who / that...

Grammar Fans: '<u>Relative Pronouns</u>'.

These are probably the <u>trickiest</u> of the <u>tricky</u> French words. Practise them lots...

1) If the person/thing you are talking about is the <u>subject</u> of the verb, i.e. the person/thing that <u>does the verb</u>, then you use '<u>qui</u>'.

| Un professeur <u>qui</u> aime bien sa classe. | = A teacher <u>who</u> likes his class. |

subject      verb

It's the teacher that's <u>doing the liking</u>, so it's <u>QUI</u>.

2) If the person/thing you are talking about is the <u>object</u> of the verb, i.e. the person/thing that <u>has something done to it</u>, then you use '<u>que</u>'.

| Un professeur <u>que</u> sa classe aime bien. | = A teacher <u>that</u> his class likes. |

object    subject    verb

It's the teacher that is <u>being liked</u> (NOT doing the liking), so it's <u>QUE</u>.

**EXAMPLES:**

| Où est le bâtiment qu'on a vu? | = Where is the building we saw? |

The building is not doing the seeing — so QUE.

| Où est le chien qui courait? | = Where is the dog that was running? |

The dog was doing the running — so QUI.

## Des mots que je déteste...

Not the easiest stuff in the world, but after a while you should get a <u>feel</u> for <u>qui</u> and <u>que</u>.
<u>Definitely</u> worth learning these examples by heart, and then making up <u>a few of your own</u>.

## PRONOUNS — I, You, Him, Them, and En & Y

Pronouns are words that replace nouns — things like 'you', 'she' or 'them'.

# je, tu, il, elle — I, you, he, she

You need 'I', 'you', 'he' and 'she' most often — for the subject (main person/thing) in a sentence...

Paul finally has a new job. **(He)** shaves poodles at the poodle parlour.

'He' is a **pronoun**. It means you don't have to say 'Paul' again.

**THE SUBJECT PRONOUNS**

| | | | |
|---|---|---|---|
| *I* | je | nous | *we* |
| *you* (informal singular) | tu | vous | *you* (plural or formal) |
| *he/it* | il | ils | *they* (masc. or masc. & fem.) |
| *she/it* | elle | elles | *they* (all fem.) |
| *one/we* | on | | |

Le chien mange le chat. = The dog eats the cat.

**(Il)** mange le chat. = It eats the cat.

The French often use 'on' when they're talking about 'we'. E.g. 'On mange' = 'We eat', 'On va aller au cinéma' = 'We are going to go to the cinema.' It's a very useful pronoun.

# me, te, le, la — me, you, him, her

These are for the person/thing in a sentence that's having the action done to it (the direct object).

Dave lave le chien. = Dave washes the dog.

Dave **(le)** lave. = Dave washes it.

**THE DIRECT OBJECT PRONOUNS**

| | | | |
|---|---|---|---|
| *me* | me | nous | *us* |
| *you* (inf. sing.) | te | vous | *you* (plural or formal) |
| *him/it* | le | les | *them* |
| *her/it* | la | | |

# There are special words for to me, to her, to them

For things that need 'to' or 'for'— like writing to someone — use the indirect object pronouns.

**THE INDIRECT OBJECT PRONOUNS**

| | | | |
|---|---|---|---|
| *to me* | me | nous | *to us* |
| *to you* (inf. sing.) | te | vous | *to you* (informal plural or formal) |
| *to him/her/it* | lui | leur | *to them* |

Le chien donne la chemise à Dave. = The dog gives the shirt to Dave.

Le chien **(lui)** donne la chemise. = The dog gives the shirt to him.

# Two Top Words — 'En' & 'Y'

**EN — MEANING 'OF IT'**

EN — this pronoun usually translates as 'of it', 'of them', 'some' or 'any'.

If a verb needs de after it, like 'avoir besoin de' you translate 'it' or 'them' as 'en':

e.g.: J'ai besoin de la banane.  J'en ai besoin.

I need the banana.  ➡ I need it.

**Y — MEANING 'THERE'**

e.g.: J'y vais.     I'm going there.

It's also used to mean 'it' or 'them' after verbs followed by à, e.g.: penser à — to think about.

e.g.:     Je n'y pense plus.

I don't think about it any more.

It's also used in several common expressions.

Il y a...     There is/There are...

Ça y est!     That's it! — as in 'I've finished!'

# Paul and Dave — loving your work...

You're not going to get very far in the exams if you can't understand things like I, you, he, she and we. The good news is that it's pretty darn easy. You don't even have to learn any sentences on this page — just a few words you probably already know. You've got no excuse whatsoever. Hm.

# Me, You, Him, Them, Mine, Yours...

You'll need to learn the pronouns here too. Yuck...

## Stick all Object Pronouns Before the Verb

These pronouns usually go <u>before</u> the verb. If you're using <u>two</u> object pronouns in the same sentence, they <u>both</u> go before the verb, but they go in a <u>special order</u>. This is a bit tricky, so get it learnt:

| 1 | 2 | 3 | 4 | 5 | 6 |
|---|---|---|---|---|---|
| me te nous vous | le la les | lui leur | y | en | (verb) |

Examples: Il <u>me les</u> donne.  He gives <u>them to me</u>.
Je <u>le lui</u> ai donné.  I gave <u>it to him</u>.

If you're using a <u>negative</u>, the '<u>ne</u>' goes <u>before</u> the object pronoun(s), and the '<u>pas</u>' after the verb.

Example: Je ne <u>les</u> mange pas.  I don't eat <u>them</u>.

## Special words for me, you, him, her...

In some sentences, you need to <u>emphasise</u> exactly who is being talked about. For example, you can say 'he's taller', but you can make the sentence clearer using an <u>emphatic pronoun</u>, e.g. 'he's taller than <u>you</u>'. There are <u>four occasions</u> when you need to use emphatic pronouns in French:

### EMPHATIC PRONOUNS

| me | moi | us | nous |
|---|---|---|---|
| you (informal sing.) | toi | you (plural or formal) | vous |
| him/it | lui | they (masc. or masc. & fem.) | eux |
| her/it | elle | they (all fem.) | elles |
| one | soi | | |

| | | |
|---|---|---|
| 1) Telling people to do something to you or to themselves. | *Écoutez-<u>moi</u>!* | = Listen to <u>me</u>! |
| 2) Comparing things. | *Il est plus grand que <u>toi</u>.* | = He is taller than <u>you</u>. |
| 3) After words like 'with', 'for', 'from'... (prepositions). | *Nous allons avec <u>eux</u>.* | = We're going with <u>them</u>. |
| 4) Where the words are on their own, or after 'c'est'. | *Qui parle? Moi! C'est moi!* | = Who's speaking? Me! It's me! |

For more on this, see page 112.

For more on comparing, see pages 92-93.

For more on prepositions, see pages 94-95.

When French people want to be <u>even clearer</u> about who's being talked about, e.g. 'I made this cake <u>myself</u>,' they use one of these words instead of a normal emphatic pronoun. They all mean '...<u>self</u>' (myself, yourself, himself etc.).

moi-même, toi-même, lui-même, elle-même, soi-même, nous-mêmes, vous-mêmes, eux-mêmes, elles-mêmes

## C'est le mien / la mienne... — It's mine...

You'll only need to <u>recognise</u> these — you won't have to use them.

### POSSESSIVE PRONOUNS

| | Singular Masc. | Fem. | Plural Masc. | Fem. |
|---|---|---|---|---|
| mine: | le mien | la mienne | les miens | les miennes |
| yours (informal sing.) | le tien | la tienne | les tiens | les tiennes |
| his / hers: | le sien | la sienne | les siens | les siennes |
| ours: | le nôtre | la nôtre | les nôtres | les nôtres |
| yours (plural or formal): | le vôtre | la vôtre | les vôtres | les vôtres |
| theirs: | le leur | la leur | les leurs | les leurs |

*Donne-moi <u>la</u> brosse, c'est <u>la</u> mienne.*
= Give me the brush, it's mine.

*Donne-lui <u>le</u> ballon, c'est <u>le</u> sien.*
= Give him the ball, it's his.

## Special words for me — you don't deserve them...

This stuff is pretty <u>grisly</u>, I'll admit. You have to understand these when you see or hear them, and if you can <u>use</u> them, your teacher will be really impressed. Which means you'll pick up more marks in the assessments. Which is the whole point. You know the drill by now — <u>cover</u> and <u>scribble</u>.

# This & That and Which

Pointing things out in shops, and generally making it clear which thing you're on about, is important.

## How to say this thing or these things

Use 'ce', 'cet'... in front of another word for saying things like 'this man', 'these apples' — i.e. when you're using 'this' as a describing word.

> Grammar Fans:
> 'Demonstrative Adjectives'.

| masculine singular | masculine singular before vowel or 'h' which takes 'l' | feminine singular | plural |
|---|---|---|---|
| ce | cet | cette | ces |

**EXAMPLES:**

ce stylo: *this pen*    cet oiseau: *this bird*
cette maison: *this house*    ces pommes: *these apples*

## Je veux celui-là — I want that one

> Grammar Fans:
> These are the 'Demonstrative Pronouns'.

The words in the box below also mean 'this'. You'll only need to recognise them, but you'll have to use the stuff in the blue box on the right.

| masculine singular | masculine plural | feminine singular | feminine plural |
|---|---|---|---|
| celui | ceux | celle | celles |

> If you're not pointing something out, you can use these ones:
> ceci = this    cela = that    ça = that
> **EXAMPLES:**
> Cela n'est pas vrai. — That isn't true.
> Lisez ceci. — Read this.

1) You often see these words with '-ci' or '-là' on the end.
2) When it ends '-ci' it means 'this one' or 'this one here'. '-là' makes it mean 'that one' or 'that one there'.

> J'ai deux chiens. *Celui-ci* est mignon, mais *celui-là* est méchant.

= I have two dogs. This one here's nice, but that one there's nasty.

3) On their own, these words can mean 'the one(s)'.

> J'aime bien cette chanson, mais je préfère *celle* qu'on a écoutée hier soir.

= I like this song, but I prefer the one we listened to yesterday evening.

## Dont — of which...

> Grammar Fans:
> This is a 'Relative Pronoun'.

1) 'Dont' can be translated as 'of which' or 'about which'.
2) This is difficult. But don't panic — you only need to recognise it.
3) Dont is used if the verb in the sentence is followed by 'de' e.g. 'avoir peur de', 'avoir besoin de'.

> Le monstre dont j'ai peur est là.

= The monster which I'm scared of is there.

> Le livre dont j'ai besoin est fantastique.

= The book which I need is fantastic.

4) You also see it where we would say 'whose'.

> Le garçon dont le père est médecin.

= The boy whose father is a doctor.
(Literally 'The boy of whom the father is a doctor.')

## So, what are you studying — oh, this and that...

OK, so the bits about 'which' get pretty tricky. What am I saying... very tricky. But the stuff about 'this' and 'that' is pretty straightforward, so it's not as bad as it seems at first. Keep at it — practice might not make perfect, but it does make it a lot better, and that's the point.

# Joining Words — Longer Sentences
**CONJUNCTIONS**

Everyone knows <u>long</u> sentences are <u>clever</u> — and clever people are <u>popular</u> when it's assessment-marking time. So learn these joining words to <u>help</u> you make longer sentences, and get <u>more marks</u> for being smart.

## Et = And

*J'aime jouer au football.* **AND** *J'aime jouer au rugby.* = *J'aime jouer au football <u>et</u> au rugby.* = I like playing football <u>and</u> rugby.

= I like playing football. = I like playing rugby.

**ANOTHER EXAMPLE:** *J'ai un frère <u>et</u> une sœur.* = I have a brother <u>and</u> a sister.

## Ou = Or
This is different from '<u>où</u>' (with an accent), which means '<u>where</u>' — see page 4.

*Il joue au football tous les jours.* **OR** *Il joue au rugby tous les jours.* = *Il joue au football <u>ou</u> au rugby tous les jours.*

= He plays football every day. = He plays rugby every day. = He plays football <u>or</u> rugby every day.

**ANOTHER EXAMPLE:** *Je voudrais être médecin <u>ou</u> ingénieur.* = I would like to be a doctor <u>or</u> an engineer.

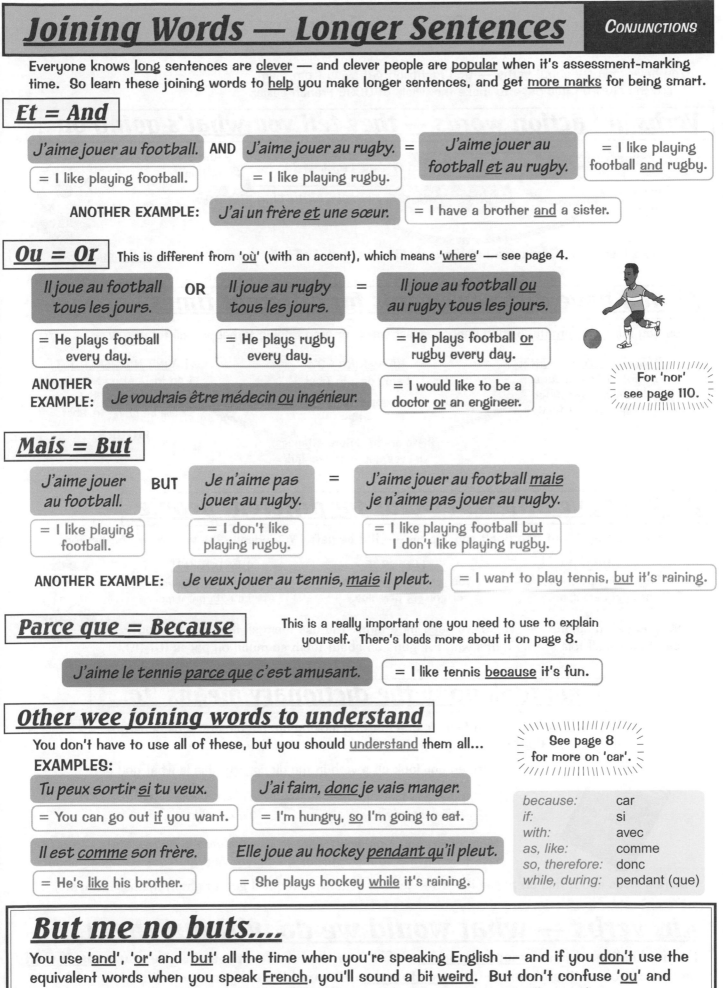

For 'nor' see page 110.

## Mais = But

*J'aime jouer au football.* **BUT** *Je n'aime pas jouer au rugby.* = *J'aime jouer au football <u>mais</u> je n'aime pas jouer au rugby.*

= I like playing football. = I don't like playing rugby. = I like playing football <u>but</u> I don't like playing rugby.

**ANOTHER EXAMPLE:** *Je veux jouer au tennis, <u>mais</u> il pleut.* = I want to play tennis, <u>but</u> it's raining.

## Parce que = Because
This is a really important one you need to use to explain yourself. There's loads more about it on page 8.

*J'aime le tennis <u>parce que</u> c'est amusant.* = I like tennis <u>because</u> it's fun.

## Other wee joining words to understand

You don't have to use all of these, but you should <u>understand</u> them all...
**EXAMPLES:**

*Tu peux sortir <u>si</u> tu veux.* *J'ai faim, <u>donc</u> je vais manger.*

= You can go out <u>if</u> you want. = I'm hungry, <u>so</u> I'm going to eat.

See page 8 for more on 'car'.

*Il est <u>comme</u> son frère.* *Elle joue au hockey <u>pendant qu</u>'il pleut.*

= He's <u>like</u> his brother. = She plays hockey <u>while</u> it's raining.

| | |
|---|---|
| because: | car |
| if: | si |
| with: | avec |
| as, like: | comme |
| so, therefore: | donc |
| while, during: | pendant (que) |

## But me no buts....

You use '<u>and</u>', '<u>or</u>' and '<u>but</u>' all the time when you're speaking English — and if you <u>don't</u> use the equivalent words when you speak <u>French</u>, you'll sound a bit <u>weird</u>. But don't confuse '<u>ou</u>' and '<u>où</u>'. Try to <u>recognise</u> all the <u>extra</u> words in the last bit too, and, better still, <u>use</u> them.

**VERBS, TENSES AND THE INFINITIVE**

# The Lowdown on Verbs

You have to know about <u>verbs</u> — you just can't get away from them.
Learn the stuff on this page to make the whole of GCSE French <u>easier</u>.

## Verbs are action words — they tell you what's going on

Rob's grandma Ethel plays football every Saturday.

These are <u>verbs</u>.

Alex's grandma prefers knitting socks.

And so is this.

There's a load of stuff you need to know about verbs, but it all boils down to these <u>two things</u>...

## 1) You have different words for different times

You say things <u>differently</u> if they happened last week, or aren't going to happen till tomorrow.

**HAS ALREADY HAPPENED**
I went to Tibet last year.
I have been to Tibet.
I had been to Tibet.

**PAST**

**HAPPENING NOW**
I am going to Tibet.

**PRESENT**

**HASN'T HAPPENED YET**
I go to Tibet on Monday.
I will go to Tibet.
I will be going to Tibet.

**FUTURE**

These are all different <u>tenses</u>, in case you're interested.

## 2) You have different words for different people

You say 'he plays', but you <u>don't</u> say '<u>I plays</u>' — it'd be daft. You change the verb to fit the person.

**ME DOING IT**
I <u>am</u> eating parsnips
or I <u>eat</u> parsnips.

**YOU DOING IT**
You <u>are</u> eating parsnips
or you <u>eat</u> parsnips.

**HIM DOING IT**
He <u>is</u> eating parsnips
or he <u>eats</u> parsnips.

OK, you get the picture — verbs are <u>dead important</u>. You use them all the time, so you need to learn all this stuff. That's why I've gone on about them so much on pages 101-116.

## The word you look up in the dictionary means 'to...'

When you want to say 'I dance' in French, you start by looking up 'dance' in the dictionary.
But you can't just use the first word you find — there's more to it than that...

When you look up a verb <u>in the dictionary</u>, this is what you get:

For grammar fans, this is called the <u>infinitive</u>.

to give: donner
to go: aller

Most of the time you won't want to use the verb in its <u>raw state</u> — you'll have to <u>change</u> it so it's right for the <u>person</u> and <u>time</u> you're talking about.

There's loads about this on pages 101-116 — learn it all now, and you'll get it right in the assessments.

## Ah, verbs — what would we do without them...

I'm not kidding — this is <u>mega-important</u> stuff. Over the next few pages I'll give you <u>loads of stuff</u> on verbs because there's loads you <u>need to know</u>. Some of it's easy, some of it's tricky — but if you <u>don't understand</u> the things on <u>this page</u> before you start, you'll have <u>no chance</u>.

# Verbs in the Present Tense

The present tense mostly describes things that are <u>happening now</u>. You'll probably need it more than any other form of the verb, so it's <u>really important</u>.

## The Present tense describes What's Happening Now

Present tense verbs describe either something that's happening <u>now</u>, e.g. 'I am brushing my teeth' or something which happens <u>repeatedly</u>, e.g. 'I brush my teeth every day'. There are <u>3 easy steps</u> to put a verb into the present tense:

1) Get the <u>infinitive</u> of the verb you want, e.g. '<u>regarder</u>'

2) Knock off the <u>last two letters</u>: regard̶e̶r̶ This gives you the <u>stem</u>.

3) Add the new <u>ending</u>. This depends on the kind of verb and the person doing the verb (see below).
E.g. Il regard**e**, vous regard **ez**, ils regard **ent**.

| Examples of Present Tense Stems | | | |
|---|---|---|---|
| Infinitive | regarder | finir | vendre |
| Stem | regard | fin | vend |

## Endings for -er verbs

To form the present tense of <u>regular</u> '-er' verbs, add the endings shown to the verb's stem — e.g.:

The first bit ('regard') doesn't change.

*regarder = to watch*

*See page 5 for when to use '<u>tu</u>' and when to use '<u>vous</u>'.*

| | | | | | |
|---|---|---|---|---|---|
| *I watch* = | je | regard **e** | nous | regard **ons** = | *we watch* |
| *you (informal singular) watch* = | tu | regard **es** | vous | regard **ez** = | *you (formal or plural) watch* |
| *he/it watches* = | il | regard **e** | ils | regard **ent** = | *they (masc. or mixed masc. and fem.) watch* |
| *she/it watches* = | elle | regard **e** | elles | regard **ent** = | *they (fem.) watch* |
| *one watches/we watch* = | on | regard **e** | | | |

<u>IMPORTANT</u>: 'il', 'elle' and 'on' <u>always</u> have the same ending, and so do 'ils' & 'elles'.

## Endings for -ir verbs

To form the present tense of <u>regular</u> '-ir' verbs, add the endings shown to the verb's stem — e.g.:

The first bit ('fin') doesn't change.

*finir = to finish*

| | | | | | |
|---|---|---|---|---|---|
| *I finis* = | je | fin **is** | nous | fin **issons** = | *we finish* |
| *you (inf. sing.) finish* = | tu | fin **is** | vous | fin **issez** = | *you (formal or plural) finish* |
| *he/she/it/one finishes* = | il/elle/on | fin **it** | ils/elles | fin **issent** = | *they finish* |

## Endings for -re verbs

To form the present tense of <u>regular</u> '-re' verbs, add the endings shown to the verb's stem — e.g.:

The first bit ('<u>vend</u>') doesn't change.

*vendre = to sell*

| | | | | | |
|---|---|---|---|---|---|
| *I sell* = | je | vend **s** | nous | vend **ons** = | *we sell* |
| *you (inf. sing.) sell* = | tu | vend **s** | vous | vend **ez** = | *you (formal or plural) sell* |
| *he/she/it/one sells* = | il/elle/on | vend | ils/elles | vend **ent** = | *they sell* |

<u>NOTE</u>: For <u>il/elle/on</u> there's <u>no</u> ending for '-re' verbs.

## The present tense — not just for Christmas...

You use the present tense for both '<u>I do</u> something' and '<u>I am doing</u> something'. Make sure you avoid disasters like 'Je suis... jouer... le tennis' for 'I am playing tennis'. Ouch. Roger Federer wouldn't say that, French-speaking Swiss pro that he is. He'd say '<u>Je joue au tennis</u>'.

**PRESENT TENSE**

# Verbs in the Present Tense

Verbs that <u>don't</u> follow the <u>same pattern</u> as regular verbs are called '<u>irregular verbs</u>' (crazy, I know). Most of the <u>really useful verbs</u> are irregular — d'oh. Anyway, here are <u>a few</u> you'll need most...

## Some of the most useful verbs are irregular

These are some of the <u>most important</u> verbs in the world, so you <u>really must</u> learn <u>all</u> the bits of them.

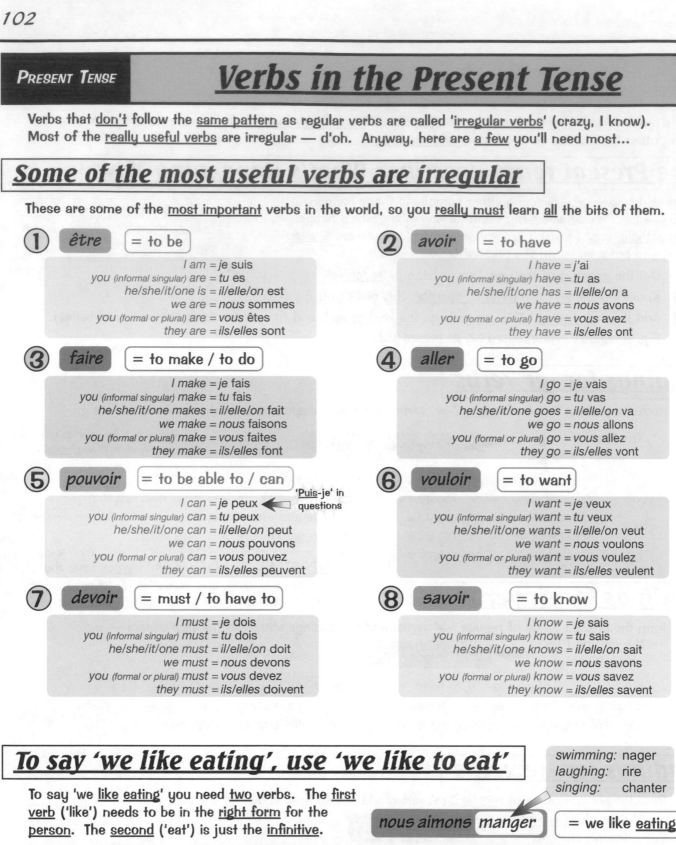

① *être*  = to be

I am = *je* suis
you (informal singular) are = *tu* es
he/she/it/one is = *il/elle/on* est
we are = *nous* sommes
you (formal or plural) are = *vous* êtes
they are = *ils/elles* sont

② *avoir*  = to have

I have = *j'*ai
you (informal singular) have = *tu* as
he/she/it/one has = *il/elle/on* a
we have = *nous* avons
you (formal or plural) have = *vous* avez
they have = *ils/elles* ont

③ *faire*  = to make / to do

I make = *je* fais
you (informal singular) make = *tu* fais
he/she/it/one makes = *il/elle/on* fait
we make = *nous* faisons
you (formal or plural) make = *vous* faites
they make = *ils/elles* font

④ *aller*  = to go

I go = *je* vais
you (informal singular) go = *tu* vas
he/she/it/one goes = *il/elle/on* va
we go = *nous* allons
you (formal or plural) go = *vous* allez
they go = *ils/elles* vont

⑤ *pouvoir*  = to be able to / can

I can = *je* peux ← 'Puis-je' in questions
you (informal singular) can = *tu* peux
he/she/it/one can = *il/elle/on* peut
we can = *nous* pouvons
you (formal or plural) can = *vous* pouvez
they can = *ils/elles* peuvent

⑥ *vouloir*  = to want

I want = *je* veux
you (informal singular) want = *tu* veux
he/she/it/one wants = *il/elle/on* veut
we want = *nous* voulons
you (formal or plural) want = *vous* voulez
they want = *ils/elles* veulent

⑦ *devoir*  = must / to have to

I must = *je* dois
you (informal singular) must = *tu* dois
he/she/it/one must = *il/elle/on* doit
we must = *nous* devons
you (formal or plural) must = *vous* devez
they must = *ils/elles* doivent

⑧ *savoir*  = to know

I know = *je* sais
you (informal singular) know = *tu* sais
he/she/it/one knows = *il/elle/on* sait
we know = *nous* savons
you (formal or plural) know = *vous* savez
they know = *ils/elles* savent

## To say 'we like eating', use 'we like to eat'

swimming: nager
laughing: rire
singing: chanter

To say 'we <u>like eating</u>' you need <u>two</u> verbs. The <u>first</u> verb ('like') needs to be in the <u>right form</u> for the <u>person</u>. The <u>second</u> ('eat') is just the <u>infinitive</u>.

*nous aimons* **manger**  = we like <u>eating</u>

Sometimes the first verb has a <u>preposition</u> (see pages 94-95) — a small but important word that comes <u>before the second verb</u>:

*il <u>arrête de</u> fumer*  = he is stopping smoking    *je <u>commence à</u> parler*  = I start speaking

In the infinitive, you say: '<u>arrêter de faire</u>', '<u>commencer à faire</u>', etc.

## Irregular verbs — they should eat more fibre...

Don't worry, all these verb forms will become second nature eventually. The thing is that the irregular verbs tend to be the ones that are <u>most used</u> in French, so you <u>can't</u> just ignore them.

# Talking About the Future

You'll need to talk about things that are going to happen at some point in the future. There are two ways you can do it — and the first one's a piece of cake, so I'd learn that first if I were you.

## 1) You can use 'I'm going to' to talk about the Future

This is pretty easy, so there's no excuse for not learning it.

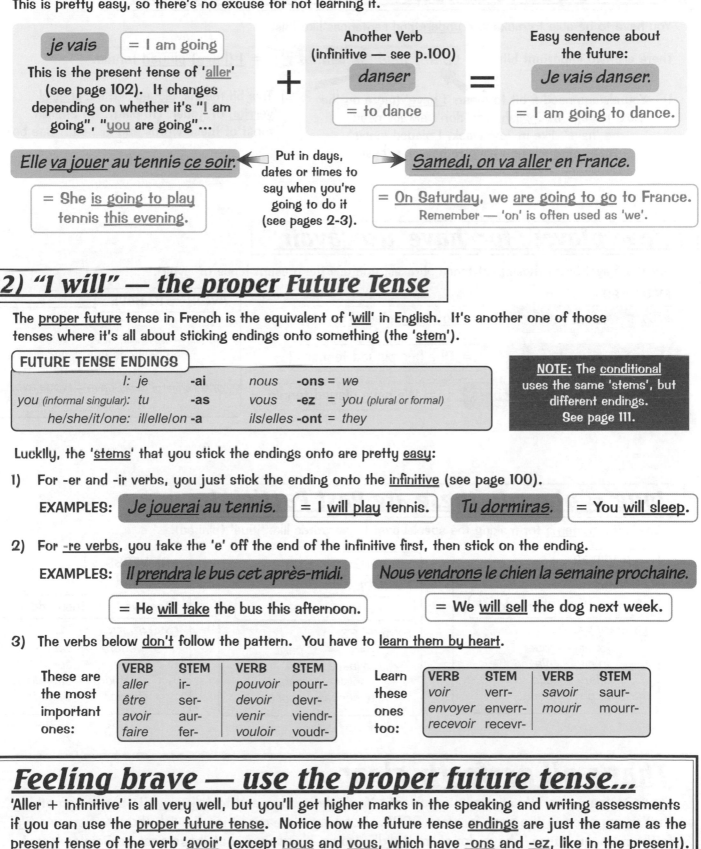

| je vais | = I am going |

This is the present tense of 'aller' (see page 102). It changes depending on whether it's "I am going", "you are going"...

**+**

Another Verb (infinitive — see p.100)

| danser |

= to dance

**=**

Easy sentence about the future:

| Je vais danser. |

= I am going to dance.

*Elle va jouer au tennis ce soir.*

= She is going to play tennis this evening.

Put in days, dates or times to say when you're going to do it (see pages 2-3).

*Samedi, on va aller en France.*

= On Saturday, we are going to go to France.
Remember — 'on' is often used as 'we'.

## 2) "I will" — the proper Future Tense

The proper future tense in French is the equivalent of 'will' in English. It's another one of those tenses where it's all about sticking endings onto something (the 'stem').

**FUTURE TENSE ENDINGS**

| | | | | |
|---|---|---|---|---|
| I: *je* | **-ai** | *nous* | **-ons** | = we |
| you (informal singular): *tu* | **-as** | *vous* | **-ez** | = you (plural or formal) |
| he/she/it/one: *il/elle/on* **-a** | | *ils/elles* **-ont** | | = they |

**NOTE:** The conditional uses the same 'stems', but different endings. See page 111.

Luckily, the 'stems' that you stick the endings onto are pretty easy:

1) For -er and -ir verbs, you just stick the ending onto the infinitive (see page 100).

   **EXAMPLES:** *Je jouerai au tennis.* = I will play tennis. *Tu dormiras.* = You will sleep.

2) For -re verbs, you take the 'e' off the end of the infinitive first, then stick on the ending.

   **EXAMPLES:** *Il prendra le bus cet après-midi.* *Nous vendrons le chien la semaine prochaine.*

   = He will take the bus this afternoon. = We will sell the dog next week.

3) The verbs below don't follow the pattern. You have to learn them by heart.

These are the most important ones:

| VERB | STEM | VERB | STEM |
|---|---|---|---|
| *aller* | ir- | *pouvoir* | pourr- |
| *être* | ser- | *devoir* | devr- |
| *avoir* | aur- | *venir* | viendr- |
| *faire* | fer- | *vouloir* | voudr- |

Learn these ones too:

| VERB | STEM | VERB | STEM |
|---|---|---|---|
| *voir* | verr- | *savoir* | saur- |
| *envoyer* | enverr- | *mourir* | mourr- |
| *recevoir* | recevr- | | |

# Feeling brave — use the proper future tense...

'Aller + infinitive' is all very well, but you'll get higher marks in the speaking and writing assessments if you can use the proper future tense. Notice how the future tense endings are just the same as the present tense of the verb 'avoir' (except nous and vous, which have -ons and -ez, like in the present).

## PERFECT TENSE — *Talking About the Past*

The perfect tense is used for things that happened in the past. It's a bit tricky so we've given you three pages on it. Like most grammar stuff, it's just a question of a few rules to follow, and a few bits and pieces to learn. Nothing you can't handle, I'm sure.

## *Qu'est-ce que tu as fait? — What have you done?*

You have to be able to make and understand sentences like this:

There are two important bits:    **J'ai** **joué** **au tennis.**    = I (have) played tennis.

1)  You always need a bit to mean 'I have' (more on the next page). In English, you don't always need the 'have', like in 'last week, I played tennis'. BUT in French you have to have the 'have'.

2)  This bit means 'played'. It's a special version of 'jouer' (to play). In English, most of these words end in '-ed'. See below.

## *I have played: for 'have' use 'avoir'*

For the 'have' bit of these past tense phrases, you use the present tense of 'avoir'.

**EXAMPLES**

*Tu as joué au tennis.*  = **You have** played tennis.

*Elle a joué au tennis.*  = **She has** played tennis.

*Nous avons joué au tennis.*  = **We have** played tennis.

**AVOIR = TO HAVE**

I have = j'ai
you (informal singular) have = tu as
he/she/it/one has = il/elle/on a
we have = nous avons
you (formal or plural) have = vous avez
they have = ils/elles ont

## *Joué = played: these are Past Participles*

Learn the patterns for making the special past tense words like 'joué' (played).

**-ER VERBS**
*FORMULA*
Remove '-er', then add 'é'
*EXAMPLES*
jouer — joué
to play  played
aller — allé
to go  gone

**-IR VERBS**
*FORMULA*
Remove '-r'
*EXAMPLES*
partir — parti
to leave  left
choisir — choisi
to choose  chosen

**-RE VERBS**
*FORMULA*
Remove '-re', then add 'u'
*EXAMPLES*
vendre — vendu
to sell  sold
attendre — attendu
to wait  waited

## *That's all perfectly clear...*

Loads to learn, but it's all really important. You'll definitely need to talk or write about something that's happened in the past for your GCSE. In a way it's easier than English though, because 'j'ai fait' can mean either 'I have done', or 'I did'. So no excuses — get these past participles learnt.

# Talking About the Past

So you've met the regular verbs in the perfect tense, now for the <u>irregular verbs</u>.
And sadly, there are quite a few of them.

## Lots of verbs have irregular past participles

Some verbs <u>don't</u> follow the patterns. It's dead annoying, because a lot of the <u>most useful</u> verbs are <u>irregular</u> — you just have to learn them <u>by heart</u>:

| Verb | Past Participle | Translation |
|------|------|------|
| avoir: | eu | had |
| boire: | bu | drunk |
| conduire: | conduit | driven |
| connaître: | connu | known |
| courir: | couru | run |
| craindre: | craint | feared |
| devenir: | devenu | become |
| devoir: | dû | had to |
| dire: | dit | said |
| écrire: | écrit | written |
| être: | été | been |
| faire: | fait | did / done |

| Verb | Past Participle | Translation |
|------|------|------|
| lire: | lu | read |
| mettre: | mis | put |
| mourir: | mort | died |
| naître: | né | been born |
| ouvrir: | ouvert | opened |
| pouvoir: | pu | been able |
| prendre: | pris | taken |
| rire: | ri | laughed |
| savoir: | su | known |
| venir: | venu | come |
| voir: | vu | seen |
| vouloir: | voulu | wanted |

## Make sure you really get to grips with the perfect tense

The key to doing well in French GCSE is using a <u>variety</u> of <u>different tenses</u>, so being able to talk about the <u>past</u> is really <u>important</u>. There's one more page of stuff on the perfect tense to go, but it's worth having a good look at these example sentences and really getting your head round them before you move on.

*J'ai mangé dans un restaurant.* = <u>I have eaten / I ate</u> in a restaurant.

*Tu as mangé dans un restaurant.* = <u>You have eaten / you ate</u> in a restaurant.

*Il a mangé dans un restaurant.* = <u>He has eaten / he ate</u> in a restaurant.

This would be almost exactly the same if you were talking about a <u>girl</u> except that '<u>il</u>' would change to '<u>elle</u>'.

*Nous avons mangé dans un restaurant.* = <u>We have eaten / we ate</u> in a restaurant.

*Vous avez mangé dans un restaurant.* = <u>You have eaten / ate</u> in a restaurant.

*Ils ont mangé dans un restaurant.* = <u>They (masc.) have eaten / ate</u> in a restaurant.

This would be almost exactly the same if you were talking about <u>girls</u> except that '<u>ils</u>' would change to '<u>elles</u>'.

## Bet you're perfectly tense by now...

I know it seems like there's a lot to learn for just one tense, but I promise you that the time you spend learning this won't be wasted. It <u>always comes up</u> and it really is the key to doing well.

# Talking About the Past

One last thing — there are a <u>handful</u> of verbs which <u>don't use</u> '<u>avoir</u>' at all in the perfect tense...

## A few verbs use être instead of avoir

1) A small number of verbs use the <u>present tense</u> of '<u>être</u>' instead of the present tense of avoir when forming the <u>perfect tense</u>.

2) Just like with verbs that take 'avoir,' you use the bit of 'être' that <u>matches</u> the <u>person</u> you're talking about. E.g. He went = Il est allé.

3) The only difference with verbs that take être is that the <u>past participle</u> has to <u>agree</u> with the person it's describing. More on this below.

> **ÊTRE = TO BE**
>
> | | |
> |---:|:---|
> | *I am* = | je suis |
> | *you (informal singular) are* = | tu es |
> | *he/she/it/one is* = | il/elle/on est |
> | *we are* = | nous sommes |
> | *you (formal or plural) are* = | vous êtes |
> | *they are* = | ils/elles sont |

## 15 verbs, to be precise — learn them

| *Verb* | *Past Participle* | *Translation* |
|---|---|---|
| *aller:* | *allé* | *gone* |
| *rester:* | *resté* | *stayed* |
| *venir:* | *venu* | *come* |
| *devenir:* | *devenu* | *become* |
| *arriver:* | *arrivé* | *arrived* |
| *partir:* | *parti* | *left* |
| *sortir:* | *sorti* | *gone out* |
| *entrer:* | *entré* | *entered* |
| *monter:* | *monté* | *gone up* |
| *descendre:* | *descendu* | *gone down* |

| *Verb* | *Past Participle* | *Translation* |
|---|---|---|
| *rentrer:* | *rentré* | *gone back* |
| *retourner:* | *retourné* | *returned* |
| *tomber:* | *tombé* | *fallen* |
| *naître:* | *né* | *been born* |
| *mourir:* | *mort* | *died* |

> The être verbs are mostly about <u>movement</u>, <u>being born</u> or <u>dying</u>. You also have to use être with <u>reflexive verbs</u> — see page 109.

**EXAMPLES:** See below for why this 'e' is there.

*Je suis allé(e) au cinéma.* = <u>I have gone</u> to the cinema.

*Il est arrivé.* = <u>He has arrived</u>.

## With être as the auxiliary verb, the past participle must agree

When you use <u>être</u> to form the perfect tense, the past participle has to <u>agree</u> with the subject of the verb. This means it <u>changes</u> if the subject is <u>feminine</u> or <u>plural</u>, just like an adjective (see page 88). The agreements are underlined:

*Il est allé en ville.* = He has gone / went into town.

*Elle est all<u>é</u>e en ville.* = She has gone / went into town.

*Ils sont all<u>é</u>s en ville.* = They (masc.) have gone / went into town.

*Elles sont all<u>é</u>es en ville.* = They (fem.) have gone / went into town.

> Add <u>e</u> if the subject is <u>feminine singular</u>
> Add <u>s</u> if the subject is <u>masculine plural</u>
> Add <u>es</u> if the subject is <u>feminine plural</u>

## The 15 exceptions that prove the rule...

So, not only are loads and loads of the past participles irregular, you can't even be sure that the verb you want to put in the perfect takes '<u>avoir</u>'. Except you can — by learning which ones <u>don't</u>.

# 'Was Doing' or 'Used to Do'

Another past tense for you. The difference here is that this one's <u>not</u> for actions that were <u>completed</u> in the past, it's for actions that were <u>ongoing</u>. More on that later — here's how you <u>form</u> it.

## The stem comes from the nous form

Grammar Fans:
This is the <u>Imperfect Tense</u>.

There are 3 easy steps to make this past tense:

**1) Get the present tense 'nous' form of the verb (see p.101-102).**

**2) Knock the '-ons' off the end.**

**3) Add on the correct ending:**

The only verb that doesn't make its stem in this way is <u>être</u> (see below).

I used to have a life

### IMPERFECT TENSE ENDINGS

|  |  |  |  |  |  |
|---|---|---|---|---|---|
| I: | je | **-ais** | we: nous | **-ions** |
| you (informal sing.): | tu | **-ais** | you (pl. or formal): vous | **-iez** |
| he/she/it/one: | il/elle/on | **-ait** | they: ils/elles | **-aient** |

This bit depends on whether you're saying '<u>I</u>', '<u>you</u>', '<u>he</u>', etc.

### EXAMPLES

| In English | Present of 'nous' form | Minus the '-ons' | Add on ending | Ta-da |
|---|---|---|---|---|
| I was waiting | attendons | attend- | attend-**ais** | J'**attendais** |
| He was speaking | parlons | parl- | parl-**ait** | Il **parlait** |
| We were going | allons | all- | all-**ions** | Nous **allions** |

## Être, Avoir and Faire crop up a lot

You're more likely to come up against some verbs than others, so it's a good idea to become <u>really familiar</u> with them.

I'm afraid '<u>être</u>' is a bit different from the others (wouldn't it just be). The <u>endings</u> are the <u>same</u> though — it's just that the <u>stem</u> is '<u>ét-</u>'.

### EXAMPLES

**Ce roman <u>était</u> magnifique.**   = This novel <u>was</u> great.

**Vous <u>étiez</u> très petit à l'époque.**   = You <u>were</u> very small at the time.

| ÊTRE = TO BE | |
|---|---|
| j' étais: | I was |
| tu étais: | you (informal sing.) were |
| il/elle/on était: | he/she/it/one was |
| nous étions: | we were |
| vous étiez: | you (formal or pl.) were |
| ils/elles étaient: | they were |

And of course...

**C'était...**   = It was...   **On est allé au Canada — <u>c'était</u> formidable.**   = We went to Canada — <u>it was</u> great.

<u>All</u> the other verbs make their imperfect in the <u>normal way</u>.

'<u>Avoir</u>' is definitely one you'll need, especially because...

**Il y avait...**   = <u>There was / There were...</u>

E.g.   Il y <u>avait</u> deux stylos sur la table.
= There were two pens on the table

And you'll need '<u>faire</u>' in the imperfect tense too, especially to describe the <u>weather</u>.

E.g.   Il <u>faisait</u> beaucoup trop froid pour faire une promenade.
= It was far too cold to go for a walk.

## Another tense, another stem, more endings...

French verbs really are quite hard, and it's really easy to get confused between all the <u>stems</u> and <u>endings</u>. But remember that French teachers get <u>embarrassingly excited</u> when you get them <u>right</u>.

| IMPERFECT TENSE | *'Was Doing' or 'Used to Do'* |

So how do you know when to use the <u>perfect tense</u> (see p.104-106), and when to use the <u>imperfect tense</u>... Well there's no simple answer actually, but here are a few <u>useful pointers</u>.

## Use the imperfect for Describing the past

Basically, you use the <u>imperfect</u> to <u>describe</u> what was going on, or to <u>set the scene</u>:

> Il <u>était</u> six heures du matin. Il <u>faisait</u> très froid. J'<u>attendais</u> le train.
> = It was six o'clock in the morning. It was very cold. I was waiting for the train.

Description in the imperfect tense

And then, suddenly, <u>something happens</u>. This goes in the <u>perfect</u> tense:

> Tout à coup j'<u>ai vu</u> mon frère sur l'autre quai.
> = All of a sudden I saw my brother on the other platform.

Event in the perfect tense

| MORE EXAMPLES |
| --- |

| <u>IMPERFECT</u> | <u>PERFECT</u> |
| --- | --- |
| Quand j'<u>avais</u> dix ans, je <u>voulais</u> une console de jeux. Ma mère n'<u>était</u> pas d'accord, donc... | ...elle m'<u>a acheté</u> une bicyclette. |
| = When I was ten, I wanted a games console. My mother didn't agree, so... | = ...she bought me a bike. |

Sometimes the event comes first, and then the description:

| <u>PERFECT</u> | <u>IMPERFECT</u> |
| --- | --- |
| J'<u>ai rencontré</u> une femme... | ...qui <u>était</u> très amusante. |
| = I met a woman... | = ...who was very amusing. |

So remember — the <u>imperfect</u> is for <u>description</u>, and the <u>perfect</u> is for <u>events</u>.

## Use the imperfect for what Used To happen

The imperfect is used for talking about what you <u>used to do</u>. That could be something you did regularly:

> *J'allais au cinéma tous les jeudis.*    = <u>I used to go</u> to the cinema every Thursday.

Or something that was just the <u>general state of affairs</u>:    *Je jouais de la guitare.*    = <u>I used to play</u> the guitar.

## Depuis + imperfect — had been

'<u>Depuis</u>' is always a tricky one. You know how if you want to say "I <u>have been learning</u> French for three years", you have to use the <u>present</u> tense: "J'<u>apprends</u> le français depuis trois ans"? (If not, refresh your memory on page 72.) Well, when it's "...<u>had been</u>...", you have to use the <u>imperfect</u> tense.

> *Il pleuvait depuis deux heures quand...*    = It had been raining for two hours when...

> *J'attendais depuis deux minutes quand il est arrivé.*    = I had been waiting for two minutes when he arrived.

## Once upon a time, there was a lovely tense...

If you want to say '<u>was doing</u>', or '<u>used to do</u>', it's a pretty safe bet that you need the imperfect in French. The best way to get a feel for where to use the imperfect is to <u>learn some examples</u>.

# Myself, Yourself, etc.

Sometimes you have to talk about things you do to <u>yourself</u> — like washing yourself or getting yourself up in the morning.

## Talking about yourself — me, te, se...

*Grammar fans: these are <u>reflexive pronouns</u>.*

Here are all the different ways to say '<u>self</u>':

*You can tell <u>which</u> verbs need 'self' by checking in the <u>dictionary</u>. If you look up 'to <u>get up</u>', it'll say '<u>se lever</u>'.*

| | | | | |
|---|---|---|---|---|
| *myself:* | me | | | |
| *yourself (informal):* | te | | *ourselves:* | nous |
| *himself:* | se | *yourself (formal), yourselves:* | vous |
| *herself:* | se | *themselves, each other:* | se |
| *oneself:* | se | | | |

## Je me lave — I wash myself / have a wash

*Grammar fans call these <u>reflexive verbs</u>.*

You need to be able to talk about your '<u>daily morning routine</u>' (what you do when you get up), and other things which are about what you do to yourself.

**SE LAVER = TO WASH ONESELF**

| | | | | |
|---|---|---|---|---|
| *I wash myself:* | je me lave | | *one washes oneself:* | on se lave |
| *you wash yourself (informal):* | tu te laves | | *we wash ourselves:* | nous nous lavons |
| *he washes himself:* | il se lave | | *you wash yourself (formal) / yourselves:* | vous vous lavez |
| *she washes herself:* | elle se lave | | *they wash themselves:* | ils/elles se lavent |

There are lots of these verbs, but here are the ones you should know for the exams. Learn these:

**THE IMPORTANT REFLEXIVE VERBS**

| | | | |
|---|---|---|---|
| *to enjoy oneself:* | s'amuser | Il s'amuse: | *He's enjoying himself.* |
| *to go to bed:* | se coucher | Je me couche à onze heures: | *I go to bed at 11 o'clock.* |
| *to get up:* | se lever | Je me lève à huit heures: | *I get up at 8 o'clock.* |
| *to feel:* | se sentir | Tu te sens mal?: | *Do you feel ill?* |
| *to be called (literally = to call oneself):* | s'appeler | Je m'appelle Bob: | *I'm called Bob.* |
| | | | *(literally = I call myself Bob)* |
| *to excuse oneself / to be sorry / to apologise:* | s'excuser | Je m'excuse...: | *I'm sorry / I apologise.* |
| *to be (literally = to find oneself):* | se trouver | Où se trouve la banque?: | *Where is the bank?* |
| | | | *(literally = Where does the bank find itself?)* |
| *to be spelt:* | s'écrire | Comment ça s'écrit?: | *How is that spelt?* |
| *to be interested in:* | s'intéresser à | Je m'intéresse au tennis: | *I'm interested in tennis.* |

## Je me suis lavé(e) — I have washed myself

1) The <u>perfect tense</u> of these verbs is pretty much the same as normal (see p.104-106) except they <u>all go with 'être'</u>, not 'avoir'. The only tricky bit is working out where to put the '<u>me</u>' or '<u>te</u>' or '<u>se</u>' or whatever — and it goes right after the '<u>je</u>', '<u>tu</u>' or '<u>il</u>' etc. (In other words, it's <u>before</u> the bit of 'être'.)

*Je <u>me</u> suis lavé(e)*

Stick the '<u>me</u>' in here.    That's the bit of 'être'.

2) Like other verbs which use '<u>être</u>' for the <u>perfect tense</u>, you might have to add on an '<u>e</u>' and/or an '<u>s</u>', to <u>match who's</u> doing it. If you're <u>female</u>, make sure you add an '<u>e</u>' when you're talking about <u>yourself</u>.

**EXAMPLES:**

| *Je me suis lavée.* | *Elle s'est lavée.* | *Ils se sont lavés.* | *Elles se sont lavées.* |
|---|---|---|---|
| = I (fem.) washed myself. | = She washed herself. | = They (masc. or mixed gender) washed themselves. | = They (fem.) washed themselves. |

## Reflexive verbs are really common in French...

...even when it's not obvious that someone's doing something to themselves. Try writing down a few sentences with reflexive verbs — some in the <u>present</u> and some in the <u>perfect</u> tense. Do it <u>NOW</u>.

## NEGATIVES — *Saying 'Not', 'Never' and 'Nobody'*

This stuff's easy enough. Well, most of it is...

## Use 'ne ... pas' to say not

1) In English you change a sentence to mean the opposite by adding 'not'.

2) In French, you have to add two little words, 'ne' and 'pas'. They go either side of the verb (see p.100).

Je suis Bob. = I am Bob. ➡ Je ne suis pas Bob. = I am not Bob.

This is the verb. The 'ne' goes in front, and the 'pas' goes after.

3) For verbs in the perfect tense (see p.104-106), you stick the 'ne' and 'pas' around the bit of avoir or être.

Je n'ai pas vu ça. = I have not seen that.     Elle n'est pas arrivée. = She has not arrived.

## For an infinitive, the ne and pas go together

The 'ne' and 'pas' usually go either side of the action word (the verb).
BUT if the action word is an infinitive (see page 100) then the 'ne' and the 'pas' both go in front of it.

Je préfère voir un film. ➡ Je préfère ne pas voir un film.

= I prefer to see a film.     = I prefer not to see a film.

## ne ... jamais — never     ne ... rien — nothing

There are more negatives you need to understand, and for top marks you should use them too.

Je ne vais plus à York.

= I don't go to York any more.
(I no longer go to York.)

Je ne vais jamais à York.

= I never go to York.
(I don't ever go to York.)

Je ne vais ni à York ni à Belfast.

= I neither go to York nor to Belfast.

*not any more (no longer)*: ne ... plus     *not ever (never)*: ne ... jamais     *neither ... nor*: ne ... ni ... ni

*not anybody (nobody)*: ne ... personne     *not anything (nothing)*: ne ... rien     *no / not one*: ne ... aucun(e)
(not a single...)

= There isn't anybody here.
(There is nobody here.)

Il n'y a personne ici.

= There isn't anything here.
(There is nothing here.)

Il n'y a rien ici.

= There are no bananas.
(There is not a single banana.)

Il n'y a aucune banane.

'Y' and 'en' go between the 'ne' and the verb.

## Je n'ai pas de... — I don't have any...

After a negative, articles such as 'un/une', 'du', 'de la' or 'des' are usually replaced by just 'de'.

Je n'ai pas d'argent. = I haven't got any money.

Elle n'a plus de chocolat. = She hasn't got any more chocolate.

The 'de' is only shortened if the next word begins with a vowel or an 'h' which takes 'l'. E.g. 'd'argent', 'd'animaux'.

## Just say no — & nobody & nothing & never & not...

OK, just one more thing, then I'll be quiet. When you want 'nobody' or 'nothing' to be the subject of the sentence, you have to say "Personne ne..." or "Rien ne...". E.g. "Personne ne nous a vus" = "Nobody saw us", and "Rien ne s'est passé" = "Nothing happened" (se passer = to happen).

# Would, Could & Should

OK, I'll admit it. This <u>is</u> tricky. But it is <u>important</u>, so <u>learn</u> it.

## Je voudrais et j'aimerais... — I would like...

These two verbs are really useful in the <u>conditional</u> — you can use them lots in your speaking assessment.

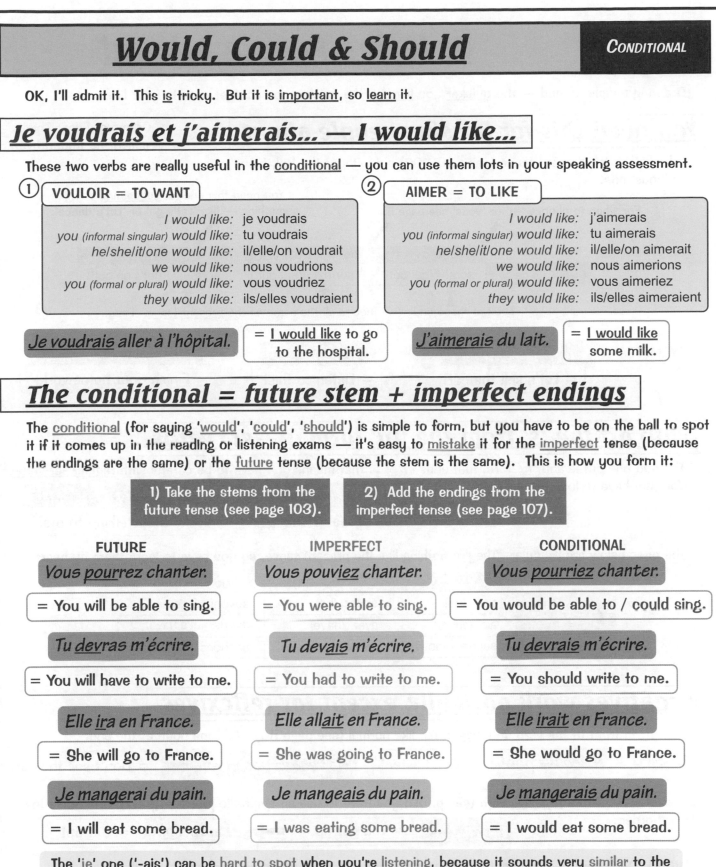

① **VOULOIR = TO WANT**

*I would like:* je voudrais
*you (informal singular) would like:* tu voudrais
*he/she/it/one would like:* il/elle/on voudrait
*we would like:* nous voudrions
*you (formal or plural) would like:* vous voudriez
*they would like:* ils/elles voudraient

② **AIMER = TO LIKE**

*I would like:* j'aimerais
*you (informal singular) would like:* tu aimerais
*he/she/it/one would like:* il/elle/on aimerait
*we would like:* nous aimerions
*you (formal or plural) would like:* vous aimeriez
*they would like:* ils/elles aimeraient

*Je voudrais aller à l'hôpital.*  = <u>I would like</u> to go to the hospital.

*J'aimerais du lait.*  = <u>I would like</u> some milk.

## The conditional = future stem + imperfect endings

The <u>conditional</u> (for saying '<u>would</u>', '<u>could</u>', '<u>should</u>') is simple to form, but you have to be on the ball to spot it if it comes up in the reading or listening exams — it's easy to <u>mistake</u> it for the <u>imperfect</u> tense (because the endings are the same) or the <u>future</u> tense (because the stem is the same). This is how you form it:

1) Take the stems from the future tense (see page 103).

2) Add the endings from the imperfect tense (see page 107).

| FUTURE | IMPERFECT | CONDITIONAL |
|---|---|---|
| *Vous <u>pourrez</u> chanter.* | *Vous <u>pouviez</u> chanter.* | *Vous <u>pourriez</u> chanter.* |
| = You will be able to sing. | = You were able to sing. | = You would be able to / could sing. |
| *Tu <u>devras</u> m'écrire.* | *Tu <u>devais</u> m'écrire.* | *Tu <u>devrais</u> m'écrire.* |
| = You will have to write to me. | = You had to write to me. | = You should write to me. |
| *Elle <u>ira</u> en France.* | *Elle <u>allait</u> en France.* | *Elle <u>irait</u> en France.* |
| = She will go to France. | = She was going to France. | = She would go to France. |
| *Je <u>mangerai</u> du pain.* | *Je <u>mangeais</u> du pain.* | *Je <u>mangerais</u> du pain.* |
| = I will eat some bread. | = I was eating some bread. | = I would eat some bread. |

The '<u>je</u>' one ('-ais') can be <u>hard to spot</u> when you're <u>listening</u>, because it sounds very <u>similar</u> to the <u>future</u> ending ('-ai'). You have to <u>think</u> about what the <u>rest</u> of the sentence means and <u>work out</u> whether the person's saying what they <u>would</u> do, or what they <u>will</u> do.

## If I were a tense, I'd be the conditional...

You often use the conditional when you have '<u>if</u>' followed by the <u>imperfect tense</u>. For example, '<u>If I had</u> a lot of money, <u>I would buy</u> seven horses' = '<u>Si j'avais</u> beaucoup d'argent, <u>j'achèterais</u> sept chevaux'. It's really useful — shame it's so tricky to form. Still, nobody said it was easy...

## IMPERATIVE
# Ordering People Around

Ordering people around — the <u>quicker</u> you <u>learn</u> it, the <u>quicker</u> you can get on with your life...

## You need this for bossing people about

*Grammar Fans: This is called the <u>Imperative</u>.*

It looks like the present tense (see p.101-102) but <u>without</u> the 'tu', 'vous' or 'nous' bits.

*For when to choose 'tu' or 'vous' see page 5.*

*You need this one for <u>suggesting</u> doing something — like 'Let's go' or 'Let's dance'.*

| | you (inf sing.): tu | you (formal or plu.): vous | let's: nous |
|---|---|---|---|
| sortir (to go out) | sors! (get out!) | sortez! (get out!) | sortons! (let's go out!) |

Look at these endings. They're all the same as the <u>present tense</u>. Easy.

**EXAMPLES**

*Vendons la voiture!*
= Let's sell the car!

*Écoute ceci!*
= Listen to this!

*Finissez vos devoirs!*
= Finish your homework!

## Whip off the 's' from the 'tu' form of '-er' verbs

The odd one out is any '<u>tu</u>' form that ends in '<u>es</u>'. That means you have to be careful with <u>regular -er verbs</u>. You just have to lose the final '<u>-s</u>':

*Regarde Jean-Paul!*
= Look at Jean-Paul!

*Arrête de me parler!*
= Stop talking to me!

The ones below are <u>irregular</u>. They're nothing like the present tense, so you have to learn them by heart.

| | you (inf. sing.): tu | you (formal or plu.): vous | let's: nous |
|---|---|---|---|
| to be: être | sois (be) | soyez (be) | soyons (let's be) |
| to have: avoir | aie (have) | ayez (have) | ayons (let's have) |
| to know: savoir | sache (know) | sachez (know) | sachons (let's know) |

## Negatives work normally, except for reflexives

Put '<u>ne</u>' in front of the verb and '<u>pas</u>' after, like normal (see page 110). Add the noun at the end.

**EXAMPLES:** *N'écoute pas!* = Don't listen! *Ne vendez pas la voiture!* = Don't sell the car!

In sentences with a <u>reflexive</u> verb (see p.109) you have to use an emphatic pronoun (p.97), and fiddle the word order...

**E.g.** *Tu <u>te</u> lèves.* = You get up. ➡ *Lève-<u>toi</u>!* = Get up!

**WATCH OUT** though — in negative sentences, you use normal pronouns and normal word order.

**E.g.** *Tu ne te lèves pas.* = You don't get up. ➡ *Ne te lève pas!* = Don't get up!

## If it's imperative, it must be important...

Hopefully you haven't found this too horrendous. But <u>do</u> be careful about dropping the '<u>s</u>' from the '<u>tu</u>' form of '<u>-er</u>' verbs — that catches out many a weary traveller. Oh, and <u>negatives</u> aren't obvious, so take another look at those before you whizz on blithely to the next page.

# Know and Can

Sooo many people get these verbs confused — so learn them right now.

## 'To know information' is 'Savoir'

1) Savoir means 'to know' in the sense of knowing information (e.g. knowing what time the bus leaves).

**DIFFERENT FORMS OF SAVOIR**

| | |
|---|---|
| I know | je sais |
| you (informal singular) know | tu sais |
| he/she/it/one knows | il/elle/on sait |
| we know | nous savons |
| you (formal or plural) know | vous savez |
| they know | ils/elles savent |

*Elle sait la réponse.* = She knows the answer.

*Je ne sais pas si nous avons des bananes.*

= I don't know if we have any bananas.

2) Savoir followed by an infinitive means 'to know how to do something', in the sense of a skill...

EXAMPLES: *Je sais conduire.* = I can drive. *Elle ne sait pas lire.* = She can't read.

## 'To be familiar with' is 'Connaître'

Connaître means to know a person or place — to 'be familiar with'.
If someone asks you whether you know their mate Bob, this is the one to use.

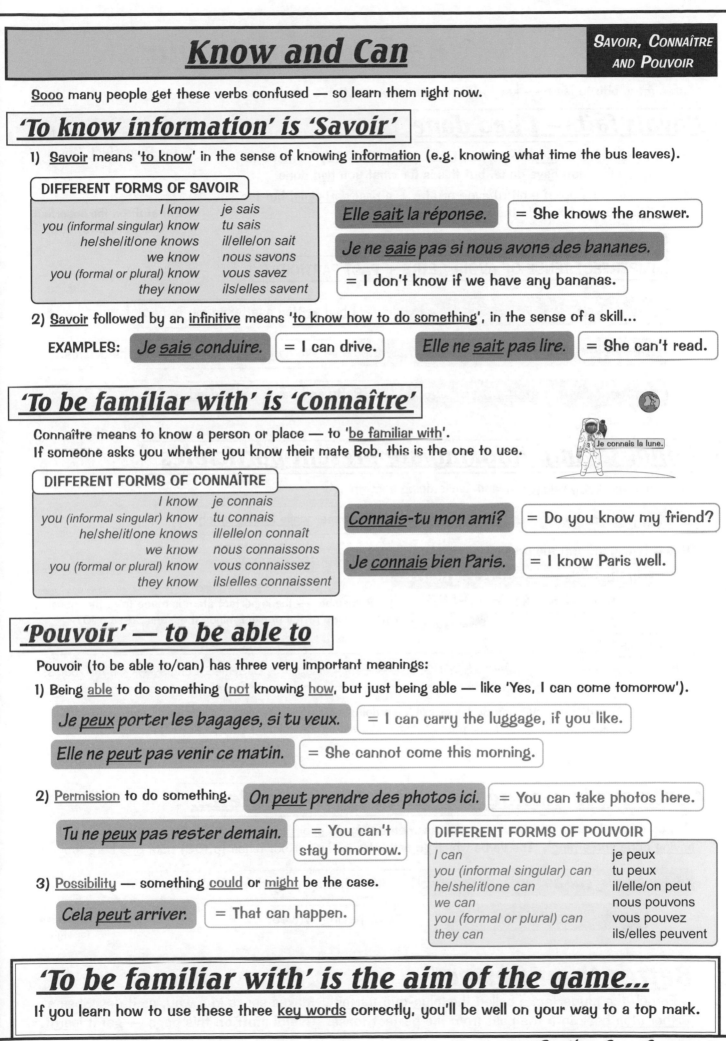

Je connais la lune.

**DIFFERENT FORMS OF CONNAÎTRE**

| | |
|---|---|
| I know | je connais |
| you (informal singular) know | tu connais |
| he/she/it/one knows | il/elle/on connaît |
| we know | nous connaissons |
| you (formal or plural) know | vous connaissez |
| they know | ils/elles connaissent |

*Connais-tu mon ami?* = Do you know my friend?

*Je connais bien Paris.* = I know Paris well.

## 'Pouvoir' — to be able to

Pouvoir (to be able to/can) has three very important meanings:

1) Being able to do something (not knowing how, but just being able — like 'Yes, I can come tomorrow').

*Je peux porter les bagages, si tu veux.* = I can carry the luggage, if you like.

*Elle ne peut pas venir ce matin.* = She cannot come this morning.

2) Permission to do something. *On peut prendre des photos ici.* = You can take photos here.

*Tu ne peux pas rester demain.* = You can't stay tomorrow.

**DIFFERENT FORMS OF POUVOIR**

| | |
|---|---|
| I can | je peux |
| you (informal singular) can | tu peux |
| he/she/it/one can | il/elle/on peut |
| we can | nous pouvons |
| you (formal or plural) can | vous pouvez |
| they can | ils/elles peuvent |

3) Possibility — something could or might be the case.

*Cela peut arriver.* = That can happen.

## 'To be familiar with' is the aim of the game...

If you learn how to use these three key words correctly, you'll be well on your way to a top mark.

# Had Done and '-ing'

Three more bits to learn — keep at it, the grammar section's nearly over...

## J'avais fait — I had done

*Grammar fans: this is the Pluperfect Tense.*

1) The pluperfect is <u>like</u> the perfect tense (see p.104-106) — that's for saying what you <u>have</u> done, but this is for what you <u>had</u> done.

2) It's still made up of a bit of <u>avoir</u> or <u>être</u> + a <u>past participle</u>, but the bit of avoir or être is in the <u>imperfect tense</u>.

*For stuff on the imperfect tense, see p.107-108.*

**FORMING THE PLUPERFECT**

**IMPERFECT TENSE OF AVOIR / ÊTRE + PAST PARTICIPLE**

*J'avais écrit une lettre à mon père.* = I <u>had written</u> a letter to my father.

*Nous étions allés voir un film au cinéma.* = We <u>had gone</u> to see a film at the cinema.

*Betty et Sarah étaient arrivées.* = Betty and Sarah <u>had arrived</u>.

## Doing, saying, thinking are present participles

<u>En</u> + the <u>present participle</u> means 'while doing something':

*Il lit le journal en déjeunant.* = He reads the paper <u>while having lunch</u>.

This is how you form the present participle:

**FORMING THE PRESENT PARTICIPLE**

**IMPERFECT STEM + '-ANT'**

*Remember — the imperfect stem is made from the 'nous' form of the present minus the '-ons'. See p.107.*

**EXAMPLES**

PLAYING: *jouons + ant = jouant*    SAYING: *disons + ant = disant*    BLUSHING: *rougissons + ant = rougissant*

<u>CAREFUL THOUGH</u> — you translate things like 'I am doing' with <u>normal tenses</u>, e.g. "je fais", and things like 'I like doing' with the present tense followed by the infinitive (see page 100).

## Après avoir mangé... — After having eaten...

This could easily crop up in the exam/assessments. '<u>Après avoir + past participle</u>' means '<u>after having done something</u>'. The verbs which go with <u>être</u> in the perfect tense (p.106) take <u>être</u> here too.

*Après avoir joué au foot, j'ai mangé.* = After having played football, I ate.

*Après être arrivé(e), j'ai...* = After having arrived, I...

*Extra marks for style*

## Better than perfect...

In French the pluperfect's called the '<u>plus-que-parfait</u>'. Makes sense in a way, as it describes a <u>further step</u> back into the past from the perfect tense. Useful stuff on this page — <u>get it learnt</u>.

# The Passive

The stuff on this page all sounds quite grammary, but in fact the passive in French is not very different from how we form it in English. And you only need to recognise this stuff, not use it.

## La tasse est cassée — The cup is broken

1) In most sentences, there's a person or thing doing the verb.
   In a passive sentence, the person or thing is having something done to it.

2) The passive in French is made up of a person or thing + être + past participle.

3) The past participle has to agree with the person or thing that is having the action done to it.

| Elle est vue par son mari. | = She is seen by her husband. |

'est' is a present tense form of the verb 'être' — to see the rest of it in the present, go to page 102.

See p.105-106 for more past participles.

## In the Past and Future, only the 'être' bit Changes...

1) You also need to recognise the passive when it's describing what happened in the past or what will happen in the future.

2) Don't worry though — the passive in the different tenses is formed in basically the same way as in the present. The only thing that changes is the tense of 'être'.

The **IMPERFECT PASSIVE** describes what happened to someone in the past. It's formed using the imperfect tense of être and a past participle:

| L'homme était battu. | = The man was beaten. | Ils étaient tués. | = They were killed. |

The **PERFECT PASSIVE** tells you about an event in the past that lasted for a fixed amount of time. It's formed using the perfect tense of être and a past participle:

| Un homme a été suivi par un camion. | = A man has been followed by a lorry. |

| Les chiens ont été volés par le voisin. | = The dogs have been stolen by the neighbour. |

The future passive is made up of part of the future tense of être + past participle:

| Elles seront tuées. | = They will be killed. |

| Tu seras puni(e). | = You will be punished. |

Don't forget that with all tenses of the passive, if it's talking about something feminine or plural the past participle has to agree.

One last thing — there's a reason why you'll need to recognise this but not use it. French doesn't use the passive as much as it's used in English. In French, they often use an active sentence with 'on' instead.

I wasn't seen.

= On ne m'a pas vu(e).

## 'Injured', 'beaten', 'killed', 'punished' — what a day...

The thing to understand about the passive is that it looks much more complicated than it actually is — usually it can be translated into English word for word, which is more than can be said for most French sentences you'll come across. And better still, the French usually use 'on' instead...

## IMPERSONAL VERBS AND THE SUBJUNCTIVE
# Impersonal Verbs & the Subjunctive

Some pretty <u>meaty stuff</u> on this page. But don't despair — one <u>final push</u> and you'll have finished the grammar section.

## Impersonal verbs only work with 'il'

Impersonal verbs always have '<u>il</u>' as the subject. For example:

> *Il faut aller au collège tous les jours.*    = <u>It is necessary to</u> go to school every day.

You also use impersonal verbs to talk about the <u>weather</u>:

> *Il a plu hier, et aujourd'hui il neige.*    = <u>It rained</u> yesterday, and today <u>it's snowing</u>.

Some impersonal verbs <u>combine</u> with other verbs in the <u>infinitive</u>:

> *Il est nécessaire de courir.*    = <u>It is necessary to</u> run.

*For more on infinitives, see page 100 and the bottom of page 102.*

> *Il me semble raisonnable d'arrêter.*    = <u>It seems</u> reasonable <u>to me</u> to stop.

*See p.96 for indirect object pronouns.*

## You may see the subjunctive instead of the infinitive

Not all <u>impersonal verbs</u> are followed by the infinitive — some are followed by the <u>subjunctive</u> instead. You just need to understand what <u>common verbs</u> look and sound like in the subjunctive in case they come up in your <u>listening</u> or <u>reading</u> exam. The <u>expressions</u> that use the subjunctive that you're most likely to see are:

> *Il faut qu'il parte demain.*    = <u>It is necessary</u> for him to <u>leave</u> tomorrow.

> *Il semble qu'il ne vienne pas.*    = <u>It seems</u> that he's not <u>coming</u>.

> *Bien qu'elle ait deux enfants...*    = <u>Although</u> she <u>has</u> two children...

> *Pour qu'il fasse ses devoirs...*    = <u>So that</u> he <u>does</u> his homework...

> *Avant que vous partiez...*    = <u>Before</u> you <u>leave</u>...

And these are the <u>verbs</u> you really need to <u>recognise</u> in the subjunctive:

*'<u>Avoir</u>' and '<u>être</u>' in the subjunctive are the same as the <u>imperative</u> (those command words you met on p.112).*

| SUBJUNCTIVE FORMS | | | | | |
|---|---|---|---|---|---|
| *Avoir* | j'aie | tu aies | il/elle/on ait | nous ayons | vous ayez | ils/elles aient |
| *Être* | je sois | tu sois | il/elle/on soit | nous soyons | vous soyez | ils/elles soient |
| *Faire* | je fasse | tu fasses | il/elle/on fasse | nous fassions | vous fassiez | ils/elles fassent |
| *Pouvoir* | je puisse | tu puisses | il/elle/on puisse | nous puissions | vous puissiez | ils/elles puissent |

# It's nothing personal...

Basically, if you see a <u>funny-looking</u> verb after the word '<u>que</u>', it's probably the <u>subjunctive</u>. You won't be expected to use it, but don't let it throw you if it comes up in the exam. Usually it'll be <u>obvious</u> what verb it's from, but there are a few banana skins, like '<u>être</u>'. Best get them <u>learnt</u>.

# Revision Summary

It's the last time you'll see the shocking words above. That's right, this is the final French 'Revision Summary'. Woohoo. Thank you for your time, and enjoy.

1) Give the words for both '<u>the</u>' and '<u>a</u>' (where appropriate) which have to accompany these:
   a) maison   b) chien   c) chaussure   d) soleil   e) travail   f) jeu   g) jeux   h) journaux

2) Je vais à la maison...  Change this sentence to tell people you're going to:
   a) le cinéma   b) l'église   c) la banque   d) le stade   e) les magasins   f) les Alpes

3) What is the French word for:  a) my horse   b) our house   c) his clothes   d) her house

4) "Janie is cool.  Janie is cooler than Jimmy.  She is the coolest."  Translate these three sentences into French, then swap "cool" for each of the following words and write them out all over again:
   a) formidable   b) intelligent(e)   c) célèbre   d) pratique   e) bavard(e)

5) Write a French sentence for each of the following French words.  Then put them all together... et voilà... you have your very own (probably weird) French poem.  You truly are the next Prévert...
   a) à   b) en   c) dans   d) pour   e) depuis   f) de

6) Place the missing <u>qui</u>'s and <u>que</u>'s in the following text and then translate it, please...
   J'ai rencontré un homme __ adorait les sports.  Cet homme __ j'ai rencontré, __ adorait les sports, n'aimait pas les escargots __ je lui avais achetés, surtout ceux __ venaient de la France.

7) Replace the underlined parts of these sentences with either 'y' or 'en':
   a) J'ai besoin <u>du chocolat</u>.  b) Je vais aller <u>au cinéma</u>.  c) Je prends six kilos <u>de bonbons</u>, s.v.p.

8) What are the French words for:
   a) and   b) or   c) but   d) because   e) with   f) while   g) therefore

9) How do you say the following in French:
   a) I have   b) she has   c) we have   d) they have   e) I am   f) he is   g) we are   h) they are

10) What does each of these French phrases mean in English?   a) Je mange un gâteau
    b) J'ai mangé un gâteau          c) Je mangeais un gâteau          d) J'avais mangé un gâteau
    e) Je vais manger un gâteau      f) Je mangerai un gâteau          g) Je mangerais un gâteau

11) Sadly, growing up means learning to do things for yourself.  Use reflexive verbs to say:
    a) We wash ourselves.   b) She went to bed.   c) They had fun.   d) I'm interested in French.

12) Ah, negativity.  We'll have none of that here.  Well, apart from these phrases.  Say these three in French:   a) I don't go out.      b) I never go out.      c) I don't go out any more.

13) Going commando.  Turn these sentences from the present tense to the imperative:
    a) Tu arrêtes de faire ça.      b) Vous êtes tranquille.          c) Nous allons au Portugal.
    d) Tu te lèves.      e) Vous ne vous inquiétez pas.      f) Nous ne regardons pas le film.

14) Translate:  a) He reads the paper while taking a shower.   b) I talk after having eaten.
    c) They play Scrabble while walking the dog.   d) We work after having listened to the radio.

15) Final question.  What does 'Il faut que tu apprennes toutes les choses dans ce livre avant de le jeter' mean?

# Do Well in Your Exam

Here are some little gems of advice, whichever exam board you're studying for.

## Read the Questions carefully

Don't go losing easy marks — it'll break my heart.
Make sure you definitely do the things on this list:

> 1) Read all the instructions properly.
> 2) Read the question properly.
> 3) Answer the question — don't waffle.

## Don't give up if you don't Understand

If you don't understand, don't panic. The key thing to remember is that you can still do well in the exam, even if you don't understand every French word that comes up. Just use one of the two methods below:

### If you're reading or listening — look for lookalikes

1) Some words look or sound the same in French and English — they're called cognates.

2) These words are great because you'll recognise them when you see them in a text.

3) Be careful though — there are some exceptions you need to watch out for.
   Some words look like an English word but have a totally different meaning:

| | | | | | |
|---|---|---|---|---|---|
| sensible: | *sensitive* | la journée: | *day* | le car: | *coach* |
| grand(e): | *big* | la pièce: | *room, coin or play* | le crayon: | *pencil* |
| large: | *wide* | la cave: | *cellar* | les affaires: | *business, items* |
| mince: | *slim* | la veste: | *jacket* | le pain: | *bread* |
| joli(e): | *pretty* | le médecin: | *doctor* | les baskets: | *trainers* |

> Words like these are called 'faux amis' — false friends.

## Make use of the Context

You'll likely come across the odd word that you don't know, especially in the reading exam. Often you'll be able to find some clues telling you what the text is all about.

> 1) The type of text, e.g. newspaper article, advertisement, website
> 2) The title of the text
> 3) Any pictures
> 4) The verbal context

Say you see the following in the reading exam, and don't know what any of these words mean:

"...des vêtements en  polyester , en  soie , en  laine  et en  coton ."

1) Well, the fact that this is a list of things all starting with 'en ...' coming after the French word for 'clothes' suggests they're all things that clothes can be made out of.

2) You can guess that 'polyester' means 'polyester', and 'coton' means 'cotton'.

3) So it's a pretty good guess that the two words you don't know are different types of fabric.
   (In fact, 'soie' means 'silk' and 'laine' means 'wool'.)

4) Often the questions won't depend on you understanding these more difficult words. It's important to be able to understand the gist though, and not let these words throw you.

## Friend or faux?

Don't get caught out by words that look like English words, but in fact mean something different.
Generally speaking, if a word doesn't seem to fit into the context of the question, have a re-think.

# Do Well in Your Exam

These pages could <u>improve</u> your <u>grade</u> — they're all about exam technique.

## Look at how a word is made up

You may read or hear a sentence and not understand <u>how the sentence works</u>. You need to remember all the <u>grammary bits</u> in Section 7 to give you a good chance at <u>piecing it all together</u>.

1) A word that ends in '<u>-é</u>', '<u>-u</u>' or '<u>-i</u>' may well be a <u>past participle</u>. Look for a bit of '<u>avoir</u>' or a bit of '<u>être</u>' nearby to work out who's done what.

2) A word that ends in '<u>r</u>' or '<u>er</u>' might be an <u>infinitive</u>. If you take off the 'er', it might look like an English word which may tell you what the verb means.

> E.g. 'confirmer' = to <u>confirm</u>

3) If you see '<u>-ment</u>' at the end of a word, it could well be an <u>adverb</u> (see page 91). Try replacing the '-ment' with '<u>-ly</u>' and see if it makes sense.

> E.g. 'généralement' ➡ 'généralely' = <u>generally</u>

4) '<u>Dé-</u>' at the beginning of a word is often '<u>dis-</u>' in the equivalent word in English.

> E.g. 'décourager' = to <u>discourage</u>

5) Sometimes <u>letters with accents</u> show that there may have been an '<u>s</u>' at some point in the past. This may help you find the corresponding English word.

> E.g. 'tempête' = <u>tempest</u>  'mât' = <u>mast</u>  'forêt' = <u>forest</u>

6) A word beginning with '<u>in-</u>' might be a <u>negative prefix</u>.

> E.g. 'inconnu' = 'in+connu = <u>unknown</u>

A prefix is a part of a word that comes before the main bit of the word.

## Take notes in the listening exam

1) You'll have <u>5 minutes</u> at the start of the listening exam to have a <u>quick look</u> through the paper. This'll give you a chance to see <u>how many questions</u> there are, and you might get a few clues from the questions about what <u>topics</u> they're on, so it won't be a horrible surprise when the recording starts.

2) You'll hear each extract <u>twice</u>. Different people have different strategies, but it's a good idea to jot down a few details that you think might come up in the questions, especially things like:

Dates
Numbers
Names

3) But... don't forget to <u>keep listening</u> to the gist of the recording while you're making notes.

4) You won't have a <u>dictionary</u> — but you probably wouldn't have time to use it anyway.

## And don't forget to keep your ears clean...

The examiners aren't above sticking a few tricky bits and pieces into the exam to see how you <u>cope</u> with them. Using all your expert knowledge, you should stand a pretty good chance of working it out. And if you can't make an <u>educated</u> guess, make an <u>uneducated</u> guess... but try <u>something</u>.

# How to Use Dictionaries

Don't go mad on dictionaries — it's the path to <u>ruin</u>. However, you're allowed to use one in the writing task, so it's good to know how to make the <u>most</u> of it.

## Don't translate Word for Word — it DOESN'T work

If you turn each word of this phrase into English, you get <u>rubbish</u>.

*Il y a une pomme.*    **NO!**    *It there has an apple.*

It's the <u>same</u> the other way round — turn English into French word by word, and you get <u>balderdash</u> — <u>don't do it</u>.

*I am reading.*    *Je suis lisant.*

## If it Doesn't make Sense, you've got it Wrong

Some words have several meanings — don't just pick the first one you see.
Look at the <u>meanings</u> listed and <u>suss out</u> which one is what you're looking for.

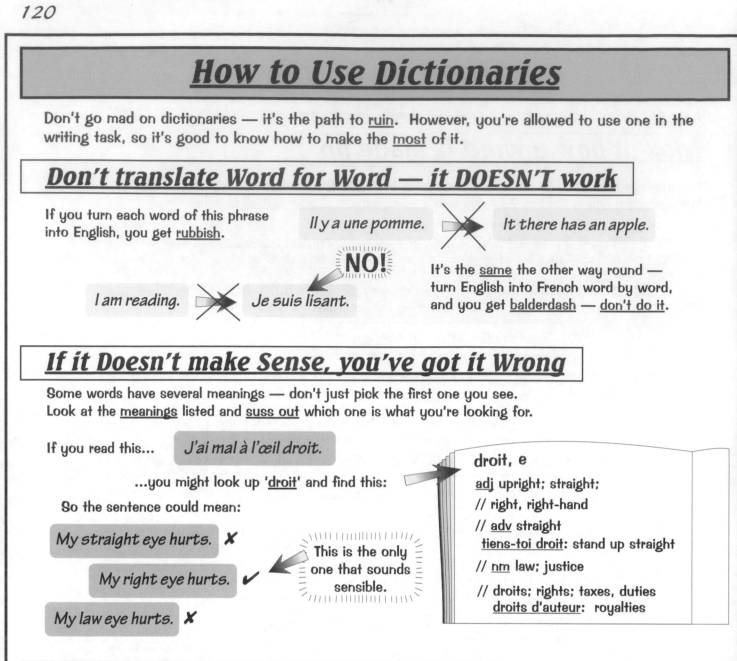

If you read this...    *J'ai mal à l'œil droit.*

...you might look up '<u>droit</u>' and find this:

So the sentence could mean:

*My straight eye hurts.* ✗

*My right eye hurts.* ✔

*My law eye hurts.* ✗

This is the only one that sounds sensible.

**droit, e**
<u>adj</u> upright; straight;
// right, right-hand
// <u>adv</u> straight
   <u>tiens-toi droit</u>: stand up straight
// <u>nm</u> law; justice
// droits; rights; taxes, duties
   <u>droits d'auteur</u>: royalties

## Verbs change according to the person

When you look up a <u>verb</u> in the dictionary, you'll find the <u>infinitive</u> (the 'to' form, like '<u>to</u> run', '<u>to</u> sing' etc.). But you may need to say '<u>I</u> run', or '<u>we</u> sing' — so you need to change the verb <u>ending</u>.

Say you need to say '<u>I work</u>'.

For the low-down on verbs and all their different endings, see the grammar section.

1) If you looked up '<u>work</u>', you'd find the word '<u>travailler</u>', meaning 'to work'.
2) But '<u>travailler</u>' is the <u>infinitive</u> — you can't put 'je travailler'.
3) You need the '<u>I</u>' (je) form of the verb — 'je <u>travaille</u>'.
4) Check the <u>tense</u> — e.g. you might want the future: 'je travaillerai'.

If you're looking up a <u>French</u> verb, look for its <u>infinitive</u> (it'll probably end in 'er', 'ir' or 're'). If you want to know what 'nous poussons' means, you'll find '<u>pousser</u>' (to push, or to grow) in the dictionary. So 'nous poussons' must mean '<u>we push</u>' or '<u>we grow</u>'.

## Dictionaries — useful for holding doors open*...

Don't get put off dictionaries by this page. They're lovely really. Just make sure your writing technique isn't to look up every single word and then bung them down in order. Cos it'll be rubbish.

*Do Well in Your Exam*

# Hints for Writing

Here are a few <u>general hints</u> about how you should approach the writing tasks.

## Write about what you know

1) You <u>won't</u> be asked to write about 19th century French novelists — it'll be easier than that.

2) You will <u>need</u> to cover certain specific things that the question asks you to, but there'll be plenty of scope to be <u>imaginative</u>.

3) Usually the writing tasks will give you some <u>flexibility</u> so you can base your answer on something you know about.

*Que sais-je?*

## You get marks for saying When and Why...

1) Saying <u>when</u> and <u>how often</u> you did things gets you big bonus marks. Learn <u>times</u>, <u>dates</u> and <u>numbers</u> carefully (pages 1-3).

2) Make sure you talk about what you've done <u>in the past</u> (see pages 104-108) or what you will do <u>in the future</u> (page 103).

3) Give <u>descriptions</u> where possible, but keep things <u>accurate</u> — a short description in <u>perfect French</u> is better than a longer paragraph of nonsense.

4) <u>Opinions</u> (pages 7-8) also score highly. Try to <u>vary them</u> as much as possible.

So, if I add one more drop we'll go back in time two hours...

...two hours later...

## ...and Where and Who With...

Most teachers are really quite nosy, and love as many details as you can give. It's a good idea to ask yourself all these '<u>wh-</u>' questions, and write the bits that show your French off in the <u>best light</u>. Also, it doesn't matter if what you're writing isn't strictly true — as long as it's <u>believable</u>.

## Use your dictionary, but sparingly

1) The time to use the dictionary is <u>**NOT**</u> to learn a completely new, fancy way of saying something.

2) Use it to look up a particular word that you've <u>forgotten</u> — a word that, when you see it, you'll <u>know</u> it's the right word.

3) Use it to check <u>genders</u> of nouns — that's whether words are <u>masculine</u> (le/un) or <u>feminine</u> (la/une).

4) Check any <u>spellings</u> you're unsure of.

> Most importantly, don't use the dictionary to <u>delve into the unknown</u>. If you don't <u>know</u> what you've written is <u>right</u>, it's <u>probably wrong</u>.

## Take your time

1) Don't <u>hurtle</u> into writing about something and then realise halfway through that you don't actually know the French for it.

2) <u>Plan</u> how you can cover all the things that the task mentions, and then think about the extra things you can slip in to show off your French.

Take me.

## And lastly, don't forget your pen...

I suppose the key is <u>variety</u> — lots of different <u>tenses</u>, plenty of meaty <u>vocabulary</u> and loads of <u>details</u>. This is your only chance to show what you can do, so don't waste all your <u>hard work</u>.

# Hints for Writing

Accuracy is really important in the writing assessment. Without it, your work will look like sloppy custard.

## Start with the Verb

1) Verbs really are the cornerstone of every French sentence. If you get the verb right, the rest of the sentence should fall into place.

*Verbs are doing words. See page 100.*

2) Be careful that you get the whole expression that uses the verb, not just the verb itself.

> EXAMPLE:   Say you want to write the following sentence in French:
>
> *On Sundays, we go for a walk, if the weather is nice.*
>
> Don't see 'go' and jump in with 'aller'.
> The expression for 'go for a walk' is 'faire une promenade'.
>
> You know that 'the weather is nice' is 'il fait beau', and 'if' is 'si'.
>
> Make sure your tenses and the endings of the verbs are right, then piece it all together:
>
> *Le dimanche, nous faisons une promenade, s'il fait beau.*

## Check and re-check

No matter how careful you think you're being, mistakes can easily creep into your work.
Go through the checklist below for every sentence straight after you've written it.

1) Are the verbs in the right TENSE?
   Demain, je travaillais dans le jardin. ✘          Demain, je travaillerai dans le jardin. ✓

2) Are the ENDINGS of the verbs right?
   Tu n'aime pas les carottes? ✘          Tu n'aimes pas les carottes? ✓

3) Do your adjectives AGREE as they should?
   Elle est grand. ✘          Elle est grande. ✓

4) Do your past participles AGREE?
   Ils sont parti. ✘          Ils sont partis. ✓

5) Do your adjectives come in the RIGHT PLACE?
   Une rose chemise ✘          Une chemise rose ✓

6) Have you used TU / VOUS correctly?
   Monsieur, peux-tu m'aider, s'il vous plaît? ✘          Monsieur, pouvez-vous m'aider, s'il vous plaît? ✓

Then when you've finished the whole piece of work, have another read through with fresh eyes.
You're bound to pick up one or two more mistakes.

## Do nothing without a verb...

I know there's loads to remember, and French verbs are a pain, but checking over your work is a real must. Reread your work assuming there are errors in it, rather than assuming it's fine as it is.

# Hints for Speaking

The speaking assessment fills many a student with <u>dread</u>. Remember though — it's your chance to show what you can <u>do</u>. It won't be nearly as bad as you think it's going to be. <u>Honest</u>.

## Be Imaginative

There are two tricky things about the speaking assessment — one is <u>what to say</u>, and the other is <u>how to say it</u>. No matter how good your French is, it won't shine through if you can't think of anything to say.

Say you're asked to talk about your <u>daily routine</u> (or to imagine someone else's daily routine). It would be easy to give a list of things you do when you get in from school:

> *"Je fais mes devoirs. Je regarde la télé. Je mange. Je vais au lit."*

> = I do my homework. I watch TV. I eat. I go to bed.

It makes sense, but the problem is, it's all a bit <u>samey</u>...

1) Try to think of when this <u>isn't</u> the case, and put it into a <u>DIFFERENT TENSE</u>:

> *"Mais demain ce sera différent, parce que je jouerai au hockey après le collège."*

> = But tomorrow it will be different, because I will play hockey after school.

2) Don't just talk about yourself. Talk about <u>OTHER PEOPLE</u> — even if you have to imagine them.

> *"J'ai regardé la télé avec mon frère, mais il n'aime pas les mêmes émissions que moi."*

> = I watched TV with my brother, but he doesn't like the same programmes as me.

3) Give loads of <u>OPINIONS</u> and <u>REASONS</u> for your opinions.

> *"J'aime finir mes devoirs avant de manger. Puis je peux me détendre plus tard."*

> = I like to finish my homework before eating. Then I can relax later on.

## A couple of 'DON'T's...

1) <u>DON'T</u> try to <u>avoid</u> a topic if you find it difficult — that'll mean you won't get <u>any</u> marks at all for that bit of the assessment. You'll be surprised what you can muster up if you stay calm and concentrate on what you <u>do</u> know how to say.

2) <u>DON'T</u> make up a word in the hope that it exists in French unless you're really, really stuck. Try one of the tricks on the next page first. However, if it's your <u>last resort</u>, it's worth a try.

## Have Confidence

1) Believe it or not, the teacher isn't trying to catch you out. He or she <u>wants</u> you to do <u>well</u>, and to be dazzled by all the excellent French you've learnt.

2) Speaking assessments can be pretty <u>daunting</u>. But remember it's the same for <u>everyone</u>.

3) <u>Nothing horrendous</u> is going to happen if you make a few slip-ups. Just try and focus on showing the teacher how much you've <u>learnt</u>.

## Imagine there's no speaking assessment...

It's easy if you try. But that's not going to get you a GCSE. The main thing to remember is that it's much better to have too much to say than too little. Bear in mind the <u>3 ways</u> to make your answers more <u>imaginative</u>. This will give you an opportunity to show off your <u>beautiful French</u>.

# Hints for Speaking

Nothing in life ever goes completely according to plan. So it's a good idea to prepare yourself for a few hiccups in the speaking assessment. (Nothing to do with glasses of water.)

## Try to find another way of saying it

There may be a particular word or phrase that trips you up. There's always a way round it though.

1) If you can't remember a French word, use an alternative word or try describing it instead.

2) E.g. if you can't remember that 'grapes' are 'les raisins' and you really need to say it, then describe them as 'the small green or red fruits', or 'les petits fruits verts ou rouges'.

3) You can fib to avoid words you can't remember — if you can't remember the word for 'dog' then just say you've got a cat instead. Make sure what you're saying makes sense though — saying you've got a pet radio isn't going to get you any marks, trust me.

4) If you can't remember the word for a cup (la tasse) in your speaking assessment, you could say 'glass' (le verre) instead — you'll still make yourself understood.

## If the worst comes to the worst, ask for help in French

1) If you can't think of a way around it, you can ask for help in the speaking assessment — as long as you ask for it in French.

2) If you can't remember what a chair is, ask your teacher; "Comment dit-on 'chair' en français?" It's better than wasting time trying to think of the word.

## You may just need to buy yourself some time

If you get a bit stuck for what to say, there's always a way out.

1) If you just need some thinking time in your speaking assessment or you want to check something, you can use these useful phrases to help you out:

| | | | |
|---|---|---|---|
| Ben... | Um... | Pouvez-vous répéter, s'il vous plaît? | Can you repeat, please? |
| Eh bien... | Well... | Je ne comprends pas. | I don't understand. |
| Je ne suis pas sûr(e). | I'm not sure. | Ça, c'est une bonne question. | That's a good question. |

2) Another good tactic if you're a bit stuck is to say what you've just said in a different way. This shows off your command of French, and also it might lead onto something else, e.g.:

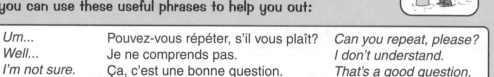

"On mange en famille... Je ne mange pas seul , sauf quand mes parents travaillent tard."

Saying the same thing a different way... leading on to another idea.

= We eat as a family... I don't eat on my own, except when my parents work late.

And don't be afraid to make mistakes — even native French speakers make 'em. Don't let a silly error shake your concentration for the rest of the assessment.

## One last thing — don't panic...

Congratulations — you've made it to the end of the book. And without accident or injury, I hope — paper cuts hurt more than people think... Anyway, enough of this idle chit-chat. Read these pages, take on board the information, use it in your GCSE, do well and then celebrate in style.

## A

à prep (à la, à l', au, aux) *at, to, in*
  à la carte *à la carte (e.g. menu)*
  à cause de conj *because of*
  à droite *on the right*
  à gauche *on the left*
  à point *medium (cooked)*
  à travers prep *across*
l' abricot m *apricot*
absolument ad *absolutely*
accompagner v *to accompany*
accro a *addicted*
l' achat m *purchase*
acheter v *to buy*
l' acteur/actrice m/f *actor/actress*
actif/active a *active*
l' activité physique f *physical activity*
les actualités fpl *news, current affairs*
l' addition f *bill (restaurant)*
l' ado m/f *adolescent*
l' adresse f *address*
l' adulte m/f *adult*
l' aéroport m *airport*
les affaires fpl *business, items*
affreux/affreuse a *awful*
(l') africain(e) a/m/f *African*
l' Afrique f *Africa*
l' âge m *age*
âgé(e) a *old, aged*
l' agence de voyages f *travel agency*
l' agent de police m *policeman/woman*
l' agneau m *lamb*
agréable a *pleasant*
agresser v *to attack*
aider v *to help*
l' ail m *garlic*
ailleurs ad *elsewhere*
aimable a *likeable, friendly*
aimer v *to like, love*
aîné(e) a *older (e.g. sister)*
ainsi ad *in this way*
l' air m *air, appearance*
  en plein air ad *outdoors*
l' aire de repos f *motorway services*
l' alcool m *alcohol*
alcoolique a *alcoholic (person)*
alcoolisé a *alcoholic (e.g. drink)*
l' alcoolisme m *alcoholism*
l' Algérie f *Algeria*
(l') algérien(ne) a/m/f *Algerian*
l' alimentation f *food, groceries*
  l' alimentation saine f *healthy eating*
l' Allemagne f *Germany*
l' allemand m *German (language)*
(l') allemand(e) a/m/f *German*
aller v *to go*
  aller bien/mieux *to be well/better*
l' aller-retour m *return ticket*
l' aller simple m *single ticket*
l' alliance f *alliance, wedding ring*
allô interj *hello (when answering phone)*
allumer v *to light, to turn on*
alors ad *then*
l' alpinisme m *mountaineering*
améliorer v *to improve*
amer, amère a *bitter*
(l') américain(e) a/m/f *American*
l' Amérique f *America*
l' ami(e) m/f *friend*
amical(e) a *friendly, amicable*
amitiés *best wishes*
l' amour m *love*
amusant(e) a *amusing, fun*
amuser v *to amuse*
  s'amuser vr *to enjoy oneself*
l' an m *year*
l' ananas m *pineapple*
l' anglais m *English (language)*
(l') anglais(e) a/m/f *English, English person*
l' Angleterre f *England*
animé(e) a *lively, animated*
l' année f *year*
l' anniversaire m *birthday*
l' annonce f *advertisement*

l' annuaire m *phone book*
annuler v *to cancel*
anonyme a *anonymous*
l' antenne f *aerial*
l' apéritif m *pre-dinner drink*
(l') août m *August*
à l'appareil *on the telephone*
l' appartement m *flat, apartment*
l' appel m *call*
appeler v *to call*
  s'appeler vr *to be called*
l' appétit m *appetite*
apprendre v *to learn*
l' apprenti(e) m/f *apprentice*
l' apprentissage m *apprenticeship*
(s') approcher (de) v(r) *to approach*
appuyer v *to press*
après prep *after*
après-demain ad *the day after tomorrow*
l' après-midi m/f *afternoon*
l' arbre m *tree*
l' argent m *money, silver*
l' argent de poche m *pocket money*
l' armoire f *wardrobe*
l' arrêt m *stop*
l' arrêt d'autobus m *bus stop*
arrêter v *to stop (something)*
  s'arrêter vr *to stop*
l' arrivée f *arrival*
l' arrondissement m *district (e.g. in Paris)*
l' ascenseur m *lift*
s' asseoir vr *to sit down*
assez ad *quite, enough*
l' assiette f *plate*
assurer v *to assure*
(l') atlantique a/m *Atlantic*
l' attaque f *attack*
attendre v *to wait*
  en attendant *while waiting*
l' attention f *attention*
  faire attention *to be careful*
atterrir v *to land*
au = à le — *see à*
au bord de prep *alongside*
au bout de prep *at the end of*
au-dessous de prep *below*
au-dessus de prep *above*
au fond de prep *at the bottom of*
au lieu de conj *instead of*
au milieu de prep *in the middle of*
au moins ad *at least*
au revoir interj *goodbye*
au secours! interj *help!*
l' auberge de jeunesse f *youth hostel*
aucun(e) *any*
  ne … aucun(e) *no …/none...*
augmenter v *to increase*
aujourd'hui ad *today*
auparavant ad *before*
aussi ad *too, as well, as*
l' Australie f *Australia*
(l') australien(ne) a/m/f *Australian*
l' auteur m *author*
l' auto f *car*
l' autobus m *bus*
l' automne m *autumn*
l' autoroute f *motorway*
autour (de) prep *around*
autre a *other*
autrement dit *in other words*
aux = à les — *see à*
en avance ad *early*
avant prep *before, in front of*
l' avantage m *advantage*
avant-hier ad *the day before yesterday*
avec prep *with*
  avec plaisir *gladly*
l' avenir m *future*
  à l'avenir ad *in the future*
l' aventure f *adventure*
l' averse f *shower (of rain)*
l' avertissement m *warning*

avertir v *to warn*
l' avion m *plane*
l' avis m *opinion*
  à mon avis *in my opinion*
l' avocat m *lawyer*
avoir v *to have*
  avoir besoin de *to need*
  avoir envie de *to want*
  avoir raison *to be right*
  avoir tort *to be wrong*
(l') avril m *April*

## B

le baby-sitting m *babysitting*
  faire du baby-sitting *to babysit*
le bac m *baccalauréat (equivalent of A-levels)*
les bagages mpl *luggage*
la bague f *ring*
la baguette f *baguette, stick*
se baigner vr *to bathe*
le bain m *bath*
le baiser m *kiss*
le balcon m *balcony*
le ballon m *ball (big, e.g. football)*
la banane f *banana*
la bande f *group*
la bande dessinée f *comic strip*
la banlieue f *suburbs*
la banque f *bank*
le baptême m *christening*
barbant(e) a *boring*
la barbe f *beard*
bas(se) a *low*
  en bas ad *downstairs*
le basket m *basketball*
les baskets mpl *trainers*
le bateau m *boat*
le bâtiment m *building*
la batterie f *drum kit*
battre v *to beat*
bavard(e) a *talkative*
bavarder v *to chat / gossip*
beau/belle a *beautiful*
  faire beau *to be nice weather*
beaucoup ad *a lot*
beaucoup (de) a *lots of, many*
le beau-fils m *son-in-law, stepson*
le beau-frère m *brother-in-law, stepbrother*
le beau-père m *father-in-law, stepfather*
le bébé m *baby*
(le/la) belge a/m/f *Belgian*
la Belgique f *Belgium*
la belle-fille f *daughter-in-law, stepdaughter*
la belle-mère f *mother-in-law, stepmother*
la belle-sœur f *sister-in-law, stepsister*
le besoin m *need*
  avoir besoin de *to need*
bête a *stupid*
le béton m *concrete*
le beurre m *butter*
la bibliothèque f *library*
bien ad *well*
bien cuit(e) a *well done (meat)*
bien équipé(e) a *well-equipped*
bien entendu a *understood*
bien payé(e) a *well paid*
bien sûr ad *of course*
bientôt ad *soon*
  à bientôt interj *see you soon*
la bienvenue f *welcome*
la bière f *beer*
le bifteck m *steak*
le bijou m *jewel, gem*
la bijouterie f *jewellery*
le billet m *ticket, banknote*
la biologie f *biology*
le biscuit m *biscuit*
le bistro m *bistro*
blanc(he) a *white*
bleu(e) a *blue*
le bloc sanitaire m *shower block*
le/la bloggeur/bloggeuse m/f *blogger*
blond(e) a *blond(e)*
le blouson m *jacket*

le bœuf m *beef*
boire v *to drink*
le bois m *wood*
la boîte f *tin, can, box*
la boîte aux lettres f *postbox*
la boîte aux lettres électronique (blé) f *inbox*
le bol m *bowl*
bon(ne) a *good*
bon anniversaire interj *happy birthday*
bon appétit interj *enjoy your meal*
bon marché a *cheap*
bon voyage interj *have a good journey*
bon week-end interj *have a good weekend*
le bonbon m *sweet*
le bonheur m *happiness*
bonjour interj *good day, hello*
bonne année interj *Happy New Year*
bonne chance interj *good luck*
bonne fête interj *have a good party*
bonne idée interj *good idea*
bonne nuit interj *good night*
bonnes vacances interj *enjoy your holiday*
bonsoir interj *good evening*
le bord m *edge*
  au bord de la mer *by the sea*
le/la boucher/bouchère m/f *butcher*
la boucherie f *butcher's*
bouclé(e) a *curly*
la boucle d'oreille f *earring*
le/la boulanger/boulangère m/f *baker*
la boulangerie f *baker's*
les boules fpl *bowls (ball game)*
le boulot m *work, job*
la boum f *party*
la bouteille f *bottle*
la boutique f *small shop*
le bouton m *button, spot*
le bowling m *bowling*
la brasserie f *brasserie*
bravo interj *bravo, well done*
le bricolage m *DIY*
briller v *to shine*
la brique f *brick*
  en brique a *made out of brick*
(le/la) britannique a/m/f *British, British person*
se bronzer vr *to sunbathe*
le brouillard m *fog*
le bruit m *noise*
brun(e) a *brown*
brutaliser v *to bully*
bruyant(e) a *noisy, loud*
le buffet m *sideboard, buffet*
le bureau de renseignements m *information service*

## C

c'est-à-dire conj *that is to say*
ça pron *that*
ça dépend *that depends*
ça fait combien? *how much does that come to?*
ça m'énerve *I don't mind*
ça m'est égal *I don't mind*
ça me fait rire *that makes me laugh*
ça me plaît *I like that*
ça ne me dit rien *that doesn't mean anything to me*
ça s'écrit comment? *how do you spell that?*
ça suffit *that's enough*
ça va(?) *I'm okay (how are you?)*
  ça ne va pas *I'm not great*
cacher v *to hide*
le cadeau m *present*
le cadre m *frame*
le café m *coffee, café*
le cahier m *notebook, exercise book*
la caisse f *counter, checkout*
le/la caissier/caissière m/f *cashier*
la calculatrice f *calculator*
calme a *calm*

le caméscope m *video camera*
le camion m *lorry*
la campagne f *countryside, campaign*
le Canada m *Canada*
(le/la) canadien(ne) a/m/f *Canadian*
le canard m *duck*
le/la candidat(e) m/f *candidate*
le canoë-kayak m *canoe*
la cantine f *canteen, dining hall*
car conj *because, since*
le car m *coach*
le car de ramassage m *school bus*
le caractère m *character, personality*
la caravane f *caravan*
le carnet m *notebook, book of tickets*
le cartable m *schoolbag, satchel*
la carotte f *carrot*
carré(e) a *square*
le carrefour m *crossroads*
la carrière f *career*
la carte f *map, card, menu*
  la carte bancaire f *bank card*
  la carte de crédit f *credit card*
  la carte d'identité f *ID card*
  la carte postale f *postcard*
le carton m *cardboard*
le casque m *helmet*
le casse-croûte m *snack, lunch*
casse-pieds a *pain in the neck*
casser v *to break*
la casserole f *saucepan*
la cassette f *cassette tape*
la cathédrale f *cathedral*
la cave f *cellar*
le CDI (centre de documentation et d'information) m *school library*
ce, cet, cette, ces pron *this*
la ceinture f *belt*
cela pron *that (i.e. that thing)*
célèbre a *famous*
célibataire a *single (not married)*
(le) cent a/m *hundred*
le centimètre m *centimetre*
le centre m *centre*
  le centre commercial m *shopping centre*
  le centre de recyclage m *recycling centre*
  le centre sportif m *sports centre*
le centre-ville m *city centre*
cependant conj *however*
les céréales fpl *cereal*
la cerise f *cherry*
certainement ad *certainly*
le certificat m *certificate*
le CES = collège d'enseignement secondaire m *secondary school*
la chaîne f *TV channel*
la chaise f *chair*
la chaleur f *heat*
la chambre f *bedroom*
  la chambre double/à deux lits/de famille f *double/twin/family room*
  la chambre pour une personne f *room for one person*
  la chambre d'hôte f *bed and breakfast*
le champ m *field*
le champignon m *mushroom*
la chance f *luck, chance*
  par chance ad *luckily*
la chanson f *song*
chanter v *to sing*
le/la chanteur/chanteuse m/f *singer*
le chapeau m *hat*
chaque a *each*
le charbon m *coal*
la charcuterie f *delicatessen, pork butcher's*
chargé(e) a *loaded, laden*
le chariot m *trolley*
le chat m *cat*
le château m *castle, palace*
chaud(e) a *warm, hot*

---

nouns — **m**: masculine    **f**: feminine    **pl**: plural      **v**: verb      **vr**: reflexive verb      **a**: adjective

le chauffage central m central heating
le chauffeur m driver, chauffeur
la chaussette f sock
la chaussure f shoe
le/la chef m/f boss/chef
le chemin de fer m railway
la chemise f shirt
le chemisier m blouse
cher/chère a, cher ad dear, expensive
chercher v to search for, to look for
le cheval m horse
les cheveux mpl hair
chez prep chez moi/toi at my/your house
chic a stylish
le chien m dog
la chimie f chemistry
la Chine f China
(le/la) chinois(e) a/m/f Chinese, Chinese person
les chips mpl crisps
le chocolat m chocolate
le chocolat chaud m hot chocolate
choisir v to choose
le choix m choice
le chômage m unemployment
la chose f thing
le chou m cabbage
chouette a great, cool
le chou-fleur m cauliflower
(le/la) chrétien(ne) a/m/f Christian
le cidre m cider
le ciel m sky, heaven
le cinéma m cinema
(le) cinq a/m five
cinquante a/m fifty
cinquième a fifth
la circulation f traffic
le citron m lemon
clair(e) a light (colour), clear
la classe f class
le clavier m keyboard
la clé f key
le/la client(e) m/f customer
le climat m climate
la climatisation f air-conditioning
cliquer v to click
le club des jeunes m youth club
le coca m cola
le cochon d'Inde m guinea-pig
le code postal m postal code
le cœur m heart
le/la coiffeur/coiffeuse m/f hairdresser
le coin m corner
collectionner v to collect
le collège m school (secondary)
le/la collègue m/f colleague
la colline f hill
la colonie de vacances f holiday camp
combien(?) ad how much, how many(?)
c'est combien? how much is it?
pour combien de temps? for how long?
la comédie f comedy
comique a funny
commander v to order
comme prep like
comme ci comme ça ad so-so
le commencement m start
commencer v to start
comment(?) ad/interj how, (pardon?)
le commerce m business
le/la commerçant(e) m/f shopkeeper
le commissariat m police station
comparer v to compare
complet/complète a full, complete
compliqué(e) a complicated
composer v to compose
composé(e) de composed of
composter v to stamp (ticket)
compréhensif/compréhensive a understanding

comprendre v to understand
le comprimé m tablet (to swallow)
compris(e) a inclusive
le/la comptable m/f accountant
compter sur v to count on
le comptoir m counter
le/la concierge m/f caretaker
le concombre m cucumber
le concours m competition
le/la conducteur/conductrice m/f driver
conduire v to drive
la confiance f confidence
confirmer v to confirm
la confiserie f sweetshop
la confiture f jam
le confort m comfort
confortable a comfortable
la connaissance f knowledge
connaître v to know (e.g. a person)
consacrer v to devote
le conseil m advice
la consigne f left luggage
la console de jeu m games console
la consommation (modérée) f (moderate) consumption
construire v to build
contacter v to contact
content(e) a happy
le contrat m contract
contre prep against
contrôler v to control
le/la copain/copine m/f friend
copier v to copy
la correspondance f connection
le/la correspondant(e) m/f correspondent, penfriend
corriger v to correct
la côte f coast
le côté m side
à côté de prep next to
la côtelette f cutlet
le coton m cotton
la couche d'ozone f ozone layer
coucher v to put to bed
se coucher vr to go to bed
la couleur f colour
de quelle couleur? what colour?
à l'heure ad on time
le couloir m corridor
le coup m knock, blow
donner un coup de main to give someone a hand
coupable a guilty
la cour f yard, playground
couramment ad fluently
courir v to run
le courrier électronique m email
le cours m lesson
le cours professionnel m vocational training course
la course f running
les courses fpl shopping
faire les courses to go shopping
court(e) a short
le couteau m knife
coûter v to cost
couvert(e) a overcast (weather)
la couverture f blanket, cover
la cravate f tie
le crayon m pencil
la crème f cream
la crème solaire f suncream
la crêpe f pancake
la crevette f prawn
la crise cardiaque f heart attack
critiquer v to criticize
croire v to believe
la croisière f cruise
le croissant m croissant
cru(e) a raw
les crudités fpl raw salad items
la cuillère f spoon
le cuir m leather
la cuisine f kitchen
la cuisinière f (à gaz / électrique) stove, cooker (gas / electric)
cultiver v to cultivate, to grow
le cybercafé m cybercafe

le cyclisme m cycling

D
d'abord ad first (of all)
d'accord inter OK, I agree
d'habitude ad normally, usually
d'occasion a used, secondhand
la dame f lady
dangereux/dangereuse a dangerous
dans prep in, into
danser v to dance
la date f date (of year)
de prep (du, de la, de l', des) of, from, some
de bonne heure ad early
de chaque côté ad from each side
de l'autre côté on the other side
de mauvaise humeur in a bad mood
de nouveau again
de rien don't mention it
de temps en temps ad from time to time
de tous côtés ad from all sides
le déboisement m deforestation
se débrouiller vr to get on with, to manage
le début m start, début
(le) décembre m December
les déchets mpl rubbish
déchirer v to tear
décider v to decide
décoller v to take off
déçu(e) a disappointed
défense de forbidden to
dégoûtant(e) a disgusting
le degré m degree
la dégustation f tasting
en dehors ad outside
déjà ad already
le déjeuner m lunch,
délicieux/délicieuse a delicious
demain ad tomorrow
à demain interj see you tomorrow
la demande d'emploi f job application
demander v to ask
déménager v to move house
demi(e) a half
le demi-frère m half-brother
la demi-pension f half-board
la demi-sœur f half-sister
démodé(e) a old-fashioned
le départ m departure
dépenser v to spend
déprimé(e) a depressed
depuis prep since, for
déranger v to disturb
dernier/dernière a last, previous
dérouler v to unwind
dérouler en bas/en haut v to scroll up/down (on computer)
derrière prep behind
des = de les — see de
désagréable a unpleasant, disagreeable
le désavantage m disadvantage
descendre v to go down
se déshabiller vr to get undressed
désintoxiquer v to treat for drug/ alcohol addiction
désirer v to desire
désolé(e) a sorry
le dessin m art, drawing
le dessin animé m cartoon
dessiner v to draw
le détail m detail
(se) détendre vr to relax
détester v to hate
le détritus m litter
détruire v to destroy
la dette f debt
(le) deux a/m two
deuxième a second
devant prep in front of
devenir v to become
la déviation f diversion
deviner v to guess
devoir v to have to

les devoirs mpl homework
la différence f difference
différent(e) a different
difficile a difficult
la difficulté f difficulty
(le) dimanche m Sunday
le dîner m supper
le diplôme m degree
dire v to say
que veut dire...? what does ... mean?
le/la directeur/directrice m/f headteacher, director
diriger v to direct
discuter v to discuss, to talk
disparaître v to disappear
disponible a available
se disputer vr to argue
le disque compact m compact disc
les distractions fpl leisure activities
distribuer v to distribute
le distributeur automatique m cashpoint
divorcé(e) a divorced
(le) dix a/m ten
dix-sept a/m seventeen
dix-huit a/m eighteen
dix-neuf a/m nineteen
la dizaine f about ten, ten or so
le docteur m doctor (academic)
le documentaire m documentary
le dommage m shame, pity
quel dommage interj what a shame
donc ad therefore
donner v to give
donner sur v to look onto
dont pron of which, of whom
dormir v to sleep
le dortoir m dormitory
la douane f customs
doubler v to repeat a year, to overtake
la douche f shower
doué(e) a gifted
la douleur f pain
douter v to doubt
Douvres Dover
doux, douce a soft, mild (weather)
la douzaine f dozen, about twelve
le douze a/m twelve
le drapeau m flag
la drogue f drug(s)
se droguer vr to take drugs
droit(e) a straight, right
tout droit ad straight on
la droite f right
les droits de l'homme mpl human rights
drôle a funny
du = de le — see de
d'un côté on one hand
dur(e) a/ad hard, harsh
durer v to last

E
l' eau f water
l'eau minérale f mineral water
l'eau potable / non potable f drinking water / non-drinking water
l' échange m exchange
échanger v to exchange, to swap
l' écharpe f scarf
les échecs mpl chess
l' échelle f ladder
échouer (à) v to fail (at)
l' éclair m lightening
l' éclaircie f sunny spell
l' école f school
l'école primaire f primary school
l'école secondaire f secondary school
les économies fpl savings
faire des économies to save money
(l') écossais(e) a/m/f Scottish, Scot
l' Écosse f Scotland
écouter v to listen

l' écran m screen
l'écran tactile m touch screen
écrire v to write
l' écrivain m writer
l' Édimbourg Edinburgh
l' éducation physique f P.E.
effacer v to erase
l' effet de serre m greenhouse effect
effrayant(e) a frightening
égal(e) a equal
l' égalité f equality
l' église f church
égoïste a selfish
l' électricien(ne) m/f electrician
électrique a electric
électronique a electrical, electronic
élégant(e) a elegant
l' élève m/f pupil
l' emballage m package, packaging
emballer v to wrap, package
embêtant(e) a annoying
l' embouteillage m traffic jam
l' émission f programme (e.g. TV)
l'émission jeunesse f children's programme
l'émission musicale f music programme
l'émission sportive f sports programme
empêcher v to prevent
l' emplacement m pitch (for tent)
l' emploi m job
l' emploi du temps m timetable, schedule
l' employé(e) m/f employee
l' EMT (éducation manuelle et technique) f D&T
en prep in, to, by (e.g. by plane), made of (e.g. of wool)
enchanté(e) a delighted (e.g. to meet someone)
encore ad still, yet, another
encore du/de la a more
encore une fois ad once more
pas encore ad not yet
encourager v to encourage
endommager v to damage
l' endroit m place, area
l' enfant m/f child
enfin ad at last
l' enlèvememt m kidnapping
l' ennui m trouble, boredom
(s') ennuyer vr to get bored
ennuyeux/ennuyeuse a boring, annoying
l' enquête f inquiry
enregistrer v to record
enrichissant(e) a enriching
l' enseignement m teaching
enseigner v to teach
ensemble ad together
ensoleillé(e) a sunny
ensuite ad next
entendre v to hear
s'entendre vr to get on
l' enthousiasme m enthusiasm
entouré(e) a surrounded
(s') entraîner vr to train
entre prep between
l' entrée f entrance, admission, first course
l'entrée libre f free entry
entrer v to go in
l' entretien m interview
envahir v to invade
l' enveloppe f envelope
l' envie f want, desire
environ ad around
l' environnement m environment
envoyer v to send
épais(e) a thick
épicé(e) a spicy
l' épicerie f grocery
l' épicier/épicière m/f grocer
épouser v to marry
l' épreuve f test
l' EPS = éducation physique et sportive f P.E.

ad: adverb   prep: preposition   pron: pronoun   interj: interjection   conj: conjunction

French—English Dictionary

épuiser v  to exhaust
équilibré(e) a  balanced
l' équipe f  team
l' équitation f  riding (horses)
l' erreur f  mistake
l' escalade f  climbing
l' escalier m  staircase
l' escargot m  snail
l' escrime f  fencing (sport)
l' espace m  space
les espaces verts mpl
    green spaces
l' Espagne f  Spain
(l') espagnol m  Spanish (language)
(l') espagnol(e) a/m/f
    Spanish, Spaniard
espérer v  to hope
l' espoir m  hope
l' esprit m  spirit
essayer v  to try
l' essence f  petrol
l' est m  east
et conj  and
l' étage m  storey, floor
l' étagère f  shelf
l' état m  state
les États-Unis mpl
    United States
l' été m  summer
éteindre v  to turn off, put out
l' étoile f  star
étonnant(e) a  surprising
étonné(e) a  surprised
étrange a  strange
l' étranger/étrangère m/f  stranger,
    foreigner
à l'étranger ad  abroad
être v  to be
    être remboursé(e)  to be
    refunded/reimbursed
étroit(e) a  narrow
l' étude f  study
l' étudiant(e) m/f  student
étudier v  to study
l' événement m  event
évidemment ad  evidently
éviter v  to avoid
l' examen m  exam
les exclus mpl  social outcasts
l' excursion scolaire f  school trip
s' excuser vr  to apologise
    excusez-moi interj  sorry
l' exemple m  example
    par exemple for example
l' explication f  explanation
expliquer v  to explain
l' exposition f  exhibition
extra a  fantastic

## F

la fac f  university
en face (de) ad/prep  opposite
fâché(e) a  angry
facile a  easy
le/la facteur/factrice m/f  postman/
    woman
la faculté f  faculty, department
faible a  weak
la faim f  hunger
faire v  to do, make
    faire attention
    to pay attention, be careful
    faire du babysitting
    to babysit
    faire du jardinage
    to do gardening
    faire du lèche-vitrine
    to go window-shopping
    faire le ménage
    to do the housework
    faire la vaisselle
    to do the washing up
la famille f  family
(le/la) fana a/m/f  fanatical, fan
fantastique a  fantastic
la farine f  flour
fatigant(e) a  tiring
fatigué(e) a  tired
faut  see il faut
la faute f  fault
le fauteuil m  armchair

faux/fausse a  false, wrong
favori(e) a  favourite
les félicitations fpl  congratulations
féliciter v  to congratulate
la femme f  woman
    la femme de ménage f
    chambermaid, housekeeper
la fenêtre f  window
le fer m  iron
férié  see jour férié
la ferme f  farm
fermé(e) a  closed
fermer v  to shut
la fermeture (annuelle) f  closing,
    closure (for holidays)
le/la fermier/fermière m/f  farmer
la fête f  party, feast, saint's day
fêter v  to celebrate
le feu m  fire
    le feu d'artifice m  firework
    les feux rouges m  traffic lights
la feuille f  sheet (of paper), leaf
feuilleter v  to flick through
le feuilleton m  soap opera
(le) février m  February
les fiançailles fpl  engagement
le/la fiancé(e) m/f  fiancé(e)
fier / fière a  proud
la fille f  girl, daughter
le film m  film
    film d'aventures m  adventure film
    film de guerre m  war film
    film d'horreur m  horror film
    film policier m  detective film
    film romantique m  romantic film
    film de science-fiction m  science
    fiction film
le fils m  son
la fin f  end
finir v  to finish
les fléchettes fpl  darts
la fleur f  flower
le/la fleuriste m/f  florist
le foie m  liver
la foire f  fair, market
    la foire d'exposition f  exhibition
la fois f  time
    à la fois  at the same time
foncé(e) a  dark
la fontaine f  fountain
la forêt f  forest
la formation f  training
    programme de formation m
    training scheme
la forme f  shape
    en bonne forme  in good shape
formidable a  great
le formulaire m  form
fort(e) a  strong, loud
fou/folle a  mad
le four m  oven
le four à micro-ondes m  microwave
la fourchette f  fork
frais/fraîche a  fresh
la fraise f  strawberry
la framboise f  raspberry
le français m  French (language)
(le/la) français(e) a/m/f
    French, French person
la France f  France
franchement ad
    frankly, honestly
frapper v  to strike
le frère m  brother
le frigo m  fridge
frisé(e) a  curly (e.g. hair)
les frites fpl  chips
froid(e) a  cold
le fromage m  cheese
la frontière f  border
les fruits de mer mpl  seafood
fumer v  to smoke
(le/la) fumeur/fumeuse m/f  smoker
(non-)fumeur a  (non-)smoking

## G

gâcher v  to spoil, to waste
gagner v  to win, to earn
le gallois m  Welsh (language)

(le/la) gallois(e) a/m/f
    Welsh, Welsh person
le gant m  glove
le garçon m  boy
garder v  to keep
la gare f  station
    la gare routière f
    coach station
(se) garer v  to park
le gâteau m  cake
(la) gauche f/a  left
le gaz m  gas
    le gaz carbonique m
    carbon dioxide
    les gaz d'échappement mpl
    exhaust fumes
le gazon m  grass, lawn
geler v  to freeze
gêner v  to bother
en général ad  generally, usually
généralement ad  generally
génial(e) a  great, of genius
le genre m  type, kind, sort
les gens mpl  people
gentil(le) a  nice, kind
la géographie f  geography
le gigot d'agneau m  leg of lamb
le gîte m  self-catering cottage
la glace f  ice cream
le goût m  taste
goûter v  to taste
le goûter m  tea, snack
le gramme m  gram
grand(e) a  big, great
la Grande-Bretagne f
    Great Britain
la grand-mère f  grandmother
le grand-père m  grandfather
les grands-parents mpl  grandparents
gras(se) a  fatty
le gratin dauphinois m  potatoes with
    cheese topping
gratuit(e) a  free (no cost)
grave a  serious
le grenier m  attic
la grille de sécurité f  safety gate
gris(e) a  grey
gros(se) a  fat, big
le groupe m  group
la guerre f  war
le guichet m  ticket office
la guitare f  guitar
le gymnase m  gymnasium
la gymnastique f  gymnastics

## H

l' habitant(e) m/f  inhabitant
habiter v  to live in
l' habitude f  habit
s' habituer à vr  to get used to
la haie f  hedge
le haricot vert m  green bean
haut(e) a  high
    en haut ad  upstairs
la hauteur f  height
hélas interj  alas
l' herbe f  grass
hésiter v  to hesitate
l' heure f  hour
    à l'heure ad  on time
    à quelle heure  at what time?
    à tout à l'heure
    see you later
    de bonne heure ad  early
    les heures d'affluence fpl
    rush hours
    quelle heure est-il?  what time
    is it?
heureux/heureuse a  happy
hier ad  yesterday
l' histoire f  history, story
historique a  historical
l' hiver m  winter
l' HLM f = habitation à loyer modéré
    council house / flat
l' homme m  man
l' homme au foyer m  house husband
la honte f  shame
l' hôpital m  hospital
l' horaire m  timetable

l' horloge m  clock
hors d'haleine a  out of breath
l' hors-d'œuvre m  starter
l' hospitalité f  hospitality
l' hôtel m  hotel
l' hôtel de ville m  town hall
l' hôtesse de l'air f  air hostess
l' huile f  oil
(le) huit a/m  eight
l' huître f  oyster
humide a  damp (weather)
humilier v  to humilate
l' hypermarché m  hypermarket

## I

ici ad  here
l' icône f  icon
l' idée f  idea
l' identité f  identity
idiot(e) a  idiot, idiotic
il faut  (we) must,
    it is necessary to
il me faut  I need
il me reste  I've got ... left
il n'y a pas  there isn't/aren't
il s'agit de  it's about, it's a question
    of
il y a  there is, there are, ago
l' île f  island
illégal(e) a  illegal
illustration f  illustration
l' immeuble m  building, flats
l' immigré(e) m/f  immigrant
impatient(e) a  impatient
l' imperméable m  raincoat
imprimer v  to print
l' incendie m  fire
les incivilités fpl  antisocial behaviour
(l') inconnu(e) a/m/f  stranger,
    unknown (person)
l' inconvénient m  disadvantage
incroyable  unbelievable
l' Inde f  India
(l') indien(ne) a/m/f  Indian
indiquer v  to indicate
individuel(le) a  individual
industriel(le) a  industrial
l' infirmier/infirmière m/f  nurse
l' informaticien(ne) m/f  computer
    scientist
l' informatique f  IT
l' ingénieur m  engineer
l' inondation f  flood
inquiet/inquiète a  worried
s' inquiéter vr  to worry
l' instituteur/institutrice m/f  primary
    school teacher
l' instruction civique f  citizenship
interdit(e) a  prohibited
intéressant(e) a  interesting
intéresser v  to interest
s' intéresser à vr  to be interested in
l' interprète m/f  interpretor
inutile a  useless
(l') irlandais(e) a/m/f  Irish, Irish
    person
l' Irlande f  Ireland
l' Irlande du Nord f  Northern Ireland
l' Italie f  Italy
(l') italien(ne) a/m/f  Italian
ivre a  drunk

## J

jaloux/jalouse a  jealous
jamais — ne...jamais ad  never
le jambon m  ham
(le) janvier m  January
le Japon m  Japan
(le/la) japonais(e) a/m/f
    Japanese, Japanese person
le jardin m  garden
    le jardin zoologique m  zoological
    garden
le jardinage m  gardening
le/la jardinier/jardinière m/f  gardener
jaune a  yellow
le jean m  jeans
jeter v  to throw (away)
le jeu m  game
    jeu de cartes m  card game
    jeu de société m  board game

jeu vidéo m  video game
(le) jeudi m  Thursday
jeune a  young
la jeunesse f  youth
joli(e) a  pretty
jouer v  to play
le jouet m  game, toy
le jour m  day
le jour de l'an m  New Year's Day
le jour férié m  public holiday
le journal m  newspaper
la journée f  day
joyeux/joyeuse a  happy
le judo m  judo
le jugement m  judgement
juif/juive a  Jewish
(le) juillet m  July
(le) juin m  June
le/la jumeau/jumelle m/f  twin
jumelé(e) a  twin, twinned
la jupe f  skirt
le jus m  juice
    le jus de fruit m  fruit juice
    le jus d'orange m  orange juice
jusqu'à prep  until, as far as
juste a  just, fair

## K

le kilo m  kilo(gram)
le kilomètre m  kilometre

## L

là ad  there
    là-bas ad  over there
le laboratoire m  laboratory
le lac m  lake
laid(e) a  ugly
la laine f  wool
laisser v  to leave
le lait m  milk
la laitue f  lettuce
la lampe f  lamp
lancer v  to throw
la langue f  language, tongue
    les langues vivantes fpl
    modern languages
le lapin m  rabbit
large a  wide, broad
le lavabo m  washbasin
laver v  to wash
    laver la voiture v  to wash the
    car
le lave-vaisselle m  dishwasher
la leçon f  lesson
le lecteur m  reader, scanner
    le lecteur DVD m  DVD player
    le lecteur MP3 m  mp3 player
la lecture f  reading
le légume m  vegetable
le lendemain m  the next day
lentement ad  slowly
la lessive f  washing powder,
    washing
la lettre f  letter
lever v  to raise
    se lever vr  to get up
les libertés civiques fpl  civil liberties
la librairie f  bookshop
libre a  free
    le libre-service m
    self-service restaurant
licencier v  to dismiss,
    to make redundant
le lien m  link
le lieu m  place
la ligne f  line
la limonade f  lemonade
lire v  to read
la liste f  list
le lit m  bed
    les lits superposés mpl
    bunk beds
le litre m  litre
le livre m  book
la livre sterling f  pound sterling
livrer v  to deliver
la location f  rental, hire
    la location de voitures f
    car rental
le logement m  accommodation

---

nouns — **m**: masculine   **f**: feminine   **pl**: plural       **v**: verb       **vr**: reflexive verb       **a**: adjective

loger v *to stay*
la loi f *law*
loin (de) ad/prep *far (from)*
le loisir m *leisure*
Londres *London*
longtemps ad *for a long time*
la longueur f *length*
louer v *to hire*
lourd(e) a *heavy*
le loyer m *rent*
la lumière f *light*
(le) lundi m *Monday*
les lunettes fpl *glasses*
    les lunettes de soleil fpl *sunglasses*
lutter v *to fight*
le lycée m *secondary school*
    le lycée technique m *secondary school for vocational training*

# M

le/la maçon(ne) m/f *builder*
Madame f *Mrs, madam*
Mademoiselle f *Miss*
le magasin m *shop*
le magnétoscope m *video recorder*
(le) mai m *May*
maigre a *thin*
le maillot m *vest*
le maillot de bain m *swimming costume*
maintenant ad *now*
la mairie f *town hall*
mais conj *but*
la maison f *house*
    la maison des jeunes f *youth club*
    la maison individuelle f *detached house*
    la maison jumelée f *semi-detached house*
    la maison de la presse f *newsagent's*
mal ad *badly*
    avoir mal v *to be in pain, to hurt*
    plus mal ad *worse*
    le plus mal ad *worst*
mal équipé(e) a *ill-equipped*
mal payé(e) a *badly paid*
(le/la) malade a/m/f *ill, ill person*
la maladie f *illness*
maladroit(e) a *clumsy*
malgré prep *despite*
malheureux/malheureuse a *unhappy, unlucky*
la maman f *mum*
la Manche f *the Channel*
manger v *to eat*
la manifestation f *demonstration*
le mannequin m *model (person), mannequin*
manquer v *to miss*
le manteau m *coat*
le maquillage m *make-up*
le/la marchand(e) m/f *shopkeeper*
    le/la marchand(e) de fruits et de légumes m/f *greengrocer*
le marché m *market*
marcher v *to walk, to work*
(le) mardi m *Tuesday*
la marée f *tide*
le mari m *husband*
le mariage m *marriage*
marié(e) a *married*
se marier vr *to get married*
le Maroc m *Morocco*
(le/la) marocain(e) a/m/f *Moroccan*
marquer v *to mark, write down*
    marquer un but v *to score a goal*
marrant(e) a *funny*
marre — en avoir marre v *to have had enough*
marron a *brown (eyes, hair)*
(le) mars m *March*
la maternelle f *reception class*
les mathématiques fpl *maths*
les maths fpl *maths*
la matière f *subject*
les matières grasses fpl *fat content*
le matin m *morning*

la matinée f — faire la grasse matinée *to have a lie-in*
mauvais(e) a *bad*
    faire mauvais *to be bad weather*
le/la mécanicien(ne) m/f *mechanic*
méchant(e) a *nasty, naughty*
le médecin m *doctor*
le médicament m *medicine*
la Méditerranée f *Mediterranean Sea*
meilleur(e) a *better*
    le meilleur(e) a *the best*
    meilleurs vœux *best wishes*
le membre m *member, limb*
même ad *even*
même a *same*
même si conj *even if*
menacer v *to threaten*
mener v *to lead*
mentir v *to lie*
le menu m *set menu*
    menu à prix fixe m *fixed-price menu*
    menu touristique m *tourist menu*
la mer f *sea*
merci interj *thank you*
(le) mercredi m *Wednesday*
la mère f *mother*
merveilleux/merveilleuse a *marvellous*
mesurer v *to measure*
le métal m *metal*
la météo f *weather forecast*
le métier m *job, profession*
le mètre m *metre*
le métro m *underground (tube)*
mettre v *to put*
    mettre à la poste *to post*
    mettre de l'argent à côté *to put money aside*
    se mettre en colère *to get angry*
    mettre en ligne *to put online*
    se mettre en route *to take to the road*
le meuble m *piece of furniture*
le midi m *midday*
mieux ad *better*
    le mieux ad *best*
mignon(ne) a *cute, sweet, nice*
le million m *million*
mince a *slim*
le minuit m *midnight*
la minute f *minute*
    dans une minute *in a minute*
le miroir m *mirror*
la mi-temps f *half, half-time (of football match), part time (job)*
mixte a *mixed (e.g. school)*
la mobylette f *moped*
moche a *ugly, rotten*
la mode f *fashion*
    à la mode a *in fashion, fashionable*
moderne a *modern*
moins ad *less*
    le moins ad *the least*
    moins ... que *less ... than*
    au moins ad *at least*
le mois m *month*
la moitié f *half*
le moment m *moment, time*
    en ce moment ad *at the moment*
le monde m *world*
mondial(e) a *global*
le moniteur m *instructor, computer monitor*
la monnaie f *change (money)*
monoparental(e) a *single-parent (family)*
Monsieur m *Mr / sir*
la montagne f *mountain*
monter v *to rise*
la montre f *watch*
montrer v *to show*
la moquette f *fitted carpet*
le moral m *morale*
le morceau m *piece*
la mort f *death*

la mosquée f *mosque*
le mot m *word*
    les mots croisés mpl *crossword*
la moto f *motorbike*
mouillé(e) a *wet*
mourir v *to die*
moyen(ne) a *medium*
le mur m *wall*
la musculation f *weight training*
    faire de la musculation *to do some weight training*
le musée m *museum*
la musique f *music*
    musique pop/rock/classique f *pop/rock/classical music*
(le/la) musulman(e) a/m/f *Muslim*

# N

nager v *to swim*
la naissance f *birth*
naître v *to be born*
la natation f *swimming*
la nationalité f *nationality*
nautique a *nautical*
né(e) a *born*
ne ... aucun *not a single*
ne ... jamais *never*
ne … pas *not*
ne … personne *no one*
ne ... plus *no longer*
ne ... que *only*
ne ... rien *nothing*
nécessaire a *necessary*
la neige f *snow*
neiger v *to snow*
nerveux/nerveuse a *nervous*
nettoyer v *to clean*
(le) neuf a/m *nine*
le neveu m *nephew*
le nez m *nose*
ni… ni... *neither… nor...*
la nièce f *niece*
le niveau m *level*
les noces fpl *wedding*
(le) Noël m *Christmas*
    joyeux Noël interj *Merry Christmas*
noir(e) a *black*
la noix f *nut*
le nom m *name*
    le nom de famille m *surname*
le nombre m *number*
    nombre de a *many*
non interj *no*
non plus ad *neither, either (e.g. I haven't any either)*
    moi non plus ad *me neither*
le non-fumeur/non-fumeuse m/f *non-smoker*
le nord m *north*
normalement ad *normally*
la nostalgie f *nostalgia*
la note f *mark, grade*
la nourriture f *food*
nouveau/nouvelle a *new*
le Nouvel An m *New Year*
(le) novembre m *November*
le nuage m *cloud*
nuageux/nuageuse a *cloudy*
la nuit f *night*
nul(le) a *useless*
nulle part ad *nowhere*
le numéro m *number*
le numéro de téléphone m *telephone number*

# O

l' obésité f *obesity*
obligatoire a *compulsory*
occupé(e) a *engaged, busy*
(l') octobre m *October*
l' odeur f *smell, fragrance*
l' œuf m *egg*
l' office de tourisme m *tourist office*
l' offre d'emploi f *job offer*
l' oignon m *onion*
l' oiseau m *bird*
l' ombre f *shade, shadow*
on pron *one, you*

l' oncle m *uncle*
(l') onze a/m *eleven*
    optimiste a *optimistic*
l' or m *gold*
l' orage m *storm*
    orageux/orageuse a *stormy*
l' orchestre m *orchestra*
ordinaire a *ordinary*
l' ordinateur m *computer*
les ordures fpl *rubbish*
l' organisation caritative f *charitable organisation*
organiser v *to organise*
l' os m *bone*
ou conj *or*
où(?) pron/ad *where(?)*
    d'où? *where from?*
    où, ça? *where's that?*
    où est? *where is?*
oublier v *to forget*
l' ouest m *west*
oui interj *yes*
ouvert(e) a *open*
l' ouvre-boîtes m *tin-opener*
l' ouvrier/ouvrière m/f *worker*
ouvrir v *to open*

# P

la page d'accueil f *home page*
le pain m *bread*
le pain grillé m *toast*
la paire f *pair*
la paix f *peace*
le palais m *palace*
le pamplemousse m *grapefruit*
le panneau m *sign, notice*
le pantalon m *trousers*
le papa m *dad*
le papier m *paper*
(les) Pâques fpl *Easter*
le paquet m *parcel, packet*
par prep *by, per*
    par chance ad *luckily*
    par contre ad *on the other hand*
    par exemple ad *for example*
paraître v *to appear*
le parapluie m *umbrella*
le parc m *park*
    le parc d'attractions m *amusement park*
parce que conj *because*
pardon interj *excuse me*
les parents mpl *parents*
paresseux/paresseuse a *lazy*
parfait(e) a *perfect*
parfois ad *sometimes*
le parfum m *flavour, perfume*
la parfumerie f *perfume shop*
le parking m *car park*
parler v *to talk*
parmi prep *amongst*
à part ad/prep *on one side, separately, except for*
partager v *to share*
le/la partenaire (idéal(e)) m/f *(ideal) partner*
partir v *to depart, leave*
    à partir de prep *from*
partout ad *everywhere*
pas encore ad *not yet*
pas mal de a *quite a few*
le passage à niveau m *level crossing*
le/la passant(e) m/f *passer-by*
le passé m *past*
le passeport m *passport*
passer v *to pass*
    passer un examen *to take an exam*
    passer le temps à *to spend time doing*
le passe-temps m *hobby*
passionnant(e) a *exciting*
le pâté m *pâté*
les pâtes fpl *pasta*
le patin à roulettes m *roller skate*
le patinage m *skating*
patiner v *to skate*
la patinoire f *ice rink*
la pâtisserie f *cake/pastry shop*

le/la patron(ne) m/f *boss*
la pause f *break, pause*
pauvre a *poor*
la pauvreté f *poverty*
le pays m *country*
le paysage m *countryside*
le pays de Galles m *Wales*
le péage m *toll*
la pêche f *fishing, peach*
pédagogique a *educational*
à peine ad *barely*
la pelouse f *lawn*
pendant (+ que) prep (conj) *during, while*
pénible a *hard, tiring*
penser v *to think*
la pension complète f *full board*
perdre v *to lose*
le père m *father*
permettre v *to allow*
le permis (de conduire) m *permit, (driving) licence*
la personnalité f *personality*
la personne f *person*
les personnes défavorisées fpl *disadvantaged people*
peser v *to weigh*
pessimiste a *pessimistic*
petit(e) a *small, short*
le/la petit(e)-ami(e) m/f *boyfriend/girlfriend*
le petit déjeuner m *breakfast*
le petit-fils m *grandson*
la petite-fille m *granddaughter*
les petits pois mpl *peas*
le pétrole m *oil, petroleum*
peu ad *little, few*
la peur f *fear*
peut-être ad *perhaps*
la photocopie f *photocopy*
la physique f *physics*
la pièce f *room, play*
la pièce d'identité f *proof of identity*
le pied m *foot*
    à pied ad *on foot*
le piercing (à l'oreille) m *(ear) piercing*
(le/la) piéton(ne) m/f/a *pedestrian*
la pile f *battery*
piquant(e) a *spicy*
le pique-nique m *picnic*
la piqûre f *bite, sting*
pire a *worse*
    le pire a *worst*
la piscine f *swimming pool*
la piste f *track, trail*
    la piste cyclable f *cycle lane, cycle track*
pittoresque a *picturesque, vivid*
le placard m *cupboard*
la place f *square, room, space, seat*
le plafond m *ceiling*
la plage f *beach*
(se) plaindre vr *to complain*
plaire (+ à) v *to please*
le plaisir m *pleasure*
le plan de ville m *map of the town*
la planche à voile f *windsurfing*
la planche de surf f *surfboard*
la plante f *plant*
le plastique m *plastic*
le plat m *dish*
    le plat du jour m *dish of the day*
    le plat principal m *main course*
la platine laser f *laser disc player*
plein(e) (de) a *full (of)*
pleurer v *to cry*
pleuvoir v *to rain*
le plombier m *plumber*
la plongée sous-marine f *deep sea diving*
la pluie f *rain*
plus ad *more*
    le plus ad *the most*
    plus tard ad *later*
    plus ... que *more ... than*
la poche f *pocket*
la pointure f *size (of shoe)*
la poire f *pear*
le poisson m *fish*

---

**ad**: adverb    **prep**: preposition    **pron**: pronoun    **interj**: interjection    **conj**: conjunction